THE SKEPTICAL
ROMANCER

THE SKEPTICAL ROMANCER

Selected Travel Writings

W. Somerset Maugham

Edited and Introduced by Pico Iyer

VINTAGE CLASSICS
Vintage Books
A Division of Random House, Inc.
New York

FIRST VINTAGE CLASSICS EDITION, FEBRUARY 2011

The Library of Congress has cataloged the Everyman's Library edition
as follows:
Maugham, W. Somerset (William Somerset), 1874–1965.
The skeptical romancer : selected travel writing / W. Somerset
Maugham ; edited and introduced by Pico Iyer.
p. cm.
1. Maugham, W. Somerset (William Somerset), 1874–1965—Travel.
2. Maugham, W. Somerset (William Somerset), 1874–1965—
Notebooks, sketchbooks, etc. 3. Authors, English—20th century—
Biography. Title.
PR6025.A86 S49 2009
2009279509

Vintage ISBN: 978-0-307-47318-9

Book design by Barbara de Wilde and Carol Devine Carson

C O N T E N T S

Introduction xi

A Very Young Traveller in Spain (from *The Land of the
    Blessed Virgin*)

The Spirit of Andalusia 3
The Churches of Ronda 4
The Mosque at Cordova 5
The Court of Oranges 7
Seville 9
The Giralda 13
Gaol 14
Corrida de Toros 19
Wind and Storm 22
Jerez 24
Cadiz 27
Adios 29

Sketches of China (from *On a Chinese Screen*)

My Lady's Parlour 35
The Cabinet Minister 36
Dinner Parties: Legation Quarter 38
The Inn 41
Her Britannic Majesty's Representative 43
The Last Chance 44
Henderson 45
Romance 47
The Song of the River 50
The Stranger 51
The Philosopher 55
The Missionary Lady 62

The Plain 63
A Student of the Drama 65
A City Built on a Rock.. 68

Across Southeast Asia (from *The Gentleman in the Parlour*)

Pagan 73
Mandalay 76
The Nuns at Mengon 78
On the Trail 79
The Salween 81
The Market 84
Keng Tung 87
The Solitary 89
Siam 92
Bangkok 95
Buddha 100
The Fever 105
Angkor 107
A Last Day in Angkor 110
Saigon and Tourane 112
Huë 116
A Night on the River 118
A Classmate in Haiphong 119

A Life in Retrospect (from *The Partial View*, comprising *The Summing Up* and *A Writer's Notebook*)

Early Travels 143
Mobility 146
Capri 154
At War 154
Hawaii 161
The Missionary and Miss Thompson 165
A Castaway 166
Tahiti 167
Russia 177
The Nevsky Prospekt 181
Opium Dream 184
The Sultan 185

CONTENTS

A Dream	..	..	..	..	..	.. 186
India ..	..	..	..	..	..	.. 187
Benares ..	..	..	..	..	..	.. 192
The Taj ..	..	..	..	..	..	.. 193
Madura ..	..	..	..	..	..	.. 193
In Texas ..	..	..	..	..	..	.. 195

INTRODUCTION

When one travelled in the East, it was astonishing how often one came across men who had modelled themselves on the creatures of his imagination.
– W. Somerset Maugham, of Rudyard Kipling

What makes a great traveler? Those of us who spend much of our lives on the road – or on the page – often beguile an idle hour or two with the question. The ideal companion should be open to every person or encounter that comes his way, perhaps – but not too ready to be taken in by them. She should be worldly, shrewd, her feet firmly on the ground; and yet she should be ready to surrender, if only for a moment, to the magic and excitement of what she could never see or do at home. He should be curious, observant, fun, wry and kind; he should be able to spin a spell-binding tale before the Royal Geographic Society in London and then throw it all over for a crazy romance in the South Seas.

The heart of the conundrum, really, is that the people we like to spend time with on the road are often sensible, and yet aware of the limits of sense, and the virtue of being senseless every now and again. They're rooted enough to be up for every possibility. They shouldn't have an agenda or overwhelming prejudices, and they should be as able to see to the heart of the natives of any country as to their fellow travelers. Maybe what they really offer is a happy blend of steadiness and surprise.

I draw up such lists myself, often, and then I look across the room and realize that there's one person I know who fits the bill ideally. Somerset Maugham was celebrated in the England of his day as one of its most successful dramatists and is cherished, even now, almost half a century after his death, as a spinner of classic tales of exploration and flight that Hollywood seems to turn into fresh movies every year. *Of Human Bondage, The Razor's Edge, The Moon and Sixpence* all define Maugham for many as a cool, even feline observer of the human tragi-comedy who could be at once startled and amused by the stories he

picked up and set in colonial Asia or the Pacific. The person
behind them, we sense, was someone always hungry for the
new, and ready to follow any opening or character he met,
down any alleyway, in search of a story, yes, but also in search
of a sense of escape and even transcendence.

Maugham's voice and presence have so much the feeling of
Edwardian England and the silk dressing-gown, however, that
it's easy to forget sometimes that he was born in Paris, and
that his early letters were all written in perfect French (for
English schoolboys the secret language of romance). He studied
in Heidelberg for two years as a teenager, he went to live in
Seville for sixteen months in his early twenties and, having
already mastered Greek, Latin, French, German, Italian and
Russian, he set about learning Spanish. He served in World
War I as volunteer ambulance driver and nurse, even though
he had four plays on at the time in London's West End – and
then became the West's main source of intelligence in Russia
during the weeks leading up to the Bolshevik Revolution. By
the 1920s, before most people, even those of means, were traveling very widely, he was going to Borneo, to China, to the South
Seas and Japan, and, having spent early sojourns in Paris and
Capri, he passed the last thirty-nine years of his life in the south
of France. There he had another memento of the larger world,
a secret symbol to repel the evil eye, painted on his outside wall
– the same symbol he slipped on to the cover of his books.

The writer who would at once take his reader on journeys
to India, Samoa, Hong Kong and yet somehow always set
him at his ease, the man of high culture who often asserted,
"The best use of culture is to talk nonsense with distinction,"
is best revealed for me in his early novel, *The Merry-Go-Round*,
published when he was thirty. That book, typically, unfolds an
interlocking set of love stories – stories of great passion and
drama – as they are seen by two slightly detached observers:
one is a fifty-seven-year-old spinster, Miss Ley, who takes in
everything with a wise serenity and pronounces grandly, and
somewhat skeptically, on human folly and illusion. The other
is a burning young medical student, Frank Hurrell, who cannot
contain his hunger for experience. "My whole soul aches for
the East, for Egypt and India and Japan," he cries out at one

point. "I want to know the corrupt, eager life of the Malays and the violent adventures of the South Sea Islands...I want to see life and death, and the passions, the virtues and vices, of men face to face, uncovered." The language is purple, but the sentiments are as alive and quickening as anything in Hesse or Kerouac, and it's hard not to recall that Maugham was himself a medical student, who learned early about human suffering, and longed, as he told us, "for fresh air, action, violence," to be away from the hushed drawing-rooms of England. Even when young, in short, he could summon the perspective of both an elderly, disengaged observer and an eager romantic – and show himself as close to woman as to man.

*

In practice, only four of the seventy-eight books Maugham turned out are generally placed on the shelves marked "Travel": his classic account of a journey from Rangoon to Haiphong, *The Gentleman in the Parlour*, brought out in 1930; a series of sketches and snapshots called *On a Chinese Screen*, from 1922; a very early, boyish series of wanderings around southern Spain, *The Land of the Blessed Virgin*, published in 1905, that he delighted in mocking and repudiating in later works for its flowery style and juvenile effusions; and a meditation on some figures in Spanish history – explicitly not "a book of travel," though often categorized as such, *Don Fernando*, in 1935. Yet travel lay behind much of his work, if only because, as Miss Ley says, "Curiosity is my besetting sin," and as is written of Frank Hurrell, his "deliberate placidity of expression masked a very emotional temperament." When it came to his masterly appraisal of his life, *The Summing Up*, and to his *A Writer's Notebook* (joined with *The Summing Up* to make *The Partial View*), it's hard not to notice how many of Maugham's central, formative experiences came on the road, or through it.

More than that, his young book on Spain, though certainly ornate, and without the crisp definition that marks the mature Maugham style, shows us the master traveler as he would always be, under the surface, and before he became an institution and the famous writer "Somerset Maugham." What we see in it is an ardent, dewy, rebellious boy – a "romancer by profession,"

as he puts it – anxious to be away from England's enclosedness
and gray, and at home already in the south, the world of sunshine and abandon. Later he will develop a more measured,
poised voice that has the sound of skepticism trying to keep
its boyishness at bay; but here, in this unselfconscious work, is
already an original and grown-up sensibility, compounded of a
susceptible heart, a careful mind and a spirit that is eager to
tangle with the essential questions of life and all its meanings.

What hit me, rereading many of his books to put this collection together, is that Maugham breaks almost every law you
might lay down in *Travel Writing 101*: he generalizes wildly, he
claims not to be interested in the places he's visiting, he admits
that he's only hunting for material and often his digressions go
on so long that we lose all sense of where we are (in the middle
of Southeast Asia, he spins out a long story, not clearly relevant,
of a novelist in London). He likens trees in a Thai village to "the
sentences of Sir Thomas Browne," tells us that Asian clothes
are much less interesting and various than those you'd see in
Piccadilly and cheerfully admits, in the middle of wildly color-
ful and unvisited landscapes, that his great delight, traveling
through Asia, is reading F. H. Bradley's *Appearance and Reality*.

Yet the cumulative effect of all these transgressions is to give
us the impression, as not every traveler does, that he's having
fun. He never seems bored and he seldom loses his temper.
The sentences, scrupulously clear and relaxed and unpreten-
tious, seem to come to us from a cozy armchair (or the sedan
on which he's sometimes being carried), and he at once wins
our trust with his lack of design and earns our affection precisely by telling us that he's lazy, unfair and uninterested, a
great believer in breaking all the rules. It's as if he's simply
taking his mind and imagination for a walk, and as they forage,
as any dogs might do, he never quite knows where they'll take
him. The air of casual ease is so distinct, you may overlook the
fact that he's sleeping for days in an open rowboat, has a
temperature of 105 (just before offering a brilliant appraisal of
Buddhism), went on a sixty-day march when he was close to
fifty years old.

It might almost seem that circumstances conspired to make
Maugham a traveler (and that kindred spirit, an explorer on

the page, drawn to everything farthest from himself). He was born in a country not his own, and when he went to England, at the age of ten, after the sudden death of both his parents, he felt a foreigner there. His training as a medical student encouraged, no doubt, his gift for listening, and for drawing people out, concentrating attentively on their stories and bringing to them a mix of compassion and discernment even as he linked them to certain textbook patterns. His lifelong stammer, moreover, made him even more of a listener, always more eager to hear others' symptoms than to tell his own; reading him, I am often reminded of the old adage you still hear everywhere in Asia about men being given two ears, two eyes and only one mouth, so as to remember they should see and hear at least twice as much as they say.

Maugham's father, when the novelist was a boy, had traveled to Greece, Turkey and Morocco, bringing back stories and memories to beguile his youngest child; his mother, when young, "could prattle Hindustani much better than English," because her own father had served in India. Maugham was a product of Empire, after a fashion, therefore, but never an admirer of it (he could barely speak English when he moved to his ostensible motherland). Where many people travel in order to become something – and to escape the failures that surround them at home – Maugham seemed to travel in order to become nobody, just an anonymous gentleman in a parlor in an inn, and to flee the successes that, he always said, could cripple a man as much as failure could. And as a playwright and a novelist, his business was, explicitly, to get into other people's minds and lives and voices; traveling, he seemed unable to believe in his own prejudices and always eager to be turned on his head.

He knew the "world," in the sense of fashionable society, but he was never much taken with it; his early works, like his first book *Liza of Lambeth*, were criticized for paying too much attention to the poor and desperate. His work as a spy – like many a writer, he must have been a natural – doubtless intensified his habit of picking up information, reading the secret codes of life, observing without being observed in turn. Though sometimes caricatured as a homosexual who lived in a world of privileged men, he had four extended affairs with women (one of whom he married), and thus knew both sides of the table in that sense, too. One of his siblings became Lord Chancellor, a pillar of the British establishment; the other was a gay writer of sorts who never rode on a train – he had a kind of vertigo – and took his own life, with nitric acid, in front of his younger brother's eyes.

Always as keen and lucid an observer of himself as of everyone else, Maugham saw that travel was in his blood and in his destiny, a place where his needs and his preferences converged. His stammer, he said, made him "a wanderer on the face of the earth" and his interest in everything prevented him from ever staying long in one place. His protagonist in *The Moon and Sixpence*, Charles Strickland, is "eternally a pilgrim, haunted by a divine nostalgia," a little as Frank Hurrell and then Larry Darrell, the hero of *The Razor's Edge*, are; Maugham wrote one novel, *The Explorer*, based partly on the adventures of Stanley and a play, *East of Suez*, based on Kipling's "Ship me somewhere east of Suez, where the best is like the worst."

"I was ever looking forward, generally to something I proposed to do in some place other than that in which I found myself," he wrote in a piece called "On the Approach of Middle Age" (included in the anthology of unpublished pieces, *A Traveller in Romance*). And his autobiography confesses to us that "I never felt entirely myself till I had put at least the Channel between my native country and me." At ninety, he spoke of going to Marrakesh – "I shall not stop my travelling" – as if what kept him young and awake, even then, was his abiding feeling that he "would sooner be a fool of twenty-five than a philosopher of fifty."

*

Maugham, then, was a born subversive who, in his unorthodox way, was always looking for the road less traveled and the humble pleasure overlooked. "For my part," he wrote with typical assurance in his memoirs, "I would much sooner spend a month on a desert island with a veterinary surgeon than with a prime minister." More than that, he was a habitual counter-moralist, who could not restrain himself from pricking at piety and preaching wherever he found it, and yet, unusually, was constantly interested in wisdom and philosophy and mysticism while professing no interest in religion. His official assessments of himself were never quite straightforward – they always diminished his skills too much – and yet you get tantalizing glimpses of him in the travelers he records, like the one in China who "collected neither plants nor beasts, but men." Most of all, his creed, insofar as he had one, was to try everything – to smoke opium and to visit prisons as well as chapels – and his advice to young wanderers at the end of his life was to do everything, to go everywhere, to explore the vicissitudes of the world. "A novelist must preserve a child-like belief in the importance of things which common-sense considers of no great consequence," he wrote, late in life. "He must never entirely grow up."

Yet a great traveler is also measured not just by how clearly he sees the world around him, and excavates the past; but by how much, in doing this, he manages to describe the future. The wayfarer with his eyes open and his senses alert sees beneath all the details he observes outlines of those features that will never change, the way he catches in the girl of fourteen the grandmother of a later age. In this regard Maugham stands up as well as any traveler of the twentieth century. Go to Chiang Mai tomorrow and you will meet a man who threw over his comfortable life in London for the less visible benefits of a cozy room in the wilderness, with a local girl who "understands" him even if she does not speak much of his language. In the same neighborhood, you'll meet a missionary, warning all visitors from London against such girls – and such a life – and an Englishwoman not very comfortable with the fascinations of the East and the positions into which they have thrust her. The Thais you see will be charming, supple, infinitely gracious and attentive and perfectly attuned both to reading a visitor's needs and to meeting them, for mutual benefit.

Go to a bar in Honolulu, visit the new China being "definitively" covered in so many current books and you'll meet the same – and find, moreover, that somehow Maugham has caught what is really going on better than that foreign correspondent (or roaming moralist) living in Shanghai in the twenty-first century, and so eagerly reporting on "what's new." Places have characters as much as people do, and it is the rare – the invaluable – traveler who, in wandering around China in the 1920s, can not only give you China of the year 2010, but the societies of Hong Kong, Paris, Buenos Aires, and the expat circles you will find in them even now. Maugham was never just a neutral observer, and some readers today may object to the fact he'd never heard of "political correctness"; he makes free with his opinions, writes off whole cultures in a sentence, calls a Chinaman a Chinaman and a thief a thief. Like any good companion he keeps you alive with the very energy and fullness of his judgments. I relish his writing even when – sometimes especially when – I'm sure that he's wrong, and his finding "insipid" food in Thailand and calling the Thais "not a comely race" prompts me to try to formulate an answer.

The point, really, is that Maugham was not interested in the exotic as such – though he responded to its magnetism and always gravitated to the unknown; in every place he went, he was digging up the familiar, and recalling the anatomy teacher who had taught him, dissecting bodies, that "the normal is the rarest thing in the world." Over and over he shows us how "ordinary"-seeming men hide the most extraordinary lives, while extraordinary men cannot hold our interest for long. His interest in people was so consuming, in fact, and agile that he asks us to deepen what we understand by the word "extraordinary." And abroad, freed of the clutter and distraction of home, we see many things – especially our own people – more clearly and more tellingly than we would at home. For Maugham, always pragmatic, travel was a great way of claiming the freedom he craved (from society and from habit) and of getting away from everything that he knew much too well (or that knew him much too well). It also allowed him to collect more types and tales in a week than he could find in a year in London.

For many there was something of the Chinese sage in Maugham, sitting at a little distance from the human drama, taking it all in with a smile and committed to a creed of detachment and a sense of the impermanence of the world. "A mysterious Asiatic influence pervades the face of this Anglo-Saxon grand seigneur," the French painter Edouard MacAvoy recorded. "Today he wears a pure Buddhist mask. He has wisdom, renunciation, profound peace born of complete dis-illusionment, a skeptical gaiety." And yet what gives his writing its life and charm is that he always knew that succumbing to illusions, in love or travel, is one of the greatest pleasures that life affords (and he gave himself up to what went against his better judgment constantly). His voice is never more British than when he went to China, dining with the lords of the foreign community and remarking on the occasional local as if that person were an exotic creature observed in its native habitat; and yet his Olympian view of things, his remaining unfazed – in fact tickled – by the constant changes in the world make him seem more of a Confucian than many of the Confucians he meets. He could understand and give unusually deep and sympathetic accounts of Confucianism or Buddhism – of mysticism or hedonism – because he could find, when he needed to, those elements in himself.

These are all rarer qualities than one might suppose: D. H. Lawrence, for example, traveled everywhere at the same time as Maugham did, and caught Ceylon, Australia, New Mexico with a vividness and immediacy that few travelers have matched in the eighty years since. Without even trying to, Lawrence could pick up the smells, shapes, instincts of a place, grow bewitched by them and then become violently disen-chanted – all inside a week. He had every gift, you could say, except patience and moderation. Aldous Huxley, meanwhile, who later became one of the most open-minded explorers of the mind, nonetheless traveled around Asia in his *Jesting Pilate* like the acerbic young man of London salons that he was, finding in each place he visited an excuse for a witticism or a hasty dismissal. One of Maugham's great gifts, by comparison, was to give us the impression that he's always where he wants to be, unburdened by any mission or publishing contract, even if his way of taking in Burma is to play patience in his room, or to sweeten the evening with some Proust. Instead of chafing against what's around him, he seems to give in to whatever the moment brings.

One way of measuring any traveler is to see how deep and wide his influence runs, eighty years after his travel books appeared. It's hard to read Graham Greene, for example, without seeing Maugham, and his mix of worldliness and romanticism, his investigations of skepticism and faith, behind many of the scenes (they even both wrote works called *The Tenth Man*, both launched unexpected attacks on pity and both ended up on the French Riviera); and when one meets Paul Bowles's defining stories of travelers consumed by the places they visit, one can recognize Maugham as one of the few people who's been there before him. Pick up *Hotel Honolulu*, by Paul Theroux, and you're reading, essentially, one of Maugham's collections of South Sea stories, though with sexual explicitness and modern rage included; tour the world with the incomparably fluent and attentive Jan Morris and you see a distinctive English blend of tolerance and acuity that, even in its cadences often (those rich descriptive sentences that begin with adjectives), brings you back to Maugham. The most serious and searching traveler of the post-colonial world, V. S. Naipaul, managed to assist his escape from his native Trinidad by writing a schoolboy essay on Maugham – it won a competition – and, more than fifty years later, after winning the Nobel, was endowing the protagonist of two late novels with the curious name, "W. Somerset Chandran," a tribute, clearly, to the traveler by whom he seemed haunted (and whose visits to India in 1939 he there invokes).

Maugham's interest was not in sights, he says repeatedly; one of his favorite devices, in every book of travels, was to warn us that he's not very diligent about seeing the sights, sits in his room reading Jane Austen while others are busy taking in guidebook facts and, in truth, prefers less information to more. But what he was doing while he was not taking the packaged expeditions that were the stuff of other travelers was to go off "on the search for emotion," as he put it in his book on Spain, and to investigate the human costs and complications of foreignness: when he visits China, for one, what he mostly gives us are thumbnail sketches of the priest, the diplomat, the restless wife, even the inn or the illusions that are a feature of almost any foreign place. Traveling around Southeast Asia, he collects "characters" at every turn – runaways, men of the cloth, drifters with unexpected tales of betrayal and obsession, some of them (as in Greene again) settled for life in a foreign place they know will never be home, others pining for an England they know they'll never see again.

Maugham's descriptive gifts, his evergreen capacity for being swept away, mean that he does give us indelible evocations of the Taj Mahal, the Alhambra, the temples of Thailand (which he loves for both their shamelessness and dazzle – Maugham, one feels, is the rare traveler who would not have looked down on Las Vegas, but would instead have found there poignant dramas of paid love and failed resolve); but what stays in the mind from his books of travel is the people he meets, their savory stories, the detours he enjoys, the riffs he suddenly takes off on (remembering Heidelberg and the promise of youth while he's bumping around Spain, or suddenly offering us a fairy-tale in the middle of his stay in Thailand). Indeed, he is, in his unrepentant waywardness, a forerunner to those counter-culture travelers of today who say that it's always in the digression, the getting lost, the unexpected diversion that the joy of travel comes. Trains of thought can take you places that no other trains reach at all.

Again, the image many of us have of an elegantly bespoke man living near Nice and consorting with Winston Churchill, Noël Coward, Cecil Beaton obscures the central fact about Maugham, which is that he was a stowaway at heart, and the hunger for rebellion, the fondness for the wastrel, his lifelong wish to get away from the small-world circles he knew and out into the wild (or at least the unknown) was what drove his writing; in that regard, travel was both a vehicle and a metaphor. One of the works of his that many probably recognize even now is *The Moon and Sixpence*, about a thriving London stockbroker who throws it all over to go to live in Paris and Tahiti – like Gauguin – and just paint. Yet that impulse is everywhere in Maugham, playing at the edges of most of his stories: some of them concern men who have made just that flight, and cannot imagine, in Hawaii or Vietnam, how they ever could have survived the years in rainy Europe; and some of them enact the same process themselves, as you can feel Maugham stretching his limbs and (to some degree) letting down his hair, as travelers have always done, and asking, in

Thoreauvian cadences, at the end of his first book of travel, "What is the use of hurrying to pile up money when one can live on so little?"

To this day, the first hippie novel ever written – in 1944 – might be said to be *The Razor's Edge* (or at least it shares that distinction with some of Hesse's work, perhaps, a little of Henry Miller, maybe some Novalis): at sixty-nine Maugham was turning himself into an idealistic young man who was leaving the comforts of Chicago behind to seek out truth in the Himalayas. In life Maugham himself embarked on a three-month (and characteristically difficult) trip around India when he was sixty-three, seeking out swamis and yogis; and he told his friend Christopher Isherwood, a few years later, that his greatest wish, when he turned seventy, was to return to India and study Shankara.

This was not, ever, part of the popular image of the brittle, Wildean playwright and habitué of grandes dames' lounges, but it is what makes Maugham feel so fresh and even liberating today (and it is what made him so famously impatient with one of the other great observers of expatriation, Henry James, who, coming from America, was transfixed by those grandes dames' lounges). He kept a young man's eagerness for knowledge – and therefore adventure – about him always. Every morning, he said, he read some philosophy, the way others might do yoga, and he could not encounter a doctrine or vision of life, it often seems, without wanting to explore or engage it. Read his grand apologia, *The Summing Up*, and you find him as metaphysically alive and excited as that German who just spun out his creed to you over dinner in a little candlelit restaurant in Ladakh last night, or that Canadian who's traveling the East to find the heart of transcendental existence. The last words of this most flexible of souls, always open to experiment and journey, concluding *The Partial View* as he turns eighty, were "I am on the wing."

*

When I began to set about making a collection of Maugham's travels, my first – and second – instinct was just to find a way to reprint *The Gentleman in the Parlour* in its entirety; for twenty years it had led me around Asia, and whenever anyone asked me what he or she should read before coming to the continent where I have lived for almost half my life, I referred them to Maugham, whose book seemed to me as up-to-date as any of this season's offerings. But when I reread that work, I was reminded that it exists in fragments and comes in and out of focus. I had remembered many unforgettable scenes and moments; but when I went back to it, I saw that I had remembered them partly because there were lots of drab or lusterless scenes between them. In some ways it is a collection, an anthology of disparate pieces already. And *On a Chinese Screen* and *The Land of the Blessed Virgin* are likewise sketchbooks, really, that do not attempt to tell a story, or to weave a narrative, with beginning, middle and end, but simply alight on points of interest, hopping from vignette to vignette as a restless bird might do.

So the best way of doing justice to the travels was to catch them in the round, I thought, geographically divided and in single scenes and parables that remind us of Maugham's curious capacity for seeming almost middle-aged when young and often surprisingly boyish even in his later years. The power of his novels comes nearly always from their passionate engagement in the dramas they record; though the narrator is taking these in from the sidelines, he gets so involved in the convulsions that he describes that we do, too. But the strength of the travel writing lies in its disengagement, its careful observations – always relieved, again and again, by moments of transport that carry the writer away almost in spite of himself.

One of Maugham's most frequent maneuvers – he uses it in virtually every book – is to note, as he writes at the beginning of his short story "Honolulu" that "the wise man travels only in imagination" or to assert, as he did even on his early trip to Spain, "It is much better to read books of travel than to travel oneself; he really enjoys foreign lands who never goes abroad." Yet having professed this, and claimed to be a skeptic and a stay-at-home, he scrupulously fails to live up to his own advice and does just what he says he shouldn't. He does go to Honolulu, in spite of his injunction, and there meets a traveler whose story he would perhaps never have listened to if he'd met the man in London or New York. And he does travel, visibly, around the wilds (so much so that he contracted malaria, fell into some rapids, often almost died), and comes away with castaways and romances that he can put into a frame once safely back at his desk.

On his nintieth birthday – he had enjoyed Japan and Italy in his eighties – he admitted, "I have wandered all my life and it would be no bad thing to die while making a sentimental journey to the one place on earth where, for me, there is beauty still and a contentment that I have found nowhere else.

"I refer to Angkor Wat, in Cambodia. I have one desire left, which is to return to that lost village in the jungle in the Far East." I only wish he could have done so, and thus captured yet another place that many of us flock to today, always humbled – and excited – by the fact that this smiling watcher has been there before us, and, while not seeing all of the sights, shown us everything worth seeing.

Pico Iyer

PICO IYER is the author of many books about travel, including *Video Night in Kathmandu, The Lady and the Monk* and *The Global Soul*. His most recent book is *The Open Road* about the fourteenth Dalai Lama.

A VERY YOUNG
TRAVELLER IN SPAIN

from *The Land of the Blessed Virgin*

THE SPIRIT OF ANDALUSIA

IN LONDON NOW, as I write, the rain of an English April pours
down; the sky is leaden and cold, the houses in front of me are
almost terrible in their monotonous greyness, the slate roofs are
shining with the wet. Now and again people pass: a woman of
the slums in a dirty apron, her head wrapped in a grey shawl; two
girls in waterproofs, trim and alert notwithstanding the inclem-
ent weather, one with a music case under her arm. A train arrives
at an underground station and a score of city folk cross my
window, sheltered behind their umbrellas; and two or three
groups of workmen, silently, smoking short pipes: they walk
with a dull, heavy tramp, with the gait of strong men who are
very tired. Still the rain pours down unceasing.

And I think of Andalusia. My mind is suddenly ablaze with its
sunshine, with its opulent colour, luminous and soft; I think of
the cities, the white of Andalusia cities bathed in light; of the
desolate wastes of sand, with their dwarf palms, the broom in
flower. And in my ears I hear the twang of the guitar, the rhythmical clapping of hands and the castanets, as two girls dance in
the sunlight on a holiday. I see the crowds going to the bull-
fight, intensely living, many-coloured. And a thousand scents are
wafted across my memory; I remember the cloudless nights, the
silence of sleeping towns, and the silence of desert country;
I remember old whitewashed taverns, and the perfumed wines
of Malaga, of Jerez, and of Manzanilla. (The rain pours down
without stay in oblique long lines, the light is quickly failing, the
street is sad and very cheerless.) I feel on my shoulder the touch
of dainty hands, of little hands with tapering fingers, and on my
mouth the kisses of red lips, and I hear a joyous laugh. I remember
the voice that bade me farewell that last night in Seville, and the
gleam of dark eyes and dark hair at the foot of the stairs, as I
looked back from the gate. "*Feliz viage, mi Inglesito.*"

It was not love I felt for you, Rosarito; I wish it had been; but
now far away, in the rain, I fancy, (oh no, not that I am at last in

love,) but perhaps that I am just faintly enamoured – of your recollection.

THE CHURCHES OF RONDA

AT THE CHURCH of the *Espirito Santo*, in a little chapel behind one of the transept altars, I saw, through a huge rococo frame of gilded wood, a *Maria de los Dolores* that was almost terrifying in poignant realism. She wore a robe of black damask, which stood as if it were cast of bronze in heavy, austere folds, a velvet cloak decorated with the old lace known as *rose point d'Espagne*; and on her head a massive imperial diadem, and a golden aureole. Seven candles burned before her; and at vespers, when the church was nearly dark, they threw a cold, sharp light upon her countenance. Her eyes were in deep shadow, strangely mysterious, and they made the face, so small beneath the pompous crown, horribly life-like: you could not see the tears, but you felt they were eyes which would never cease from weeping.

I suppose it was all tawdry and vulgar and common, but a woman knelt in front of the Mother of Sorrows, praying, a poor woman in a ragged shawl; I heard a sob, and saw that she was weeping; she sought to restrain herself and in the effort a tremor passed through her body, and she drew the shawl more closely round her.

I walked away, and came presently to the most cruel of all these images. It was a *Pietà*. The Mother held on her knees the dead Son, looking in His face, and it was a ghastly contrast between her royal array and His naked body. She, too, wore the imperial crown, with its golden aureole, and her cloak was of damask embroidered with heavy gold. Her hair fell in curling abundance about her breast, and the sacristan told me it was the hair of a lady who had lost her husband and her only son. But the dead Christ was terrible, His face half hidden by the long straight hair, long as a woman's, and His body thin and all discoloured: from the wounds thick blood poured out, and their edges were swollen and red; the broken knees, the feet and hands, were purple and green with the beginning of putrefaction.

THE MOSQUE AT CORDOVA

BUT CORDOVA, FROM which Az-Zahra was about four miles distant, has visible delights that can vie with its neighbour's vanished
pomp. I know nothing that can give a more poignant emotion
than the interior of the mosque at Cordova; and yet I remember
well the splendour of barbaric and oriental magnificence which
was my first sight of St. Mark's at Venice, as I came abruptly from
the darkness of an alley into the golden light of the Piazza. But
to me at least the famous things of Italy, known from childhood
in picture and in description, afford more than anything a joyful
sense of recognition, a feeling as it were of home-coming, such
as may hope to experience the devout Christian on entering
upon his heritage in the Kingdom of Heaven. The mosque of
Cordova is oriental and barbaric too; but I had never seen nor
imagined anything in the least resembling it; there was no disillu-
sionment possible, as too often in Italy, for the accounts I had
read prepared me not at all for that overwhelming impression.
It was so weird and strange, I felt myself transported suddenly to
another world.

They were singing Vespers when I entered, and I heard the
shrill voices of choristers crying the responses; it did not sound
like Christian music. The mosque was dimly lit, the air heavy
with incense; and I saw this forest of pillars, extending every way,
as far as the eye could reach. It was mysterious and awe-inspiring
as those enchanted forests of one's childhood in which huge trees
grew in serried masses and where in cavernous darkness goblins
and giants of the fairy-tales, wild beasts and monstrous shapes,
lay in wait for the terrified traveller who had lost his way. I wandered, keeping the Christian chapels out of sight, trying to lose
myself among the columns; and now and then gained views of
horseshoe arches interlacing, decorated with Moorish tracery.

At length I came to the *Mihrab*, which is the Holy of Holies,
the most exquisite as well as the most sacred part of the mosque.
It is approached by a vestibule of which the roof is a miracle of
grace, with mosaics that glow like precious stones, ultramarine,
scarlet, emerald, and gold. The arch between the chambers is
ornamented with four pillars of coloured marble, and again with
mosaic, the gold letters of an Arabic inscription forming on the
deep sapphire of the background a decorative pattern. The

Mihrab itself, which contained the famous Koran of Othman, has seven sides of white marble, and the roof is a huge shell cut from a single block.

I tried to picture to myself the mosque before the Christians laid their desecrating hands upon it. The floor was of coloured tiles, tiles such as may still be seen in the Alhambra of Granada and in the Alcazar at Seville. The columns are of marble, of porphyry and jasper; tradition says they came from Carthage, from pagan temples in France and Christian churches in Spain; they are slender and unadorned, they must have contrasted astonishingly with the roof of larch wood, all ablaze with gold and with vermilion.

There were three hundred chandeliers; and eight thousand lamps – cast of Christian bells – hung from the roof. The Arab writer tells of gold shining from the ceiling like fire, blazing like lightning when it darts across the clouds. The pulpit, wherein was kept the Koran, was of ivory and of exquisite woods, of ebony and sandal, of plantain, citron and aloe, fastened together with gold and silver nails and encrusted with priceless gems. It needed six Khalifs and Almanzor, the great Vizier, to complete the mosque of which Arab writers, with somewhat prosaic enthusiasm, said that "in all the lands of Islam there was none of equal size, none more admirable in its workmanship, in its construction and durability."

Then the Christians conquered Cordova, and the charming civilization of the Moors was driven out by monks and priests and soldiers. First they built only chapels in the outermost aisles; but in a little while, to make room for a choir, they destroyed six rows of columns; and at last, when Master Martin Luther had rekindled Catholic piety, they set up a great church in the very middle of the mosque. The story of this vandalism is somewhat quaint, and one detail at least affords a suggestion that might prove useful in the present time; for the Town Council of Cordova menaced with death all who should assist in the work: one imagines that a similar threat from the Lord Mayor of London might have a salutary effect upon the restorers of Westminster Abbey or the decorators of St. Paul's. How very much more entertaining must have been the world when absolutism was the fashion and the preposterous method of universal suffrage had never been considered! But the Chapter, as those in power always are, was bent upon restoring, and induced Charles V. to give the necessary authority. The king, however, had not understood what they wished to do, and when later he visited Cordova and saw what had happened, he turned to the dignitaries who were pointing out the improvements and said: "You have built what you or others might have built anywhere, but you have destroyed something that was unique in the world." The words show a fine scorn; but as a warning to later generations it would have been more to the purpose to cut off a dozen priestly heads.

Yet oddly enough the Christian additions are not so utterly discordant as one would expect! Hernan Ruiz did the work well, even though it was work he might conveniently have been drawn and quartered for doing. Typically Spanish in its fine proportion, in its exuberance of fantastic decoration, his church is a masterpiece of plateresque architecture. Nor are the priests entirely out of harmony with the building wherein they worship. For an hour they had sung Vespers, and the deep voices of the canons, chaunting monotonously, rang weird and long among the columns; but they finished, and left the choir one by one, walking silently across the church to the sacristy. The black cassock and the scarlet hood made a fine contrast, while the short cambric surplice added to the costume a most delicate grace. One of them paused to speak with two ladies in *mantillas*, and the three made a picturesque group, suggesting all manner of old Spanish romance.

THE COURT OF ORANGES

AND THE THOUGHT impressed itself upon me while I lingered in that peaceful spot, that there was far more to be said for the simple pleasures of sense than northern folk would have us believe. The English have still much of that ancient puritanism which finds a vague sinfulness in the uncostly delights of sunshine, and colour, and ease of mind. It is well occasionally to leave the eager turmoil of great cities for such a place as this, where one may learn that there are other, more natural ways of living, that it is possible still to spend long days, undisturbed by restless passion, without regret or longing, content in the various show that nature offers, asking only that the sun should shine and the happy seasons run their course.

An English engineer whom I had seen at the hotel, approaching me, expressed the idea in his own graphic manner. "Down here there are a good sight more beer and skittles in life than up in Sheffield!"

One canon especially interested me, a little thin man, bent and wrinkled, apparently of fabulous age, but still something of a dandy, for he wore his clothes with a certain air, as though half a century before, byronically, he had been quite a devil with the ladies. The silver buckle on his shoes was most elegant, and he protruded his foot as though the violet silk of his stocking gave him a discreet pleasure. To the very backbone he was an optimist, finding existence evidently so delightful that it did not even need rose-coloured spectacles. He was an amiable old man, perhaps a little narrow, but very indulgent to the follies of others. He had committed no sin himself – for many years: a suspicion of personal vanity is in itself proof of a pure and gentle mind; and as for the sins of others – they were probably not heinous, and at all events would gain forgiveness. The important thing, surely, was to be sound in dogma. The day wore on and the sun now shone only in a narrow space; and this the canon perambulated, smoking the end of a cigarette, the delectable frivolity of which contrasted pleasantly with his great age. He nodded affably to other priests as they passed, a pair of young men, and one obese old creature with white hair and an expression of comfortable self-esteem. He removed his hat with a great and courteous sweep when a lady of his acquaintance crossed his path. The priests basking in the warmth were like four great black cats. It was indeed a pleasant spot, and contentment oozed into one by every pore. The canon rolled himself another cigarette, smiling as he inhaled the first sweet whiffs; and one could not but think the sovereign herb must greatly ease the journey along the steep and narrow way which leads to Paradise. The smoke rose into the air lazily, and the old cleric paused now and again to look at it, the little smile of self-satisfaction breaking on his lips.

Up in the North, under the cold grey sky, God Almighty may be a hard taskmaster, and the Kingdom of Heaven is attained only by much endeavour; but in Cordova these things come more easily. The aged priest walks in the sun and smokes his *cigarillo*. Heaven is not such an inaccessible place after all. Evidently he feels that he has done his duty – with the help of Havana tobacco – in that state of life wherein it has pleased a merciful providence to place him; and St. Peter would never be so churlish as to close the golden gates in the face of an ancient canon who sauntered to them jauntily, with the fag end of a cigarette in the corner of his mouth. Let us cultivate our cabbages in the best of all possible worlds; and afterwards – *Dieu pardonnera; c'est son métier.*

Three months later in the *Porvenir,* under the heading, "Suicide of a Priest," I read that one of these very canons of the Cathedral at Cordova had shot himself. A report was heard, said the journal, and the Civil Guard arriving, found the man prostrate with blood pouring from his ear, a revolver by his side. He was transported to the hospital, the sacrament administered, and he died. In his pockets they found a letter, a pawn-ticket, a woman's bracelet, and some peppermint lozenges. He was thirty-five years old. The newspaper moralized as follows: "When even the illustrious order to which the defunct belonged is tainted with such a crime, it is well to ask whither tends the incredulity of society which finds an end to its sufferings in the barrel of a revolver. Let moralists and philosophers combat with all their might this dreadful tendency; let them make even the despairing comprehend that death is not the highest good but the passage to an unknown world where, according to Christian belief, the ill deeds of this existence are punished and the virtuous rewarded."

SEVILLE

THE IMPRESSION LEFT by strange towns and cities is often a matter of circumstance, depending upon events in the immediate past; or on the chance which, during his earliest visit, there befell the traveller. After a stormy passage across the Channel, Newhaven, from the mere fact of its situation on solid earth, may gain a fascination which closer acquaintance can never entirely destroy; and even Birmingham, first seen by a lurid sunset, may so affect the imagination as to appear for ever like some infernal, splendid city, restless with the hurried toil of gnomes and goblins. So to myself Seville means ten times more than it can mean to others. I came to it after weary years in London, heartsick with much hoping, my mind dull with drudgery; and it seemed a land of freedom. There I became at last conscious of my youth, and it seemed a *belvedere* upon a new life. How can I forget the delight of wandering in the Sierpes, released at length from all imprisoning ties, watching the various movement as though it were a stage-play, yet half afraid that the falling curtain would bring back reality! The songs, the dances, the happy idleness of orange-gardens, the gay turbulence of Seville by night; ah! there at least I seized life eagerly, with both hands, forgetting everything but that time was short and existence full of joy. I sat in the warm sunshine, inhaling the pleasant odours, reminding myself that I had no duty to do then, or the morrow, or the day after. I lay a-bed thinking how happy, effortless and free would be my day. Mounting my horse, I clattered through the narrow streets, over the cobbles, till I came to the country; the air was fresh and sweet, and Aguador loved the spring mornings. When he put his feet to the springy turf he gave a little shake of pleasure, and without a sign from me broke into a gallop. To the amazement of shepherds guarding their wild flocks, to the confusion of herds of brown pigs, scampering hastily as we approached, he and I excited by the wind singing in our ears, we pelted madly through the country. And the whole land laughed with the joy of living.

But I love also the recollection of Seville in the grey days of December, when the falling rain offered a grateful contrast to the unvarying sunshine. Then new sights delighted the eye, new perfumes the nostril. In the decay of that long southern autumn a more sombre opulence was added to the gay colours; a different spirit filled the air, so that I realized suddenly that old romantic Spain of Ferdinand and Isabella. It lay a-dying still, gorgeous in corruption, sober yet flamboyant, rich and poverty-stricken, squalid, magnificent. The white streets, the dripping trees, the clouds gravid with rain, gave to all things an adorable melancholy, a sad, poetic charm. Looking back, I cannot dismiss the suspicion that my passionate emotions were somewhat ridiculous, but at twenty-three one can afford to lack a sense of humour.

* * *

But Seville at first is full of disillusion. It has offered abundant material to the idealist who, as might be expected, has drawn of it a picture which is at once common and pretentious. Your idealist can see no beauty in sober fact, but must array it in all the theatrical properties of a vulgar imagination; he must give to things more imposing proportions, he colours gaudily; Nature for him is ever posturing in the full glare of footlights. Really he stands on no higher level than the housemaid who sees in every woman a duchess in black velvet, an Aubrey Plantagenet in plain John Smith. So I, in common with many another traveller, expected to find in the Guadalquivir a river of transparent green, with orange-groves along its banks, where wandered ox-eyed youths and maidens beautiful. Palm-trees, I thought, rose towards heaven, like passionate souls longing for release from earthly bondage; Spanish women, full-breasted and sinuous, danced *boleros*, *fandangos*, while the air rang with the joyous sound of castanets, and toreadors in picturesque habiliments twanged the light guitar.

Alas! the Guadalquivir is like yellow mud, and moored to the busy quays lie cargo-boats lading fruit or grain or mineral; there no perfume scents the heavy air. The nights, indeed, are calm and clear, and the stars shine brightly; but the river banks see no amours more romantic than those of stokers from Liverpool or Glasgow, and their lady-loves have neither youth nor beauty.

Yet Seville has many a real charm to counter-balance these lost illusions. He that really knows it, like an ardent lover with his mistress' imperfections, would have no difference; even the Guadalquivir, so matter-of-fact, really so prosaic, has an un-imagined attractiveness; the crowded shipping, the hurrying porters, add to that sensation of vivacity which is of Seville the most fascinating characteristic. And Seville is an epitome of Andalusia, with its life and death, with its colour and vivid contrasts, with its boyish gaiety.

It is a city of delightful ease, of freedom and sunshine, of torrid heat. There it does not matter what you do, nor when, nor how you do it. There is none to hinder you, none to watch. Each takes his ease, and is content that his neighbour should do the like. Doubtless people are lazy in Seville, but good heavens! why should one be so terribly strenuous? Go into the Plaza Nueva, and you will see it filled with men of all ages, of all classes, "taking the sun"; they promenade slowly, untroubled by any mental activity, or sit on benches between the palm-trees, smoking cigarettes; perhaps the more energetic read the bull-fighting news in the paper. They are not ambitious, and they do not greatly care to make their fortunes; so long as they have enough to eat and drink — food is very cheap — and cigarettes to smoke, they are quite happy. The Corporation provides seats, and the sun shines down for nothing — so let them sit in it and warm themselves. I daresay it is as good a way of getting through life as most others.

A southern city never reveals its true charm till the summer, and few English know what Seville is under the burning sun of July. It was built for the great heat, and it is only then that the refreshing coolness of the *patio* can be appreciated. In the streets the white glare is mitigated by awnings that stretch from house to house, and the half light in the Sierpes, the High Street, has a curious effect; the people in their summer garb walk noiselessly, as though the warmth made sound impossible. Towards evening the sail-cloths are withdrawn, and a breath of cold air sinks down; the population bestirs itself, and along the Sierpes the *cafés* become suddenly crowded and noisy.

Then, for it was too hot to ride earlier, I would mount my horse and cross the river. The Guadalquivir had lost its winter russet, and under the blue sky gained varied tints of liquid gold, of emerald and of sapphire. I lingered in Triana, the gipsy-quarter, watching the people. Beautiful girls stood at the windows, so that the whole way was lined with them, and their lips were not unwilling to break into charming smiles. One especially I remember who was used to sit on a balcony at a street-corner; her hair was irreproachable in its elaborate arrangement, and the red carnation in it gleamed like fire against the night. Her face was long, fairer-complexioned than is common, with regular and delicate features. She sat at her balcony, with a huge book open on her knee, which she read with studied disregard of the passers-by; but when I looked back sometimes I saw that she had lifted her eyes, lustrous and dark, and they met mine gravely.

And in the country I passed through long fields of golden corn, which reached as far as I could see; I remembered the spring, when it had all been new, soft, fresh, green. And presently I turned round to look at Seville in the distance, bathed in brilliant light, glowing as though its walls were built of yellow flame. The Giralda arose in its wonderful grace like an arrow; so slim, so comely, it reminded one of an Arab youth, with long, thin limbs. With the setting sun, gradually the city turned rosy-red and seemed to lose all substantiality, till it became a many-shaped mist that was dissolved in the tenderness of the sky.

Late in the night I stood at my window looking at the cloudless heaven. From the earth ascended, like incense, the mellow odours of summertime; the belfry of the neighbouring church stood boldly outlined against the darkness, and the storks that had built their nest upon it were motionless, not stirring even as the bells rang out the hours. The city slept, and it seemed that I alone watched in the silence; the sky still was blue, and the stars shone in their countless millions. I thought of the city that never rested, of London with its unceasing roar, the endless streets, the greyness. And all around me was a quiet serenity, a tranquillity such as the Christian may hope shall reward him in Paradise for the troublous pilgrimage of life. But that is long ago and passed for ever.

THE GIRALDA

I LOOKED DOWN at Seville from above. A Spanish town wears always its most picturesque appearance thus seen, but it is never different; the *patios* glaring with whitewash, the roofs of brown and yellow tiles, and the narrow streets, winding in unexpected directions, narrower than ever from such a height and dark with shade, so that they seem black rivulets gliding stealthily through the whiteness. Looking at a northern city from a tall church tower all things are confused with one another, the slate roofs join together till it is like a huge uneven sea of grey; but in Seville the atmosphere is so limpid, the colour so brilliant, that every house is clearly separated from its neighbour, and sometimes there appears to be between them a preternatural distinctness. Each stands independently of any other; you might suppose yourself in a strange city of the *Arabian Nights* where a great population lived in houses crowded together, but invisibly, so that each person fancied himself in isolation.

Immediately below was the Cathedral and to remind you of

Cordova, the Court of Oranges; but here was no sunny restful-
ness, nor old-world quiet. The Court is gloomy and dark, and
the trim rows of orange-trees contrast oddly with the grey stone
of the Cathedral, its huge porches, and the flamboyant exuberance of its decoration. The sun never shines in it and no fruit
splash the dark foliage with gold. You do not think of the generations of priests who have wandered in it on the summer evenings,
basking away their peaceful lives in the sunshine; but rather of
the busy merchants who met there in the old days when it was
still the exchange of Seville, before the Lonja was built, to discuss
the war with England, or the fate of ships bringing gold from
America. At one end of the court is an old stone pulpit from
which preached St. Francis of Borga and St. Vincent Ferrer and
many an unknown monk besides. Then it was thronged with
multi-coloured crowds, with townsmen, soldiers and great
noblemen, when faith was living and strong; and the preacher,
with all the gesture and the impassioned rhetoric of a Spaniard,
poured out burning words of hate for Jew and Moor and Heretic,
so that the listeners panted and a veil of blood passed before their
eyes; or else uttered so eloquent a song in praise of the Blessed
Virgin, immaculately conceived, that strong men burst into tears
at the recital of her perfect beauty.

GAOL

I WAS CURIOUS to see the prison in Seville. Gruesome tales had
been told me of its filth and horror, and the wretched condition
of the prisoners; I had even heard that from the street you might
see them pressing against the barred windows with arms thrust
through, begging the passer-by for money or bread. Mediæval
stories recurred to my mind and the clank of chains trailed
through my imagination.

I arranged to be conducted by the prison doctor, and one
morning soon after five set out to meet him. My guide informed
me by a significant gesture that his tendencies were – bibulous,
and our meeting-place was a tavern; but when we arrived they
told us that don Felipe – such was his name – had been, taken
his morning dram and gone; however, if we went to another inn
we should doubtless find him. But there we heard he had not yet

arrived, he was not due till half-past five. To pass the time we drank a mouthful of *aguardiente* and smoked a cigarette, and eventually the medico was espied in the distance. We went towards him – a round, fat person with a red face and a redder nose, somewhat shabbily dressed.

He looked at me pointedly and said:

"I'm dry. *Vengo seco.*"

It was a hint not to be neglected, and we returned to the tavern where don Felipe had his nip.

"It's very good for the stomach," he assured me.

We sallied forth together, and as we walked he told me the number of prisoners, the sort of crimes for which they were detained – ranging from manslaughter to petty larceny – and finally, details of his own career. He was an intelligent man, and when we came to the prison door insisted on drinking my health.

The prison is an old convent, and it is a little startling to see the church façade, with a statue of the Madonna over the central porch. At the steps a number of women stood waiting with pots and jars and handkerchiefs full of food for their relatives within; and when the doctor appeared several rushed up to ask about a father or a son that lay sick. We went in and there was a melo-dramatic tinkling of keys and an unlocking of heavy doors.

The male prisoners, the adults, were in the *patio* of the con-vent, where in olden days the nuns had wandered on summer evenings, watering their roses. The iron door was opened and shut behind us; there was a movement of curiosity at the sight of a stranger, and many turned to look at me. Such as had illnesses came to the doctor, and he looked at their tongues and felt their pulse, giving directions to an assistant who stood beside him with a notebook. Don Felipe was on excellent terms with his patients, laughing and joking; a malingerer asked if he could not have a little wine because his throat was sore; the doctor jeered and the man began to laugh; they bandied repartees with one another.

There were about two hundred in the *patio*, and really they did not seem to have so bad a time. There was one large group gathered round a man who read a newspaper aloud; it was Monday morning, and all listened intently to the account of a bull-fight on the previous day, bursting into a little cry of surprise and admiration on hearing that the *matador* had been caught and tossed. Others lay by a pillar playing draughts for matches, while half a dozen more eagerly watched, giving unsolicited advice with much gesticulation. The draught-board consisted of little squares drawn on the pavement with chalk, and the pieces were scraps of white and yellow paper. One man sat cross-legged by a column busily rolling cigarettes; he had piles of them by his side arranged in packets, which he sold at one penny each; it was certainly an illegal offence, because the sale of tobacco is a government monopoly, but if you cannot break the laws in prison where can you break them? Others occupied themselves by making baskets or nets. But the majority did nothing at all, standing about, sitting when they could, with the eternal cigarette between their lips; and the more energetic watched the blue smoke curl into the air. Altogether a very happy family!

Nor did they seem really very criminal, more especially as they wore no prison uniform, but their own clothes. I saw no difference between them and the people I met casually in the street. They were just very ordinary citizens, countrymen smelling of the soil, labouring men, artisans. Their misfortune had been only to make too free a use of their long curved knives or to be discovered taking something over which another had prior claims. But in Andalusia every one is potentially as criminal, which is the same as saying that these jail-birds were estimable persons whom an unkind fate and a mistaken idea of justice had separated for a little while from their wives and families.

I saw two only whose aspect was distinctly vicious. One was a tall fellow with shifty eyes, a hard thin mouth, a cruel smile, and his face was really horrible. I asked the doctor why he was there. Don Felipe, without speaking, made the peculiar motion of the fingers which signifies robbery, and the man seeing him repeated it with a leer. I have seldom seen a face that was so utterly repellent, so depraved and wicked: I could not get it out of my head, and for a long time saw before me the crafty eyes and the grinning mouth. Obviously the man was a criminal born who would start thieving as soon as he was out of prison, hopelessly and utterly corrupt. But it was curious that his character should be marked so plainly on his face; it was a danger-signal to his fellows, and one would have thought the suspicion it aroused must necessarily keep him virtuous. It was a countenance that would make a man instinctively clap his hand to his pocket.

The other was a Turk, a huge creature, with dark scowling face and prominent brows; he made a singular figure in his bright fez and baggy breeches, looking at his fellow prisoners with a frown of hate.

But the doctor had finished seeing his patients and the iron door was opened for us to go out. We went upstairs to the hospital, a long bare ward, terribly cheerless. Six men, perhaps, lay in bed, guarded by two warders; one old fellow with rheumatism groaning in agony, two others dazed and very still, with high fever. We walked round quickly, don Felipe as before mechanically looking at their tongues and feeling their pulse, speaking a word to the assistant and moving on. The windows were shut and there was a horrid stench of illness and drugs and antiseptics.

We went through long corridors to the female side, and meanwhile the assistant told the doctor that during the night a woman had been confined. Don Felipe sat down in an office to write a certificate.

"What a nuisance these women are!" he said. "Why can't they wait till they get out of prison? How is it?"

"It was still-born."

"*Pero, hombre,*" said the doctor crossly. "Why didn't you tell me that before? Now I shall have to write another certificate. This one's no good."

He tore it up and painfully made out a second with the slow laborious writing of a man unused to holding a pen.

Then we marched on and came to another smaller *patio* where the females were. They were comparatively few, not more than twenty or thirty; and when we entered a dark inner-room to see the woman who was ill they all trooped in after us – all but one. They stood round eagerly telling us of the occurrence.

"Don't make such a noise, *por Dios*! I can't hear myself speak," said the doctor.

The woman was lying on her back with flushed cheeks, her eyes staring glassily. The doctor asked a question, but she did not answer. She began to cry, sobbing from utter weakness in a silent, unrestrained way. On a table near her, hidden by a cloth, lay the dead child.

We went out again into the *patio*. The sun was higher now and it was very warm, the blue sky shone above us without a cloud. The prisoners returned to their occupations. One old hag was doing a younger woman's hair; I noticed that even for Spain it was beautiful, very thick, curling, and black as night. The girl held a carnation in her hand to put in front of the comb when the operation was completed. Another woman suckled a baby, and several tiny children were playing about happily, while their mothers chatted to one another, knitting.

But there was one, markedly different from the others, who sat alone taking no notice of the scene. It was she who remained in the *patio* when the rest followed us into the sick room, a gipsy, tall and gaunt, with a skin of the darkest yellow. Her hair was not elaborately arranged as that of her companions, but plainly done, drawn back stiffly from the forehead. She sat there, erect and motionless, looking at the ground with an unnatural stare, silent. They told me she never spoke a word nor paid attention to the women in the court. She might have been entirely alone. She never altered her position, but sat there, sphinx-like, in that attitude of stony grief. She was a stranger among the rest, and her bronzed face, her silence gave a weird impression; she seemed to recall the burning deserts of the East and an endless past.

At last we came out, and the heavy iron door was closed behind us. What a relief it was to be in the street again, to see the sun and the trees, and to breathe the free air! A cart went by with a great racket, drawn by three mules, and the cries of the driver as he cracked his whip were almost musical; a train of donkeys passed; a man trotted by on a brown shaggy cob, his huge panniers filled with glowing vegetables, green and red, and in a corner was a great bunch of roses. I took long breaths of the free air, I shook myself to get rid of those prison odours.

I offered don Felipe refreshment and we repaired to a dram-shop immediately opposite. Two women were standing there.

"*Ole!*" said the doctor to an old toothless hag with a vicious leer. "What are you doing here? You've not been in for some time."

She laughed and explained that she was come to fetch her friend, a young woman, who had been released that morning. The doctor nodded to her, asking how long she had been in gaol.

"Two years and nine months," she said.

And she began to laugh hysterically with tears streaming down her cheeks.

"I don't know what I'm doing," she cried. "I can't understand it."

She looked into the street with wild, yearning eyes; everything seemed to her strange and new.

"I haven't seen a tree for nearly three years," she sobbed.

But the hag was pressing the doctor to drink with her; he accepted without much hesitation, and gallantly proposed her health.

"What are you going to do?" he said to the younger woman, she was hardly more than a girl. "You'd better not hang about in Seville or you'll get into trouble again."

"Oh no," she said, "I'm going to my village – *mi pueblo* – this afternoon. I want to see my husband and my child."

Don Felipe turned to me and asked what I thought of the Seville prison. I made some complimentary reply.

"Are English prisons like that?" he asked.

I said I did not think so.

"Are they better?"

I shrugged my shoulders.

"I'm told," he said, "that two years' hard labour in an English prison kills a man."

"The English are a great nation," I replied.

"And a humane one," he added, with a bow and a smile.

I bade him good-morning.

CORRIDA DE TOROS

THE DOORS ARE opened two hours before the performance. Through the morning the multitude has trooped to the Plaza San Fernando to buy tickets, and in the afternoon all Seville wends its way towards the ring. The road is thronged with people, they walk in dense crowds, pushing one another to get out of the way of broken-down shays that roll along filled with enthusiasts. The drivers crack their whips, shouting: "*Un real, un real a los Toros!*" *

* "Twopence-halfpenny to the Bulls."

The sun beats down and the sky is intensely blue. It is very hot, already people are blowing and panting, boys sell *fans* at a half-penny each. *"Abanicos a perra chica!"**

When you come near the ring the din is tremendous; the many vendors shout their wares, middlemen offer tickets at double the usual price, friends call to one another. Now and then is a quarrel, a quick exchange of abuse as one pushes or treads upon his neighbour; but as a rule all are astonishingly good-natured. A man, after a narrow escape from being run over, will shout a joke to the driver, who is always ready with a repartee. And they surge on towards the entrance. Every one is expectant and thrilled, the very air seems to give a sense of exhilaration. The people crowd in like ants. All things are gay and full of colour and life.

A *picador* passes on horseback in his uncouth clothes, and all turn to look at him.

And in the ring itself the scene is marvellous. On one side the sun beats down with burning rays, and there, the seats being cheaper, notwithstanding the terrific heat people are closely packed. There is a perpetual irregular movement of thousands of women's fans fluttering to and fro. Opposite, in the shade, are nearly as many persons, but of better class. Above, in the boxes sit ladies in mantillas, and when a beautiful woman appears she is often greeted with a burst of applause, which she takes most unconcernedly. When at last the ring is full, tier above tier crammed so that not a place is vacant, it gives quite an extra-ordinary emotion. The serried masses cease then to be a collec-tion of individuals, but gain somehow a corporate unity; you realize, with a kind of indeterminate fear, the many-headed beast of savage instincts and of ruthless might. No crowd is more picturesque than the Spanish, and the dark masculine costume vividly contrasts with the bright colours of the women, with flowers in their hair and *mantillas* of white lace.

But also the tremendous vitality of it all strikes you. Late arrivals walk along looking for room, gesticulating, laughing, bandying jokes; vendors of all sorts cry out their goods: the men who sell prawns, shrimps, and crabs' claws from Cadiz pass with large baskets: *"Bocas, bocas!"*

* "Fans, one halfpenny each !"

The water sellers with huge jars: "*Agua, quien, quiere agua? Agua!*"* The word sings along the interminable rows. A man demands a glass and hands down a halfpenny; a mug of sparkling water is sent up to him. It is deliciously cool.

The sellers of lottery tickets, offering as usual the first prize: "*Premio gordo, quien quiere el premio gordo*";† or yelling the number of the ticket: "Who wants number seventeen hundred and eighty-five for three *pesetas*?"

And the newsboys add to the din: "*Noticiero! Porvenir!*" Later on arrives the Madrid paper: "*Heraldo ! Heraldo!*"

Lastly the men with stacks of old journals to use as seats: "*A perra chica, dos periodicos a perra chica!*"‡

Suddenly there is a great clapping of hands, and looking up you find the president has come; he is supported by two friends, and all three, with comic solemnity, wear tall hats and frock coats. They bow to the public. Bull-fighting is the only punctual thing in Spain, and the president arrives precisely as the clock strikes half-past four. He waves a handkerchief, the band strikes up, a door is opened, and the fighters enter. First come the three *matadors*, the eldest in the middle, the next on his right, and the youngest on the left; they are followed by their respective *cuadrillas*, the *banderilleros*, the *capeadors*, the *picadors* on horseback, and finally the *chulos*, whose duty it is to unsaddle dead horses, attach the slaughtered bull to the team of mules, and perform other minor offices. They advance, gorgeous in their coloured satin and gold embroidery, bearing a cloak peculiarly folded over the arm; they walk with a kind of swinging motion, as ordained by the convention of a century. They bow to the president, very solemnly. The applause is renewed. They retire to the side, three *picadors* take up their places at some distance from one another on the right of the door from which issues the bull. The *alguaciles*, in black velvet, with peaked and feathered hats, on horseback, come forward, and the key of the bull's den is thrown to them. They disappear. The fighters meanwhile exchange their satin cloaks for others of less value. There is another flourish of trumpets, the gates are opened for the bull.

---

* "Water, who wants water? Water!"
† "The first prize, who wants the first prize?"
‡ "One halfpenny, two papers for one halfpenny."

Then comes a moment of expectation, every one is trembling with excitement. There is perfect silence. All eyes are fixed on the open gate.

WIND AND STORM

PRESENTLY, IN A clearing, I caught sight of three men on donkeys, walking slowly one after the other, and I galloped after to ask my way. The beasts were laden with undressed skins which they were taking to Fuentes, and each man squatted cross-legged on the top of his load. The hindermost turned right round when I asked my question and sat unconcernedly with his back to the donkey's head. He looked about him vaguely as though expecting the information I sought to be written on the trunk of an olive-tree, and scratched his head.

"Well," he said, "I should think it was a matter of seven leagues, but it will rain before you get there."

"This is the right way, isn't it?"

"It may be. If it doesn't lead to Marchena it must lead somewhere else."

There was a philosophic ring about the answer which made up for the uncertainty. The skinner was a fat, good-humoured creature, like all Spaniards intensely curious; and to prepare the way for inquiries, offered a cigarette.

"But why do you come to Ecija by so roundabout a way as Carmona, and why should you return to Seville by such a route as Marchena ?"

His opinion was evidently that the shortest way between two places was also the best. He received my explanation with incredulity and asked, more insistently, why I went to Ecija on horseback when I might go by train to Madrid.

"For pleasure," said I.

"My good sir, you must have come on some errand."

"Oh yes," I answered, hoping to satisfy him, "on the search for emotion."

At this he bellowed with laughter and turned round to tell his fellows.

"*Usted es muy guason*," he said at length, which may be translated: "You're a mighty funny fellow."

I expressed my pleasure at having provided the skinners with amusement and bidding them farewell, trotted on.

I went for a long time among the interminable olives, grey and sad beneath the sullen clouds, and at last the rain began to fall. I saw a farm not very far away and cantered up to ask for shelter. An old woman and a labourer came to the door and looked at me very doubtfully; they said it was not a *posada*, but my soft words turned their hearts and they allowed me to come in. The rain poured down in heavy, oblique lines.

The labourer took Aguador to the stable and I went into the parlour, a long, low, airy chamber like the refectory of a monastery, with windows reaching to the ground. Two girls were sitting round the *brasero*, sewing; they offered me a chair by their side, and as the rain fell steadily we began to talk. The old woman discreetly remained away. They asked about my journey, and as is the Spanish mode, about my country, myself, and my belongings. It was a regular volley of questions I had to answer, but they sounded pleasanter in the mouth of a pretty girl than in that of an obese old skinner; and the rippling laughter which greeted my replies made me feel quite witty. When they smiled they showed the whitest teeth. Then came my turn for questioning. The girl on my right, prettier than her sister, was very Spanish, with black, expressive eyes, an olive skin, and a bunch of violets in her abundant hair. I asked whether she had a *novio*, or lover; and the question set her laughing immoderately. What was her name? "Soledad – Solitude."

I looked somewhat anxiously at the weather, I feared the shower would cease, and in a minute, alas! the rain passed away; and I was forced to notice it, for the sun-rays came dancing through the window, importunately, making patterns of light upon the floor. I had no further excuse to stay, and said goodbye; but I begged for the bunch of violets in Soledad's dark hair and she gave it with a pretty smile. I plunged again into the endless olive-groves.

It was a little strange, the momentary irruption into other people's lives, the friendly gossip with persons of a different tongue and country, whom I had never seen before, whom I should never see again; and were I not strictly truthful I might here lighten my narrative by the invention of a charming and romantic adventure. But if chance brings us often for a moment into other existences, it takes us out with equal suddenness so that we scarcely know whether they were real or mere imaginings of an idle hour: the Fates have a passion for the unfinished sketch and seldom trouble to unravel the threads which they have so laboriously entangled. The little scene brought another to my mind. When I was "on accident duty" at St. Thomas's Hospital a man brought his son with a broken leg; it was hard luck on the little chap, for he was seated peacefully on the ground when another boy, climbing a wall, fell on him and did the damage. When I returned him, duly bandaged, to his father's arms, the child bent forward and put out his lips for a kiss, saying goodnight with babyish pronunciation. The father and the attendant nurse laughed, and I, being young, was confused and blushed profusely. They went away and somehow or other I never saw them again. I wonder if the pretty child, (he must be eight or ten now,) remembers kissing a very weary medical student, who had not slept much for several days, and was dead tired. Probably he has quite forgotten that he ever broke his leg. And I suppose no recollection remains with the pretty girl in the farm of a foreigner riding mysteriously through the olive-groves, to whom she gave shelter and a bunch of violets.

JEREZ

JEREZ IS THE Andalusian sunshine again after the dark clouds of Granada. It is a little town in the middle of a fertile plain, clean and comfortable and spacious. It is one of the richest places in Spain; the houses have an opulent look, and without the help of Baedeker you may guess that they contain respectable persons with incomes, and carriages and horses, with frock coats and gold watch-chains. I like the people of Jerez; their habitual expression suggests a consciousness that the Almighty is pleased with them, and they without doubt are well content with the Almighty. The main street, with its trim shops and its *cafés*, has the air of a French provincial town – an appearance of agreeable ease and dulness.

Every building in Jerez is washed with lime, and in the sunlight the brilliancy is dazzling. You realize then that in Seville the

houses are not white – although the general impression is of a
white town – but, on the contrary, tinted with various colours
from faintest pink to pale blue, pale green; they remind you of
the summer dresses of women. The soft tones are all mingled
with the sunlight and very restful. But Jerez is like a white banner
floating under the cloudless sky, the pure white banner of
Bacchus raised defiantly against the gaudy dyes of teetotalism and
its shrieking trumpets.

Jerez the White is, of course, the home of sherry, and the
whole town is given over to the preparation of the grateful juice.
The air is impregnated with a rich smell. The sun shines down
on Jerez; and its cleanliness, its prosperity, are a rebuke to harsh-
voiced contemners of the grape.

You pass *bodega* after *bodega*, cask-factories, bottle-factories.
A bottle-factory is a curious, interesting place, an immense barn,
sombre, so that the eye loses itself in the shadows of the roof;
and the scanty light is red and lurid from the furnaces, which
roar hoarsely and long. Against the glow the figures of men, half-
naked, move silently, performing the actions of their craft with
a monotonous regularity which is strange and solemn. They
move to and fro, carrying an iron instrument on which is the
molten mass of red-hot glass, and it gleams with an extraordinary
warm brilliancy. It twists hither and thither in obedience to the
artisan's deft movements; it coils and writhes into odd shapes,
like a fire-snake curling in the torture of its own unearthly
ardour. The men pass so regularly, with such a silent and exact
precision, that it seems a weird and mystic measure they perform
– a rhythmic dance of unimaginable intricacy, whose meaning
you cannot gather and whose harmony escapes you. The flames
leap and soar in a thousand savage forms, and their dull thunder
fills your ears with a confusion of sound. Your eyes become
accustomed to the dimness, and you discern more clearly the
features of those swarthy men, bearded and gnome-like. But the
molten mass has been put into the mould; you watch it withdrawn, the bottom indented, the mouth cut and shaped. And
now it is complete, but still red-hot, and glowing with an infernal
transparency, gem-like and wonderful; it is a bottle fit now for
the juice of satanic vineyards, and the miraculous potions of
eternal youth, for which men in the old days bartered their
immortal souls.

And the effect of a *bodega* is picturesque, too, though in a different way. It is a bright and cheerful spot, a huge shed with whitewashed walls and an open roof supported by dark beams; great casks are piled up, impressing you in their vast rotundity with a sort of aldermanic stateliness. The whole place is fragrant with clean, vinous perfumes. Your guide carries a glass and a long filler. You taste wine after wine, in different shades of brown; light wines to drink with your dinner, older wines to drink before your coffee; wines more than a century old, of which the odour is more delicate than violets; new wines of the preceding year, strong and rough; Amontillados, with the softest flavour in the world; Manzanillas for the gouty; Marsalas, heavy and sweet; wines that smell of wild-flowers; cheap wines and expensive wines. Then the brandies – the distiller tells you proudly that Spanish brandy is made from wine, and contemptuously that French brandy is not – old brandies for which a toper would sell his soul; new brandies like fusel-oil; brandies mellow and mild and rich. It is a drunkard's paradise.

And why should not the drinker have his paradise? The tee-totallers have slapped their bosoms and vowed that liquor was the devil's own invention. (Note, by the way, that liquor is a noble word that should not be applied to those weak-kneed abominations that insolently flaunt their lack of alcohol. Let them be called liquids or fluids or beverages, or what you will. Liquor is a word for heroes, for the British tar who has built up British glory – Imperialism is quite the fashion now.) And for a hundred years none has dared lift his voice in refutation of these dyspeptic slanders. The toper did not care, he nursed his bottle and let the world say what it would; but the moderate drinker was abashed. Who will venture to say that a glass of beer gives savour to the humblest crust, and comforts Corydon, lamenting the inconstancy of Phyllis? Who will come forward and strike an attitude and prove the benefits of the grape? (The attitude is essential, for without it you cannot hope to impress your fellow men.) Rise up in your might, ye lovers of hop and grape and rye – rise up and slay the Egyptians. Be honest and thank your stars for the cup that cheers. Bacchus was not a pot-bellied old sot, but a beautiful youth with vine-leaves in his hair, Bacchus the lover of flowers; and Ariadne was charming.

* * *

The country about Jerez undulates in just such an easy comfort-able fashion as you would expect. It is scenery of the gentlest and pleasantest type, sinuous; little hills rising with rounded lines and fertile valleys. The vines cover the whole land, Jerez creeping over the brown soil fantastically, black stumps, shrivelled and gnarled, tortured into uncouth shapes; they remind you of the creeping things in a naturalist's museum, of giant spiders and great dried centipedes and scorpions. But imagine the vineyards later, when the spring has stirred the earth with fecundity! The green shoots tenderly forth; at first it is all too delicate for a colour, it is but a mist of indescribable tenuity; and gradually the leaves burst out and trail along the ground with ever-increasing luxuriance; and then it is a rippling sea of passionate verdure.

But I liked Jerez best towards evening, when the sun had set and the twilight glided through the tortuous alleys like a woman dressed in white. Then, as I walked in the silent streets, narrow and steep, with their cobble-paving, the white houses gained a new aspect. There seemed not a soul in the world, and the loneli-ness was more intoxicating than all their wines; the shining sun was gone, and the sky lost its blue richness, it became so pale that you felt it like a face of death – and the houses looked like long rows of tombs. We walked through the deserted streets, I and the woman dressed in white, side by side silently; our footsteps made no sound upon the stones. And Jerez was wrapped in a ghostly shroud. Ah, the beautiful things I have seen which other men have not!

CADIZ

I ADMIRE THE strenuous tourist who sets out in the morning with his well-thumbed Baedeker to examine the curiosities of a foreign town, but I do not follow in his steps; his eagerness after knowledge, his devotion to duty, compel my respect, but excite me to no imitation. I prefer to wander in old streets at random without a guidebook, trusting that fortune will bring me across things worth seeing; and if occasionally I miss some monument that is world-famous, more often I discover some little dainty piece of architecture, some scrap of decoration, that repays me for all else I lose. And in this fashion the less pretentious beauties

of a town delight me, which, if I sought under the guidance of
the industrious German, would seem perhaps scarcely worth the
trouble. Nor do I know that there is in Cadiz much to attract
the traveller beyond the grace with which it lies along the blue
sea and the unstudied charm of its gardens, streets, and market-
place; the echo in the cathedral to which the gaping tripper
listens with astonishment leaves me unmoved; and in the church
of *Santa Catalina*, which contains the last work of Murillo, upon
which he was engaged at his death, I am more interested in the
tall stout priest, unctuous and astute, who shows me his treasure,
than in the picture itself. I am relieved now and again to visit a
place that has no obvious claims on my admiration; it throws me
back on the peculiarities of the people, on the stray incidents of
the street, on the contents of the shops.

Cadiz is said to be the gayest town in Andalusia. Spaniards have
always a certain gravity; they are not very talkative, and like the
English, take their pleasures a little sadly. But here lightness of
heart is thought to reign supreme, and the inhabitants have not
even the apparent seriousness with which the Sevillan cloaks a
somewhat vacant mind. They are great theatre-goers, and as
dancers, of course, have been famous since the world began. But
I doubt whether Cadiz deserves its reputation, for it always seems
to me a little prim. The streets are well-kept and spacious, the
houses, taller than is usual in Andalusia, have almost as cared-for
an appearance as those in a prosperous suburb of London; and it
is only quite occasionally, when you catch a glimpse of tawny
rock and of white breakwater against the blue sea, that by a reminiscence of Naples you can persuade yourself it is as immoral as
they say. For, not unlike the Syren City, Cadiz lies white and
cool along the bay, with gardens at the water's edge; but it has
not the magic colour of its rival, it is quieter, smaller, more restful; and on the whole lacks that agreeable air of wickedness
which the Italian town possesses to perfection. It is impossible to
be a day in Naples without discovering that it is the most
depraved city in Europe; there is something in the atmosphere
which relaxes the moral fibre, and the churchwarden who keeps
guard in the bosom of every Englishman falls asleep, so that you
feel capable of committing far more than the seven deadly sins.
Of course, you don't, but still it is comfortable to have them
within reach.

ADIOS

AND THEN THE morrow was come. Getting up at five to catch my boat, I went down to the harbour; a grey mist hung over the sea, and the sun had barely risen, a pallid, yellow circle; the fishing boats lolled on the smooth, dim water, and fishermen in little groups blew on their fingers.

And from Cadiz I saw the shores of Spain sink into the sea; I saw my last of Andalusia. Who, when he leaves a place that he has loved, can help wondering when he will see it again? I asked the wind, and it sighed back the Spanish answer: "*Quien sabe? Who knows?*" The traveller makes up his mind to return quickly, but all manner of things happen, and one accident or another prevents him; time passes till the desire is lost, and when at last he comes back, himself has altered or changes have occurred in the old places and all seems different. He looks quite coldly at what had given an intense emotion, and though he may see new things, the others hardly move him; it is not thus he imagined them in the years of waiting. And how can he tell what the future may have in store; perhaps, notwithstanding all his passionate desires, he will indeed never return.

Of course the intention of this book is not to induce people to go to Spain: railway journeys are long and tedious, the trains crawl, and the hotels are bad. Experienced globe-trotters have told me that all mountains are very much alike, and that pictures, when you have seen a great many, offer no vast difference. It is much better to read books of travel than to travel oneself; he really enjoys foreign lands who never goes abroad; and the man who stays at home, preserving his illusions, has certainly the best of it. How delightful is the anticipation as he looks over time-tables and books of photographs, forming delightful images of future pleasure! But the reality is full of disappointment, and the more famous the monument the bitterer the disillusion. Has any one seen St. Peter's without asking himself: Is that all? And the truest enjoyment arises from things that come unexpectedly, that one had never heard of. Then, living in a strange land, one loses all impression of its strangeness; it is only afterwards, in England, that one realizes the charm and longs to return; and a hundred pictures rise to fill the mind with delight. Why can one not be strong enough to leave it at that and never tempt the fates again?

The wisest thing is to leave unvisited in every country some place that one wants very much to see. In Italy I have never been to Siena, and in Andalusia I have taken pains to avoid Malaga. The guidebooks tell me there is nothing whatever to see there; and according to them it is merely a prosperous seaport with a good climate. But to me, who have never seen it, Malaga is something very different; it is the very cream of Andalusia, where every trait and characteristic is refined to perfect expression.

I imagine Malaga to be the most smiling town on the seaboard, and it lies along the shore ten times more charmingly than Cadiz. The houses are white, whiter than in Jerez; the *patios* are beautiful with oranges and palm-trees, and the dark green of the luxuriant foliage contrasts with the snowy walls. In Malaga the sky is always blue and the sun shines, but the narrow Arab streets are cool and shady. The passionate odours of Andalusia float in the air, the perfume of a myriad cigarettes and the fresh scent of fruit and flower. The blue sea lazily kisses the beach and fishing-boats bask on its bosom.

In Malaga, for me, there are dark churches, with massive, tall pillars; the light falls softly through the painted glass, regilding the golden woodwork, the angels and the saints and the bishops in their mitres. The air is heavy with incense, and women in *mantillas* kneel in the half-light, praying silently. Now and then I come across an old house with a fragment of Moorish work, reminding me that here again the Moors have left their mark.

And in Malaga, for me, the women are more lovely than in Seville; for their dark eyes glitter marvellously, and their lips, so red and soft, are ever trembling with a half-formed smile. They are more graceful than the daffodils, their hands are lovers' sighs, and their voice is a caressing song. (What was your voice like, Rosarito? Alas! it is so long ago that I forget.) The men are tall and slender, with strong, clear features and shining eyes, deep sunken in their sockets.

In Malaga, for me, life is a holiday in which there are no dull-ards and no bores; all the world is strong and young and full of health, and there is nothing to remind one of horrible things. Malaga, I know, is the most delightful place in Andalusia. Oh, how refreshing it is to get away from sober fact, but what a fool I should be ever to go there!

* * *

The steamer plods on against the wind slowly, and as the land sinks away, unsatisfied to leave the impressions hovering vaguely through my mind, I try to find the moral. The Englishman, ever somewhat sententiously inclined, asks what a place can teach him. The churchwarden in his bosom gives no constant, enduring peace; and after all, though he may be often ridiculous, it is the churchwarden who has made good part of England's greatness.

And most obviously Andalusia suggests that it might not be ill to take things a little more easily: we English look upon life so very seriously, so much without humour. Is it worth while to be quite so strenuous? At the stations on the line between Jerez and Cadiz, I noticed again how calmly they took things; people lounged idly talking to one another; the officials of the railway smoked their cigarettes; no one was in a hurry, time was long, and whether the train arrived late or punctual could really matter much to no one. A beggar came to the window, a cigarette-end between his lips.

"*Caballero!* Alms for the love of God for a poor old man. God will repay you!"

He passed slowly down the train. It waited for no reason; the passengers stared idly at the loungers on the platform, and they stared idly back. No one moved except to roll himself a cigarette. The sky was blue and the air warm and comforting. Life seemed good enough, and above all things easy. There was no particular cause to trouble. What is the use of hurrying to pile up money when one can live on so little? What is the use of reading these endless books? Why not let things slide a little, and just take what comes our way? It is only for a little while, and then the great antique mother receives us once more in her bosom. And there are so many people in the world. Think again of all the countless hordes who have come and gone, and who will come and go; the immense sea of Time covers them, and what matters the life they led? What odds is it that they ever existed at all? Let us do our best to be happy; the earth is good and sweet-smelling, there is sunshine and colour and youth and loveliness; and afterwards – well, let us shrug our shoulders and not think of it.

SKETCHES OF CHINA

from *On a Chinese Screen*

MY LADY'S PARLOUR

"I REALLY THINK I can make something of it," she said.

She looked about her briskly, and the light of the creative imagination filled her eyes with brightness.

It was an old temple, a small one, in the city, which she had taken and was turning into a dwelling house. It had been built for a very holy monk by his admirers three hundred years before, and here in great piety, practising innumerable austerities, he had passed his declining days. For long after in memory of his virtue the faithful had come to worship, but in course of time funds had fallen very low and at last the two or three monks that remained were forced to leave. It was weather-beaten and the green tiles of the roof were overgrown with weeds. The raftered ceiling was still beautiful with its faded gold dragons on a faded red; but she did not like a dark ceiling, so she stretched a canvas across and papered it. Needing air and sunlight, she cut two large windows on one side. She very luckily had some blue curtains which were just the right size. Blue was her favourite colour: it brought out the colour of her eyes. Since the columns, great red sturdy columns, oppressed her a little she papered them with a very nice paper which did not look Chinese at all. She was lucky also with the paper with which she covered the walls. It was bought in a native shop, but really it might have come from Sanderson's; it was a very nice pink stripe and it made the place look cheerful at once. At the back was a recess in which had stood a great lacquer table and behind it an image of the Buddha in his eternal meditation. Here generations of believers had burned their tapers and prayed, some for this temporal benefit or that, some for release from the returning burden of earthly existence; and this seemed to her the very place for an American stove. She was obliged to buy her carpet in China, but she managed to get one that looked so like an Axminster that you would hardly know the difference. Of course, being hand-made, it had not quite the smoothness of the English article, but it was a very decent substitute. She was able to buy a very nice lot of furniture from a member of the Legation who was leaving the country for a post in Rome, and she got a nice bright chintz from Shanghai to make loose covers with. Fortunately, she had quite a number of pictures, wedding presents and some even that she had bought herself, for she was very artistic, and these gave the room a cosy look. She needed a screen and here there was no help for it, she had to buy a Chinese one, but as she very cleverly said, you might perfectly well have a Chinese screen in England. She had a great many photographs, in silver frames, one of them of a Princess of Schleswig-Holstein, and one of the Queen of Sweden, both signed, and these she put on the grand piano, for they give a room an air of being lived in. Then, having finished, she surveyed her work with satisfaction.

"Of course, it doesn't look like a room in London," she said, "but it might quite well be a room in some nice place in England, Cheltenham, say, or Tunbridge Wells."

THE CABINET MINISTER

HE RECEIVED ME in a long room looking on to a sandy garden. The roses withered on the stunted bushes and the great old trees flagged forlorn. He sat me down on a square stool at a square table and took his seat in front of me. A servant brought cups of flowered tea and American cigarettes. He was a thin man, of the middle height, with thin, elegant hands; and through his gold-rimmed spectacles he looked at me with large, dark, and melancholy eyes. He had the look of a student or of a dreamer. His smile was very sweet. He wore a brown silk gown and over it a short black silk jacket, and on his head a billy-cock hat.

"Is it not strange," he said, with his charming smile, "that we Chinese wear this gown because three hundred years ago the Manchus were horsemen?"

"Not so strange," I retorted, "as that because the English won the battle of Waterloo Your Excellency should wear a bowler."

"Do you think that is why I wear it?"

"I could easily prove it."

Since I was afraid that his exquisite courtesy would prevent him from asking me how, I hastened in a few well-chosen words to do so.

He took off his hat and looked at it with the shadow of a sigh. I glanced round the room. It had a green Brussels carpet, with great flowers on it, and round the walls were highly carved blackwood chairs. From a picture rail hung scrolls on which were writings by the great masters of the past, and to vary these, in bright gold frames, were oil paintings which in the nineties might very well have been exhibited in the Royal Academy. The minister did his work at an American roll-top desk.

He talked to me with melancholy of the state of China. A civilization, the oldest the world had known, was now being ruthlessly swept away. The students who came back from Europe and from America were tearing down what endless generations had built up, and they were placing nothing in its stead. They had no love of their country, no religion, no reverence. The temples, deserted by worshipper and priest, were falling into decay and presently their beauty would be nothing but a memory.

But then, with a gesture of his thin, aristocratic hands, he put the subject aside. He asked me whether I would care to see some of his works of art. We walked round the room and he showed me priceless porcelains, bronzes, and Tang figures. There was a horse from a grave in Honan which had the grace and the exquisite modelling of a Greek work. On a large table by the side of his desk was a number of rolls. He chose one and holding it at the top gave it to me to unroll. It was a picture of some early dynasty of mountains seen through fleecy clouds, and with smiling eyes he watched my pleasure as I looked. The picture was set aside and he showed me another and yet another. Presently I protested that I could not allow a busy man to waste his time on me, but he would not let me go. He brought out picture after picture. He was a connoisseur. He was pleased to tell me the schools and periods to which they belonged and neat anecdotes about their painters.

"I wish I could think it was possible for you to appreciate my greatest treasures," he said, pointing to the scrolls that adorned his walls. "Here you have examples of the most perfect calligraphies of China."

"Do you like them better than paintings?" I asked.

"Infinitely. Their beauty is more chaste. There is nothing meretricious in them. But I can quite understand that a European would have difficulty in appreciating so severe and so delicate an art. Your taste in Chinese things tends a little to the grotesque, I think."

He produced books of paintings and I turned their leaves. Beautiful things! With the dramatic instinct of the collector he kept to the last the book by which he set most store. It was a series of little pictures of birds and flowers, roughly done with a few strokes, but with such a power of suggestion, with so great a feeling for nature and such a playful tenderness, that it took your breath away. There were sprigs of plum blossom that held in their dainty freshness all the magic of the spring; there were sparrows in whose ruffled plumage were the beat and the tremor of life. It was the work of a great artist.

"Will these American students ever produce anything like this?" he asked with a rueful smile.

But to me the most charming part of it was that I knew all the time that he was a rascal. Corrupt, inefficient, and unscrupulous, he let nothing stand in his way. He was a master of the squeeze. He had acquired a large fortune by the most abominable methods. He was dishonest, cruel, vindictive, and venal. He had certainly had a share in reducing China to the desperate plight which he so sincerely lamented. But when he held in his hand a little vase of the colour of lapis lazuli his fingers seemed to curl about it with a charming tenderness, his melancholy eyes caressed it as they looked, and his lips were slightly parted as though with a sigh of desire.

DINNER PARTIES: LEGATION QUARTER

THE SWISS DIRECTOR of the Banque Sino-Argentine was announced. He came with a large, handsome wife, who displayed her opulent charms so generously that it made you a little nervous. It was said that she had been *a cocotte*, and an English maiden lady (in salmon pink satin and beads) who had come early, greeted her with a thin and frigid smile. The Minister of Guatemala and the Chargé d'Affaires of Montenegro entered together. The Chargé d'Affaires was in a state of extreme agitation; he had not understood that it was an official function, he thought he had been asked to dine *en petit comité*, and he had not put on his orders. And there was the Minister of Guatemala blazing with stars! What in heaven's name was to be done? The emotion caused by what for a moment seemed almost a diplomatic incident was diverted by the appearance of two Chinese servants in long silk robes and four-sided hats with cocktails and zakouski. Then a Russian princess sailed in. She had white hair and a black silk dress up to her neck. She looked like the heroine of a play by Victorien Sardou who had outlived the melodramatic fury of her youth and now did crochet. She was infinitely bored when you spoke to her of Tolstoi or Chekov; but grew animated when she talked of Jack London. She put a question to the maiden lady which the maiden lady, though no longer young, had no answer for.

"Why," she asked, "do you English write such silly books about Russia?"

But then the first secretary of the British Legation appeared. He gave his entrance the significance of an event. He was very tall, baldish but elegant, and he was beautifully dressed: he looked with polite astonishment at the dazzling orders of the Minister of Guatemala. The Chargé d'Affaires of Montenegro, who flattered himself that he was the best dressed man in the diplomatic body, but was not quite sure whether the first secretary of the British Legation thought him so, fluttered up to him to ask his candid opinion of the frilled shirt he wore. The Englishman placed a gold-rimmed glass in his eye and looked at it for a moment gravely; then he paid the other a devastating compliment. Everyone had come by now but the wife of the French Military Attaché. They said she was always late.

"*Elle est insupportable*," said the handsome wife of the Swiss banker.

But at last, magnificently indifferent to the fact that she had kept everyone waiting for half an hour, she swam into the room. She was tall on her outrageously high heels, extremely thin, and she wore a dress that gave you the impression that she had nothing on at all. Her hair was bobbed and blonde, and she was boldly painted. She looked like a post-impressionist's idea of patient Griselda. When she moved, the air was heavy with exotic odours. She gave the Minister of Guatemala a jewelled, emaciated hand to kiss; with a few smiling words made the banker's wife feel passée, provincial, and portly; flung an improper jest at the English lady whose embarrassment was mitigated by the knowledge that the wife of the French Military Attaché was *très bien née*; and drank three cocktails in rapid succession.

Dinner was served. The conversation varied from a resonant rolling French to a somewhat halting English. They talked of this Minister who had just written from Bucharest or Lima, and that Counsellor's wife who found it so dull in Christiana or so expensive in Washington. On the whole it made little difference to them in what capital they found themselves, for they did precisely the same things in Constantinople, Berne, Stockholm and Peking. Entrenched within their diplomatic privileges and supported by a lively sense of their social consequence, they dwelt in a world in which Copernicus had never existed, for to them sun and stars circled obsequiously round this earth of ours, and they were its centre. No one knew why the English lady was there and the wife of the Swiss director said privately that she was without doubt a German spy. But she was an authority on the country. She told you that the Chinese had such perfect manners and you really should have known the Empress Dowager; she was a perfect darling. You knew very well that in Constantinople she would have assured you that the Turks were such perfect gentlemen and the Sultana Fatima was a perfect dear and spoke such wonderful French. Homeless, she was at home wherever her country had a diplomatic representative.

The first secretary of the British Legation thought the party rather mixed. He spoke French more like a Frenchman than any Frenchman who ever lived. He was a man of taste, and he had a natural aptitude for being right. He only knew the right people and only read the right books; he admired none but the right music and cared for none but the right pictures; he bought his clothes at the right tailor's and his shirts from the only possible haberdasher. You listened to him with stupefaction. Presently you wished with all your heart that he would confess to a liking for something just a little vulgar: you would have felt more at your ease if only with bold idiosyncrasy he had claimed that *The Soul's Awakening* was a work of art or *The Rosary* a masterpiece. But his taste was faultless. He was perfect and you were half afraid that he knew it, for in repose his face had the look of one who bears an intolerable burden. And then you discovered that he wrote *vers libre*. You breathed again.

THE INN

IT SEEMS LONG since the night fell, and for an hour a coolie has
walked before your chair carrying a lantern. It throws a thin
circle of light in front of you, and as you pass you catch a pale
glimpse (like a thing of beauty emerging vaguely from the ceaseless flux of common life) of a bamboo thicket, a flash of water in
a rice field, or the heavy darkness of a banyan. Now and then a
belated peasant, bearing two heavy baskets on his yoke, sidles by.
The bearers walk more slowly, but after the long day they have
lost none of their spirit, and they chatter gaily; they laugh, and
one of them breaks into a fragment of tuneless song. But the
causeway rises and the lantern throws its light suddenly on a
whitewashed wall: you have reached the first miserable houses
that straggle along the path outside the city wall, and two or three
minutes more bring you to a steep flight of steps. The bearers
take them at a run. You pass through the city gates. The narrow
streets are multitudinous and in the shops they are busy still. The
bearers shout raucously. The crowd divides and you pass through
a double hedge of serried, curious people. Their faces are impassive and their dark eyes stare mysteriously. The bearers, their
day's work done, march with a swinging stride. Suddenly they
stop, wheel to the right, into a courtyard, and you have reached
the inn. Your chair is set down.

The inn – it consists of a long yard, partly covered, with rooms
opening on it on each side – is lit by three or four oil lamps.
They throw a dim light immediately around them, but make the
surrounding darkness more impenetrable. All the front of the
yard is crowded with tables and at these people are packed, eating
rice or drinking tea. Some of them play games you do not know.
At the great stove, where water in a cauldron is perpetually heat-
ing and rice in a huge pan being prepared, stand the persons of
the inn. They serve out rapidly great bowls of rice and fill the
teapots which are incessantly brought them. Further back a
couple of naked coolies, sturdy, thickset and supple, are sluicing
themselves with boiling water. You walk to the end of the yard
where, facing the entrance but protected from the vulgar gaze
by a screen, is the principal guest chamber.

It is a spacious, windowless room, with a floor of trodden
earth, lofty, for it goes the whole height of the inn, with an open

roof. The walls are whitewashed, showing the beams, so that they remind you of a farmhouse in Sussex. The furniture consists of a square table, with a couple of straight-backed wooden armchairs, and three or four wooden pallets covered with matting on the least dirty of which you will presently lay your bed. In a cup of oil a taper gives a tiny point of light. They bring you your lantern and you wait while your dinner is cooked. The bearers are merry now that they have set down their loads. They wash their feet and put on clean sandals and smoke their long pipes.

How precious then is the inordinate length of your book (for you are travelling light and you have limited yourself to three) and how jealously you read every word of every page so that you may delay as long as possible the dreaded moment when you must reach the end! You are mightily thankful then to the authors of long books and when you turn over their pages, reckoning how long you can make them last, you wish they were half as long again. You do not ask then for the perfect lucidity which he who runs may read. A complicated phraseology which makes it needful to read the sentence a second time to get its meaning is not unwelcome; a profusion of metaphor, giving your fancy ample play, a richness of allusion affording you the delight of recognition, are then qualities beyond price. Then if the thought is elaborate without being profound (for you have been on the road since dawn and of the forty miles of the day's journey you have footed it more than half) you have the perfect book for the occasion.

But the noise in the inn suddenly increases to a din and looking out you see that more travellers, a party of Chinese in sedan chairs, have arrived. They take the rooms on each side of you and through the thin walls you hear their loud talking far into the night. With a lazy, restful eye, your whole body conscious of the enjoyment of lying in bed, taking a sensual pleasure in its fatigue, you follow the elaborate pattern of the transom. The dim lamp in the yard shines through the torn paper with which it is covered, and its intricate design is black against the light. At last everything is quiet but for a man in the next room who is coughing painfully. It is the peculiar, repeated cough of phthisis, and hearing it at intervals through the night you wonder how long the poor devil can live. You rejoice in your own rude strength. Then a cock crows loudly, just behind your head, it seems; and not far away a bugler blows a long blast on his bugle, a melancholy wail; the inn begins to stir again; lights are lit, and the coolies make ready their loads for another day.

HER BRITANNIC MAJESTY'S REPRESENTATIVE

HE WAS A man of less than middle height, with stiff brown hair *en brosse*, a little toothbrush moustache, and glasses through which his blue eyes, looking at you aggressively, were somewhat distorted. There was a defiant perkiness in his appearance which reminded you of the cock-sparrow, and as he asked you to sit down and inquired your business, meanwhile sorting the papers littered on his desk as though you had disturbed him in the midst of important affairs, you had the feeling that he was on the look out for an opportunity to put you in your place. He had cultivated the official manner to perfection. You were the public, an unavoidable nuisance, and the only justification for your existence was that you did what you were told without argument or delay. But even officials have their weakness and somehow it chanced that he found it very difficult to bring any business to an end without confiding his grievance to you. It appeared that people, missionaries especially, thought him supercilious and domineering. He assured you that he thought there was a great deal of good in missionaries; it is true that many of them were ignorant and unreasonable, and he didn't like their attitude; in his district most of them were Canadians, and personally he didn't like Canadians; but as for saying that he put on airs of superiority (he fixed his pince-nez more firmly on his nose) it was monstrously untrue. On the contrary he went out of his way to help them, but it was only natural that he should help them in his way rather than in theirs. It was hard to listen to him without a smile, for in every word he said you felt how exasperating he must be to the unfortunate persons over whom he had control. His manner was deplorable. He had developed the gift of putting up your back to a degree which is very seldom met with. He was, in short, a vain, irritable, bumptious, and tiresome little man.

During the revolution, while a lot of firing was going on in the city between the rival factions, he had occasion to go to the

Southern general on official business connected with the safety of his nationals, and on his way through the yamen he came across three prisoners being led out to execution. He stopped the officer in charge of the firing party and finding out what was about to happen vehemently protested. These were prisoners of war and it was barbarity to kill them. The officer – very rudely, in the consul's words – told him that he must carry out his orders. The consul fired up. He wasn't going to let a confounded Chinese officer talk to him in that way. An altercation ensued. The general, informed of what was occurring, sent out to ask the consul to come in to him, but the consul refused to move till the prisoners, three wretched coolies, green with fear, were handed over to his safe-keeping. The officer waved him aside and ordered his firing squad to take aim. Then the consul – I can see him fixing his glasses on his nose and his hair bristling fiercely – then the consul stepped forwards between the levelled rifles and the three miserable men, and told the soldiers to shoot and be damned. There was hesitation and confusion. It was plain that the rebels did not want to shoot a British consul. I suppose there was a hurried consultation. The three prisoners were given over to him and in triumph the little man marched back to the consulate.

"Damn it, Sir," he said furiously, "I almost thought the blighters would have the confounded cheek to shoot me."

They are strange people the British. If their manners were as good as their courage is great, they would merit the opinion they have of themselves.

THE LAST CHANCE

IT WAS PATHETICALLY obvious that she had come to China to be married, and what made it almost tragic was that not a single man in the treaty port was ignorant of the fact. She was a big woman with an ungainly figure; her hands and feet were large; she had a large nose, indeed all her features were large; but her blue eyes were fine. She was, perhaps, a little too conscious of them. She was a blonde and she was thirty. In the daytime, when she wore sensible boots, a short skirt, and a slouch hat, she was personable; but in the evening, in blue silk to enhance the colour of her eyes, in a frock cut by heaven knows what suburban dressmaker from the models in an illustrated paper, when she set herself out to be alluring she was an object that made you horribly ill-at-ease. She wished to be all things to all unmarried men. She listened brightly while one of them talked of shooting and she listened gaily when another talked of the freight on tea. She clapped her hands with girlish excitement when they discussed the races which were to be run next week. She was desperately fond of dancing, with a young American, and she made him promise to take her to a baseball match; but dancing wasn't the only thing she cared for (you can have too much of a good thing) and, with the elderly, but single, taipan of an important firm, what she simply loved was a game of golf. She was willing to be taught billiards by a young man who had lost his leg in the war, and she gave her sprightly attention to the manager of a bank who told her what he thought of silver. She was not much interested in the Chinese, for that was a subject which was not very good form in the circles in which she found herself, but being a woman she could not help being revolted at the way in which Chinese women were treated.

"You know, they don't have a word to say about who they're going to marry," she explained. "It's all arranged by go-betweens and the man doesn't even see the girl till he's married her. There's no romance or anything like that. And as far as love goes . . ."

Words failed her. She was a thoroughly good-natured creature. She would have made any of those men, young or old, a perfectly good wife. And she knew it.

HENDERSON

IT WAS VERY hard to look at him without a chuckle, for his appearance immediately told you all about him. When you saw him at the club, reading *The London Mercury* or lounging at the bar with a gin and bitters at his elbow (no cocktails for him) his unconventionality attracted your attention; but you recognized him at once, for he was a perfect specimen of his class. His unconventionality was exquisitely conventional. Everything about him was according to standard, from his square-toed serviceable boots to his rather long, untidy hair. He wore a loose low collar that showed a thick neck and loose, somewhat shabby, but well-cut clothes. He always smoked a short briar pipe. He was very humorous on the subject of cigarettes. He was a biggish fellow, athletic, with fine eyes and a pleasant voice. He talked fluently. His language was often obscene, not because his mind was impure, but because his bent was democratic. As you guessed by the look of him he drank beer (not in fact but in the spirit) with Mr. Chesterton and walked the Sussex downs with Mr. Hilaire Belloc. He had played football at Oxford, but with Mr. Wells he despised the ancient seat of learning. He looked upon Mr. Bernard Shaw as a little out of date, but he had still great hopes of Mr. Granville Barker. He had had many serious talks with Mr. and Mrs. Sydney Webb, and he was a member of the Fabian Society. The only point where he touched upon the same world as the frivolous was his appreciation of the Russian Ballet. He wrote rugged poems about prostitutes, dogs, lamp-posts, Magdalen College, public-houses and country vicarages. He held English, French, and Americans in scorn; but on the other hand (he was no misanthropist) he would not listen to a word in dispraise of Tamils, Bengalis, Kaffirs, Germans, or Greeks. At the club they thought him rather a wild fellow.

"A socialist, you know," they said.

But he was junior partner in a well-known and respectable firm, and one of the peculiarities of China is that your position excuses your idiosyncrasies. It may be notorious that you beat your wife, but if you are manager of a well-established bank the world will be civil to you and ask you to dinner. So when Henderson announced his socialistic opinions they merely laughed. When he first came to Shanghai he refused to use the jinrickshaw. It revolted his sense of personal dignity that a man, a human being no different from himself, should drag him hither and thither. So he walked. He swore it was good exercise and it kept him fit; besides, it gave him a thirst he wouldn't sell for twenty dollars, and he drank his beer with gusto. But Shanghai is very hot and sometimes he was in a hurry, so now and again he was obliged to use the degrading vehicle. It made him feel uncomfortable, but it was certainly convenient. Presently he came to use it frequently, but he always thought of the boy between the shafts as a man and a brother.

He had been three years in Shanghai when I saw him. We had

spent the morning in the Chinese city, going from shop to shop and our rickshaw boys were hot with sweat; every minute or two they wiped their foreheads with ragged handkerchiefs. We were bound now for the club and had nearly reached it when Henderson remembered that he wanted to get Mr. Bertrand Russell's new book, which had just reached Shanghai. He stopped the boys and told them to go back.

"Don't you think we might leave it till after luncheon?" I said. "Those fellows are sweating like pigs."

"It's good for them," he answered. "You mustn't ever pay attention to the Chinese. You see, we're only here because they fear us. We're the ruling race."

I did not say anything. I did not even smile.

"The Chinese always have had masters and they always will."

A passing car separated us for a moment and when he came once more abreast of me he had put the matter aside.

"You men who live in England don't know what it means to us when new books get out here," he remarked. "I read everything that Bertrand Russell writes. Have you seen the last one?"

"*Roads to Freedom*? Yes. I read it before I left England."

"I've read several reviews. I think he's got hold of some interesting ideas."

I think Henderson was going to enlarge on them, but the rickshaw boy passed the turning he should have taken.

"Round the corner, you bloody fool," cried Henderson, and to emphasize his meaning he gave the man a smart kick on the bottom.

ROMANCE

ALL DAY I had been dropping down the river. This was the river up which Chang Chien, seeking its source, had sailed for many days till he came to a city where he saw a girl spinning and a youth leading an ox to the water. He asked what place this was and in reply the girl gave him her shuttle, telling him to show it on his return to the astrologer Yen Chün-ping, who would thus know where he had been. He did so, and the astrologer at once recognized the shuttle as that of the Spinning Damsel, further declaring that on the day and at the hour when Chang Chien received the shuttle he had noticed a wandering star intrude itself between the Spinning Damsel and the Cowherd. So Chang Chien knew that he had sailed upon the bosom of the Milky Way.

I, however, had not been so far. All day, as for seven days before, my five rowers, standing up, had rowed, and there rang still in my ears the monotonous sound of their oars against the wooden pin that served as rowlock. Now and again the water became very shallow and there was a jar and a jolt as we scraped along the stones of the river bed. Then two or three of the rowers turned up their blue trousers to the hip and let themselves over the side. Shouting they dragged the flat-bottomed boat over the shoal. Now and again we came to a rapid, of no great consequence when compared with the turbulent rapids of the Yangtze, but sufficiently swift to call for trackers to pull the junks that were going up stream; and we, going down, passed through them with many shouts, shot the foaming breakers and presently reached water as smooth as any lake.

Now it was night and my crew were asleep, forward, huddled together in such shelter as they had been able to rig up when we moored at dusk. I sat on my bed. Bamboo matting spread over three wooden arches made the sorry cabin which for a week had served me as parlour and bedroom. It was closed at one end by matchboarding so roughly put together that there were large chinks between each board. The bitter wind blew through them. It was on the other side of this that the crew – fine sturdy fellows – rowed by day and slept by night, joined then by the steersman, who had stood from dawn to dusk, in a tattered blue gown and a wadded coat of faded grey, a black turban round his head, at the long oar, which was his helm. There was no furniture but my bed, a shallow dish like an enormous soup-plate, in which burned charcoal, for it was cold, a basket containing my clothes, which I used as a table, and a hurricane lamp which hung from one of the arches and swayed slightly with the motion of the water. The cabin was so low that I, a person of no great height (I comfort myself with Bacon's observation, that with tall men it is as with tall houses, the top story is commonly the least furnished) could only just stand upright. One of the sleepers began to snore more loudly, and perhaps he awoke two of the others, for I heard the sound of speaking; but presently this ceased, the snorer was quiet, and all about me once more was silence.

Then suddenly I had a feeling that here, facing me, touching me almost, was the romance I sought. It was a feeling like no other, just as specific as the thrill of art; but I could not for the life of me tell what it was that had given me just then that rare emotion.

In the course of my life I have been often in situations which, had I read of them, would have seemed to me sufficiently romantic; but it is only in retrospect, comparing them with my ideas of what was romantic, that I have seen them as at all out of the ordinary. It is only by an effort of the imagination, making myself, as it were, a spectator of myself acting a part, that I have caught anything of the precious quality in circumstances which in others would have seemed to me instinct with its fine flower. When I have danced with an actress whose fascination and whose genius made her the idol of my country, or wandered through the halls of some great house in which was gathered all that was distinguished by lineage or intellect that London could show, I have only recognized afterwards that here perhaps, though in somewhat Ouidaesque a fashion, was romance. In battle, when, myself in no great danger, I was able to watch events with a thrill of interest, I had not the phlegm to assume the part of a spectator. I have sailed through the night, under the full moon, to a coral island in the Pacific, and then the beauty and the wonder of the scene gave me a conscious happiness, but only later the exhilarating sense that romance and I had touched fingers. I heard the flutter of its wings when once, in the bedroom of a hotel in New York, I sat round a table with half a dozen others and made plans to restore an ancient kingdom whose wrongs have for a century inspired the poet and the patriot; but my chief feeling was a surprised amusement that through the hazards of war I found myself engaged in business so foreign to my bent. The authentic thrill of romance has seized me under circumstances which one would have thought far less romantic, and I remember that I knew it first one evening when I was playing cards in a cottage on the coast of Brittany. In the next room an old fisherman lay dying, and the women of the house said that he would go out with the tide. Without a storm was raging and it seemed fit for the last moments of that aged warrior of the seas that his going should be accompanied by the wild cries of the wind as it hurled itself against the shuttered windows. The waves thundered upon the tortured rocks. I felt a sudden exultation, for I knew that here was romance.

And now the same exultation seized me, and once more romance, like a bodily presence, was before me. But it had come so unexpectedly that I was intrigued. I could not tell whether it had crept in among the shadows that the lamp threw on the bamboo matting or whether it was wafted down the river that I saw through the opening of my cabin. Curious to know what were the elements that made up the ineffable delight of the moment I went out to the stern of the boat. Alongside were moored half a dozen junks, going up river, for their masts were erect; and everything was silent in them. Their crews were long since asleep. The night was not dark, for though it was cloudy the moon was full, but the river in that veiled light was ghostly. A vague mist blurred the trees on the further bank. It was an enchanting sight, but there was in it nothing unaccustomed and what I sought was not there. I turned away. But when I returned to my bamboo shelter the magic which had given it so extraordinary a character was gone. Alas, I was like a man who should tear a butterfly to pieces in order to discover in what its beauty lay. And yet, as Moses descending from Mount Sinai wore on his face a brightness from his converse with the God of Israel, my little cabin, my dish of charcoal, my lamp, even my camp bed, had still about them something of the thrill which for a moment was mine. I could not see them any more quite indifferently, because for a moment I had seen them magically.

THE SONG OF THE RIVER

YOU HEAR IT all along the river. You hear it, loud and strong, from the rowers as they urge the junk with its high stern, the mast lashed alongside, down the swift-running stream. You hear it from the trackers, a more breathless chaunt, as they pull desperately against the current, half a dozen of them, perhaps, if they are taking up a wupan, a couple of hundred if they are hauling a splendid junk, its square sail set, over a rapid. On the junk a man stands amidships beating a drum incessantly to guide their efforts, and they pull with all their strength, like men possessed, bent double; and sometimes in the extremity of their travail they crawl on the ground on all fours, like the beasts of the field. They strain, strain fiercely, against the pitiless might of the stream. The leader goes up and down the line and when he sees one who is not putting all his will into the task he brings down his split bamboo on the naked back. Each one must do his utmost or the labour of all is in vain. And still they sing a vehement, eager chaunt, the chaunt of the turbulent waters. I do not know how words can describe what there is in it of effort. It serves to express the straining heart, the breaking muscles, and at the same time the indomitable spirit of man which overcomes the pitiless force of nature. Though the rope may part and the great junk swing back, in the end the rapid will be passed; and at the close of the weary day there is the hearty meal and perhaps the opium pipe with its dreams of ease. But the most agonizing song is the song of the coolies who bring the great bales from the junk up the steep steps to the town wall. Up and down they go, endlessly, and endless as their toil rises their rhythmic cry. He, aw – ah, oh. They are barefoot and naked to the waist. The sweat pours down their faces and their song is a groan of pain. It is a sigh of despair. It is heart-rending. It is hardly human. It is the cry of souls in infinite distress, only just musical, and that last note is the ultimate sob of humanity. Life is too hard, too cruel, and this is the final despairing protest. That is the song of the river.

THE STRANGER

IT WAS A COMFORT in that sweltering heat to get out of the city. The missionary stepped out of the launch in which he had dropped leisurely down the river and comfortably settled himself in the chair which was waiting for him at the water's edge. He was carried through the village by the river side and began to ascend the hill. It was an hour's journey along a pathway of broad stone steps, under fir trees, and now and again you caught a delightful glimpse of the broad river shining in the sun amid the exultant green of the padi fields. The bearers went along with a swinging stride. The sweat on their backs shone. It was a sacred mountain with a Buddhist monastery on the top of it, and on

the way up there were rest houses where the coolies set down
the chair for a few minutes and a monk in his grey robe gave you
a cup of flowered tea. The air was fresh and sweet. The pleasure
of that lazy journey – the swing of the chair was very soothing –
made a day in the city almost worth while; and at the end of it
was his trim little bungalow where he spent the summer, and
before him the sweet-scented night. The mail had come in that
day and he was bringing on letters and papers. There were four
numbers of the *Saturday Evening Post* and four of the *Literary
Digest*. He had nothing but pleasant things to look forward to
and the usual peace (a peace, as he often said, which passeth all
understanding), which filled him whenever he was among these
green trees, away from the teeming city, should long since have
descended upon him.

But he was harassed. He had had that day an unfortunate
encounter and he was unable, trivial as it was, to put it out of
his mind. It was on this account that his face bore a somewhat
peevish expression. It was a thin and sensitive face, almost ascetic,
with regular features and intelligent eyes. He was very long and
thin, with the spindly legs of a grasshopper, and as he sat in his
chair, swaying a little with the motion of his bearers, he reminded
you, somewhat grotesquely, of a faded lily. A gentle creature. He
could never have hurt a fly.

He had run across Dr. Saunders in one of the streets of the
city. Dr. Saunders was a little grey-haired man, with a high
colour and a snub nose which gave him a strangely impudent
expression. He had a large sensual mouth and when he laughed,
which he did very often, he showed decayed and discoloured
teeth; when he laughed his little blue eyes wrinkled in a curious
fashion and then he looked the very picture of malice. There
was something faunlike in him. His movements were quick and
unexpected. He walked with a rapid trip as though he were
always in a hurry. He was a doctor who lived in the heart of the
city among the Chinese. He was not on the register, but someone had made it his business to find out that he had been duly
qualified; he had been struck off, but for what crime, whether
social or purely professional, none know; nor how he had happened to come to the East and eventually settle on the China
coast. But it was evident that he was a very clever doctor and
the Chinese had great faith in him. He avoided the foreigners

and rather disagreeable stories were circulated about him. Everyone knew him to say how do you do to, but no one asked him to his house nor visited him in his own.

When they had met that afternoon, Dr. Saunders had exclaimed:

"What on earth has brought you to the city at this time of year?"

"I have some business that I couldn't leave any longer," answered the missionary, "and then I wanted to get the mail."

"There was a stranger here the other day asking for you," said the doctor.

"For me?" cried the other, with surprise.

"Well, not for you particularly," explained the doctor. "He wanted to know the way to the American Mission. I told him; but I said he wouldn't find anyone there. He seemed rather surprised at that, so I told him that you all went up to the hills in May and didn't come back till September."

"A foreigner?" asked the missionary, still wondering who the stranger could be.

"Oh, yes, certainly." The doctor's eyes twinkled. "Then he asked me about the other missions; I told him the London Mission had a settlement here, but it wasn't the least use going there as all the missionaries were away in the hills. After all, it's devilish hot in the city. 'Then I'd like to go to one of the mission schools,' said the stranger. 'Oh, they're all closed,' I said. 'Well, then, I'll go to the hospital.' 'That's well worth a visit,' I said, 'the American hospital is equipped with all the latest contrivances. Their operating theatre is perfect.' 'What is the name of the doctor in charge?' 'Oh, he's up in the hills.' 'But what about the sick?' 'There are no sick between May and September,' I said, 'and if there are they have to put up with the native dispensers.'"

Dr. Saunders paused for a moment. The missionary looked ever so slightly vexed.

"Well?" he said.

"The stranger looked at me irresolutely for a moment or two. 'I wanted to see something of the missions before I left,' he said. 'You might try the Roman Catholics,' I said, 'they're here all the year round.' 'When do they take their holidays, then?' he asked. 'They don't,' I said. He left me at that. I think he went to the Spanish convent.'"

The missionary fell into the trap and it irritated him to think how ingenuously he had done so. He ought to have seen what was coming.

"Who was this, anyway?" he asked innocently.

"I asked him his name," said the doctor. " 'Oh, I'm Christ,' he said."

The missionary shrugged his shoulders and abruptly told his rickshaw boy to go on.

It had put him thoroughly out of temper. It was so unjust. Of course they went away from May to September. The heat made any useful activity quite out of the question, and it had been found by experience that the missionaries preserved their health and strength much better if they spent the hot months in the hills. A sick missionary was only an encumbrance. It was a matter of practical politics, and it had been found that the Lord's work was done more efficiently if a certain part of the year was set aside for rest and recreation. And then the reference to the Roman Catholics was grossly unfair. They were unmarried. They had no families to think of. The mortality among them was terrifying. Why, in that very city, of fourteen nuns who had come out to China ten years ago, all but three were dead. It was perfectly easy for them, because it was more convenient for their work to live in the middle of the city and to stay there all the year round. They had no ties. They had no duties to those who were near and dear to them. Oh, it was grossly unjust to drag in the Roman Catholics.

But suddenly an idea flashed through his mind. What rankled most was that he had left the rascally doctor (you only had to look at his face all puckered with malicious amusement to know he was a rogue) without a word. There certainly was an answer, but he had not had the presence of mind to make it; and now the perfect repartee occurred to him. A glow of satisfaction filled him and he almost fancied that he had made it. It was a crushing rejoinder, and he rubbed his very long thin hands with satisfaction. "My dear Sir," he ought to have said, "Our Lord never in the whole course of his ministry claimed to be the Christ." It was an unanswerable snub, and thinking of it the missionary forgot his ill-humour.

THE PHILOSOPHER

IT WAS SURPRISING to find so vast a city in a spot that seemed to me so remote. From its battlemented gate towards sunset you could see the snowy mountains of Tibet. It was so populous that you could walk at ease only on the walls, and it took a rapid walker three hours to complete their circuit. There was no railway within a thousand miles and the river on which it stood was so shallow that only junks of light burden could safely navigate it. Five days in a sampan were needed to reach the Upper Yangtze. For an uneasy moment you asked yourself whether trains and steamships were as necessary to the conduct of life as we who use them every day consider; for here, a million persons throve, married, begat their kind, and died; here a million persons were busily occupied with commerce, art, and thought.

And here lived a philosopher of repute, the desire to see whom had been to me one of the incentives of a somewhat arduous journey. He was the greatest authority in China on the Confucian learning. He was said to speak English and German with facility. He had been for many years secretary to one of the Empress Dowager's greatest viceroys, but he lived now in retirement. On certain days in the week, however, all through the year he opened his doors to such as sought after knowledge, and discoursed on the teaching of Confucius. He had a body of disciples, but it was small, since the students, for the most part, preferred to his modest dwelling and his severe exhortations the sumptuous buildings of the foreign university and the useful science of the barbarians: with him this was mentioned only to be scornfully dismissed. From all I heard of him I concluded that he was a man of character.

When I announced my wish to meet this distinguished person my host immediately offered to arrange a meeting; but the days passed and nothing happened. I made inquiries and my host shrugged his shoulders.

"I sent him a chit and told him to come along," he said. "I don't know why he hasn't turned up. He's a cross-grained old fellow."

I did not think it was proper to approach a philosopher in so cavalier a fashion and I was hardly surprised that he had ignored a summons such as this. I caused a letter to be sent asking, in the politest terms I could devise, whether he would allow me to call upon him and within two hours received an answer making an appointment for the following morning at ten o'clock.

I was carried in a chair. The way seemed interminable. I went through crowded streets and through streets deserted till I came at last to one, silent and empty, in which, at a small door in a long white wall, my bearers set down my chair. One of them knocked, and after a considerable time a judas was opened; dark eyes looked through; there was a brief colloquy; and finally I was admitted. A youth, pallid of face, wizened, and poorly dressed, motioned me to follow him. I did not know if he was a servant or a pupil of the great man. I passed through a shabby yard and was led into a long low room, sparsely furnished, with an American roll-top desk, a couple of blackwood chairs and two little Chinese tables. Against the walls were shelves on which were a great number of books: most of them, of course, were Chinese, but there were many, philosophical and scientific works, in English, French and German; and there were hundreds of unbound copies of learned reviews. Where books did not take up the wall space hung scrolls on which, in various calligraphies, were written, I suppose, Confucian quotations. There was no carpet on the floor. It was a cold, bare, and comfortless chamber. Its sombreness was relieved only by a yellow chrysanthemum which stood by itself on the desk in a long vase.

I waited for some time and the youth who had shown me in brought a pot of tea, two cups, and a tin of Virginian cigarettes. As he went out the philosopher entered. I hastened to express my sense of the honour he did me in allowing me to visit him. He waved me to a chair and poured out the tea.

"I am flattered that you wished to see me," he returned. "Your countrymen deal only with coolies and with compradores; they think every Chinese must be one or the other."

I ventured to protest. But I had not caught his point. He leaned back in his chair and looked at me with an expression of mockery.

"They think they have but to beckon and we must come."

I saw then that my friend's unfortunate communication still rankled. I did not quite know how to reply. I murmured something complimentary.

He was an old man, tall, with a thin grey queue, and bright large eyes, under which were heavy bags. His teeth were broken and discoloured. He was exceedingly thin, and his hands, fine and small, were withered and claw-like. I had been told that he was an opium-smoker. He was very shabbily dressed in a black gown, a little black cap, both much the worse for wear, and dark grey trousers gartered at the ankle. He was watching. He did not quite know what attitude to take up, and he had the manner of a man who was on his guard. Of course, the philosopher occupies a royal place among those who concern themselves with the things of the spirit, and we have the authority of Benjamin Disraeli that royalty must be treated with abundant flattery. I seized my trowel. Presently I was conscious of a certain relaxation in his demeanour. He was like a man who was all set and rigid to have his photograph taken, but hearing the shutter click lets himself go and eases into his natural self. He showed me his books.

"I took the Ph.D. in Berlin, you know," he said. "And afterwards I studied for some time in Oxford. But the English, if you will allow me to say so, have no great aptitude for philosophy."

Though he put the remark apologetically it was evident that he was not displeased to say a slightly disagreeable thing.

"We have had philosophers who have not been without influence in the world of thought," I suggested.

"Hume and Berkeley? The philosophers who taught at Oxford when I was there were anxious not to offend their theological colleagues. They would not follow their thought to its logical consequences in case they should jeopardize their position in university society."

"Have you studied the modern developments of philosophy in America?" I asked.

"Are you speaking of Pragmatism? It is the last refuge of those who want to believe the incredible. I have more use for American petroleum than for American philosophy."

His judgments were tart. We sat down once more and drank another cup of tea. He began to talk with fluency. He spoke a somewhat formal but an idiomatic English. Now and then he helped himself out with a German phrase. So far as it was possible for a man of that stubborn character to be influenced he had been influenced by Germany. The method and the industry of the Germans had deeply impressed him and their philosophical acumen was patent to him when a laborious professor published in a learned magazine an essay on one of his own writings.

"I have written twenty books," he said. "And that is the only notice that has ever been taken of me in a European publication."

But his study of Western philosophy had only served in the end to satisfy him that wisdom, after all, was to be found within the limits of the Confucian canon. He accepted its philosophy with conviction. It answered the needs of his spirit with a completeness which made all foreign learning seem vain. I was interested in this because it bore out an opinion of mine that philosophy is an affair of character rather than of logic: the philosopher believes not according to evidence, but according to his own temperament; and his thinking merely serves to make reasonable what his instinct regards as true. If Confucianism gained so firm a hold on the Chinese it is because it explained and expressed them as no other system of thought could do.

My host lit a cigarette. His voice at first had been thin and tired, but as he grew interested in what he said it gained volume. He talked vehemently. There was in him none of the repose of the sage. He was a polemist and a fighter. He loathed the modern cry for individualism. For him society was the unit, and the family the foundation of society. He upheld the old China and the old school, monarchy, and the rigid canon of Confucius. He grew violent and bitter as he spoke of the students, fresh from foreign universities, who with sacrilegious hands tore down the oldest civilization in the world.

"But you, do you know what you are doing?" he exclaimed. "What is the reason for which you deem yourselves our betters? Have you excelled us in arts or letters? Have our thinkers been less profound than yours? Has our civilization been less elaborate, less complicated, less refined than yours? Why, when you lived in caves and clothed yourselves with skins we were a cultured people. Do you know that we tried an experiment which is unique in the history of the world? We sought to rule this great country not by force, but by wisdom. And for centuries we succeeded. Then why does the white man despise the yellow? Shall I tell you? Because he has invented the machine gun. That is your superiority. We are a defenceless horde and you can blow us into eternity. You have shattered the dream of our philosophers that the world could be governed by the power of law and order. And now you are teaching our young men your secret. You have thrust your hideous inventions upon us. Do you not know that we have a genius for mechanics? Do you not know that there are in this country four hundred millions of the most practical and industrious people in the world? Do you think it will take us long to learn? And what will become of your superiority when the yellow man can make as good guns as the white and fire them as straight? You have appealed to the machine gun and by the machine gun shall you be judged."

But at that moment we were interrupted. A little girl came softly in and nestled close up to the old gentleman. She stared at me with curious eyes. He told me that she was his youngest child. He put his arms round her and with a murmur of caressing words kissed her fondly. She wore a black coat and trousers that barely reached her ankles, and she had a long pigtail hanging down her back. She was born on the day the revolution was brought to a successful issue by the abdication of the emperor.

"I thought she heralded the Spring of a new era," he said. "She was but the last flower of this great nation's Fall."

From a drawer in his roll-top desk he took a few cash, and handing them to her, sent her away.

"You see that I wear a queue," he said, taking it in his hands. "It is a symbol. I am the last representative of the old China."

He talked to me, more gently now, of how philosophers in long past days wandered from state to state with their disciples, teaching all who were worthy to learn. Kings called them to their councils and made them rulers of cities. His erudition was great and his eloquent phrases gave a multicoloured vitality to the incidents he related to me of the history of his country. I could not help thinking him a somewhat pathetic figure. He felt in himself the capacity to administer the state, but there was no king to entrust him with office; he had vast stores of learning which he was eager to impart to the great band of students that his soul hankered after, and there came to listen but a few, wretched, half-starved, and obtuse provincials.

Once or twice discretion had made me suggest that I should take my leave, but he had been unwilling to let me go. Now, at last, I was obliged to. I rose. He held my hand.

"I should like to give you something as a recollection of your visit to the last philosopher in China, but I am a poor man and I do not know what I can give you that would be worthy of your acceptance."

I protested that the recollection of my visit was in itself a priceless gift. He smiled.

"Men have short memories in these degenerate days, and I should like to give you something more substantial. I would give you one of my books, but you cannot read Chinese."

He looked at me with an amicable perplexity. I had an inspiration.

"Give me a sample of your calligraphy," I said.

"Would you like that?" He smiled. "In my youth I was considered to wield the brush in a manner that was not entirely despicable."

He sat down at his desk, took a fair sheet of paper, and placed it before him. He poured a few drops of water on a stone, rubbed the ink stick in it, and took his brush. With a free movement of the arm he began to write. And as I watched him I remembered with not a little amusement something else which had been told me of him. It appeared that the old gentleman, whenever he could scrape a little money together, spent it wantonly in the streets inhabited by ladies to describe whom a euphemism is generally used. His eldest son, a person of standing in the city, was vexed and humiliated by the scandal of this behaviour; and only his strong sense of filial duty prevented him from reproaching the libertine with severity. I daresay that to a son such looseness would be disconcerting, but the student of human nature could look upon it with equanimity. Philosophers are apt to elaborate their theories in the study, forming conclusions upon life which they know only at second hand, and it has seemed to me often that their works would have a more definite significance if they had exposed themselves to the vicissitudes which befall the common run of men. I was prepared to regard the old gentleman's dalliance in hidden places with leniency. Perhaps he sought but to elucidate the most inscrutable of human illusions.

He finished. To dry the ink he scattered a little ash on the paper and rising handed it to me.

"What have you written?" I asked.

I thought there was a slightly malicious gleam in his eyes.

"I have ventured to offer you two little poems of my own."

"I did not know you were a poet."

"When China was still an uncivilized country," he retorted with sarcasm, "all educated men could write verse at least with elegance."

I took the paper and looked at the Chinese characters. They made an agreeable pattern upon it.

"Won't you also give me a translation?"

"*Traduttore – traditore*," he answered. "You cannot expect me to betray myself. Ask one of your English friends. Those who know most about China know nothing, but you will at least find one who is competent to give you a rendering of a few rough and simple lines."

I bade him farewell, and with great politeness he showed me to my chair. When I had the opportunity I gave the poems to a sinologue of my acquaintance, and here is the version he made,* I confess that, doubtless unreasonably, I was somewhat taken aback when I read it.

You loved me not: your voice was sweet;
Your eyes were full of laughter; your hands were tender.
And then you loved me: your voice was bitter;
Your eyes were full of tears; your hands were cruel.
Sad, sad that love should make you
Unlovable.

I craved the years would quickly pass
That you might lose
The brightness of your eyes, the peach-bloom of your skin,
And all the cruel splendour of your youth.
Then I alone would love you
And you at last would care.

The envious years have passed full soon
And you have lost
The brightness of your eyes, the peach-bloom of your skin,
And all the charming splendour of your youth.
Alas, I do not love you
And I care not if you care.

* I owe it to the kindness of my friend Mr. P. W. Davidson.

THE MISSIONARY LADY

SHE WAS CERTAINLY fifty, but a life of convictions harassed by
never a doubt had left her face unwrinkled. The hesitations
of thought had never lined the smoothness of her brow. Her
features were bold and regular, somewhat masculine, and her
determined chin bore out the impression given you by her eyes.
They were blue, confident, and unperturbed. They summed
you up through large round spectacles. You felt that here was a
woman to whom command came easily. Her charity was above
all things competent and you were certain that she ran the
obvious goodness of her heart on thoroughly business lines.
It was possible to suppose that she was not devoid of human
vanity (and this is to be counted to her for grace) since she
wore a dress of violet silk, heavily embroidered, and a toque of
immense pansies which, on a less respectable head, would have
been almost saucy. But my Uncle Henry, for twenty-seven years
Vicar of Whitstable, who had decided views on the proper
manner of dress for a clergyman's wife, never objected to my
Aunt Sophie wearing violet, and he would have found nothing
to criticize in the missionary lady's gown. She spoke fluently,
with the even flow of water turned on at a tap. Her conversation
had the admirable volubility of a politician at the end of an
electioneering campaign. You felt that she knew what she meant
(with most of us so rare an accomplishment) and meant what
she said.

"I always think," she remarked pleasantly, "that if you know
both sides of a question you'll judge differently from what you
will if you only know one side. But the fact remains that two and
two make four and you can argue all night and you won't make
them five. Am I right or am I wrong?"

I hastened to assure her that she was right, though with these
new theories of relativity and parallel lines behaving at infinity
in such a surprising manner I was in my heart of hearts none
too sure.

"No one can eat their cake and have it," she continued,
exemplifying Benedetto Croce's theory that grammar has little
to do with expression, "and one has to take the rough with the
smooth, but as I always say to the children you can't expect to
have everything your own way. No one is perfect in this world

SKETCHES OF CHINA 63

and I always think that if you expect the best from people you'll get the best."

I confess that I was staggered, but I determined to do my part. It was only civil.

"Most men live long enough to discover that every cloud has a silver lining," I began earnestly. "With perseverance you can do most things that are not beyond your powers, and after all, it's better to want what you have than to have what you want."

I thought her eyes were glazed with a sudden perplexity when I made this confident statement; but I daresay it was only my fancy, for she nodded vigorously.

"Of course, I see your point," she said. "We can't do more than we can."

But my blood was up now and I waved aside the interruption. I went on.

"Few people realize the profound truth that there are twenty shillings in every pound and twelve pence in every shilling. I'm sure it's better to see clearly to the end of your nose than indistinctly through a brick wall. If there's one thing we can be certain about it is that the whole is greater than the part."

When, with a hearty shake of the hand, firm and characteristic, she bade me farewell, she said:

"Well, we've had a most interesting chat. It does one good in a place like this, so far away from civilization, to exchange ideas with one's intellectual equals."

"Especially other people's," I murmured.

"I always think that one should profit by the great thoughts of the past," she retorted. "It shows that the mighty dead have not lived in vain."

Her conversation was devastating.

THE PLAIN

THE INCIDENT WAS, of course, perfectly trivial, and it could be very easily explained; but I was surprised that the eyes of the spirit could blind me so completely to what was visible to the eyes of sense. I was taken aback to find how completely one could be at the mercy of the laws of association. Day after day I had marched among the uplands and today I knew that I must

come to the great plain in which lay the ancient city whither
I was bound; but when I set out in the morning there was no
sign that I approached it. Indeed the hills seemed no less sheer,
and when I reached the top of one, thinking to see the valley
below, it was only to see before me one steeper and taller yet.
Beyond, climbing steadily, I could see the white causeway that
I had followed so long, shining in the sunlight as it skirted the
brow of a rugged, tawny rock. The sky was blue and in the west
hung here and there little clouds like fishing boats becalmed
towards evening off Dungeness. I trudged along, mounting all
the time, alert for the prospect that awaited me, if not round
this bend, then round the next, and at last, suddenly, when I was
thinking of other things, I came upon it. But it was no Chinese
landscape that I saw, with its padi fields, its memorial arches and
its fantastic temples, with its farmhouses set in a bamboo grove
and its wayside inns, where, under the banyan trees, the poor
coolies may rest them of their weary loads; it was the valley of
the Rhine, the broad plain all golden in the sunset, the valley
of the Rhine with its river, a silvery streak, running through it,
and the distant towers of Worms; it was the great plain upon
which my young eyes rested, when, a student in Heidelberg,
after walking long among the fir-clad hills above the old city,
I came out upon a clearing. And because I was there first conscious of beauty; because there I knew the first glow of the
acquisition of knowledge (each book I read was an extraordinary adventure); because there I first knew the delight of
conversation (oh, those wonderful commonplaces which each
boy discovers as though none had discovered them before);
because of the morning stroll in the sunny Anlage, the cakes
and coffee which refreshed my abstemious youth at the end of
a strenuous walk, the leisurely evenings on the castle terrace,
with the smoky blue haze over the tumbled roofs of the old
town below me; because of Goethe and Heine and Beethoven
and Wagner and (why not?) Strauss with his waltzes, and the
beer-garden where the band played and girls with yellow plaits
walked sedately; because of all these things – recollections which
have all the force of the appeal of sense – to me not only does
the word *plain* mean everywhere and exclusively the valley of
the Rhine; but the only symbol for happiness I know is a wide
prospect all golden in the setting sun, with a shining stream of

silver running through it, like the path of life or like the ideal that guides you through it, and far away the grey towers of an ancient town.

A STUDENT OF THE DRAMA

HE SENT IN a neat card of the correct shape and size, deeply bordered in black, upon which, under his name, was printed *Professor of Comparative Modern Literature*. He turned out to be a young man, small, with tiny, elegant hands, with a larger nose than you see as a rule in the Chinese and gold-rimmed spectacles. Though it was a warm day he was dressed, in European clothes, in a suit of heavy tweed. He seemed a trifle shy. He spoke in a high falsetto, as though his voice had never broken, and those shrill notes gave I know not what feeling of unreality to his conversation. He had studied in Geneva and in Paris, Berlin and Vienna, and he expressed himself fluently in English, French, and German.

It appeared that he lectured on the drama and he had lately written, in French, a work on the Chinese theatre. His studies abroad had left him with a surprising enthusiasm for Scribe, and this was the model he proposed for the regeneration of the Chinese drama. It was curious to hear him demand that the drama should be exciting. He was asking for the *pièce bien faite*, the *scène à faire*, the curtain, the unexpected, the dramatic. The Chinese theatre, with its elaborate symbolism, has been what we are always crying for, the theatre of ideas; and apparently it has been perishing of dullness. It is true that ideas do not grow on every gooseberry bush, they need novelty to make them appetizing, and when they are stale they stink as badly as stale fish.

But then, remembering the description on the card, I asked my friend what books, English and French, he recommended his students to read in order to familiarize themselves with the current literature of the day. He hesitated a little.

"I really don't know," he said at last, "you see, that's not my branch, I only have to do with drama; but if you're interested I'll ask my colleague who lectures on European fiction to call on you."

"I beg your pardon," I said.

"Have you read *Les Avariés?*" he asked. "I think that is the finest play that has been produced in Europe since Scribe."

"Do you?" I said politely.

"Yes, you see our students are greatly interested in sociological questions."

It is my misfortune that I am not, and so as deftly as I could I led the conversation to Chinese philosophy, which I was desultorily reading. I mentioned Chuang-Tzu. The professor's jaw fell.

"He lived a very long time ago," he said, perplexed.

"So did Aristotle," I murmured pleasantly.

"I have never studied the philosophers," he said, "but of course we have at our university a professor of Chinese philosophy, and if you are interested in that I will ask him to come and call on you."

It is useless to argue with a pedagogue, as the Spirit of the Ocean (somewhat portentously to my mind) remarked to the Spirit of the River, and I resigned myself to discuss the drama. My professor was interested in its technique and, indeed, was preparing a course of lectures on the subject, which he seemed to think both complicated and abstruse. He flattered me by asking me what were the secrets of the craft.

"I know only two," I answered. "One is to have common-sense, and the other is to stick to the point."

"Does it require no more than that to write a play?" he inquired, with a shade of dismay in his tone.

"You want a certain knack," I allowed, "but no more than to play billiards."

"They lecture on the technique of the drama in all the important universities of America," said he.

"The Americans are an extremely practical people," I answered. "I believe that Harvard is instituting a chair to instruct grandmothers how to suck eggs."

"I do not think I quite understand you."

"If you can't write a play no one can teach you, and if you can it's as easy as falling off a log."

Here his face expressed a lively perplexity, but I think only because he could not make up his mind whether this operation came within the province of the professor of physics or within that of the professor of applied mechanics.

"But if it is so easy to write a play why do dramatists take so long about it?"

"They didn't, you know. Lope de Vega and Shakespeare and a hundred others wrote copiously and with ease. Some modern playwrights have been perfectly illiterate men and have found it an almost insuperable difficulty to put two sentences together. A celebrated English dramatist once showed me a manuscript and I saw that he had written the question: will you have sugar in your tea, five times before he could put it in this form. A novelist would starve if he could not on the whole say what he wanted to without any beating about the bush."

"You would not call Ibsen an illiterate man and yet it is well known that he took two years to write a play."

"It is obvious that Ibsen found a prodigious difficulty in thinking of a plot. He racked his brain furiously, month after month, and at last in despair used the very same that he had used before."

"What do you mean?" the professor cried, his voice rising to a shrill scream. "I do not understand you at all."

"Have you not noticed that Ibsen uses the same plot over and over again? A number of people are living in a closed and stuffy room, then someone comes (from the mountains or from over the sea) and flings the window open; everyone gets a cold in the head and the curtain falls."

I thought it just possible that the shadow of a smile might lighten for a moment the professor's grave face, but he knit his brows and gazed for two minutes into space. Then he rose.

"I will peruse the works of Henrik Ibsen once more with that point of view in mind," he said.

I did not omit before he left to put him the question which one earnest student of the drama always puts another when peradventure they meet. I asked him, namely, what he thought was the future of the theatre. I had an idea that he said, oh hell, but on reflection I believe his exclamation must have been, *ô ciel!* He sighed, he shook his head, he threw up his elegant hands; he looked the picture of dejection. It was certainly a comfort to find that all thoughtful people considered the drama's state in China no less desperate than all thoughtful people consider it in England.

A CITY BUILT ON A ROCK

THEY SAY OF it that the dogs bark when peradventure the sun shines there. It is a grey and gloomy city, shrouded in mist, for it stands upon its rock where two great rivers meet so that it is washed on all sides but one by turbid, rushing waters. The rock is like the prow of an ancient galley and seems, as though possessed of a strange, unnatural life, all tremulous with effort; it is as if it were ever on the point of forging into the tumultuous stream. Rugged mountains hem the city round about.

Outside the walls bedraggled houses are built on piles, and here, when the river is low, a hazardous population lives on the needs of the watermen; for at the foot of the rock a thousand junks are moored, wedged in with one another tightly, and men's lives there have all the turbulence of the river. A steep and tortuous stairway leads to the great gate guarded by a temple, and up and down this all day long go the water coolies, with their dripping buckets; and from their splashing the stair and the street that leads from the gate are wet as though after heavy rain. It is difficult to walk on the level for more than a few minutes, and there are as many steps as in the hill towns of the Italian Riviera. Because there is so little space the streets are pressed together, narrow and dark, and they wind continuously so that to find your way is like finding it in a labyrinth. The throng is as thick as the throng on a pavement in London when a theatre is emptying itself of its audience. You have to push your way through it, stepping aside every moment as chairs come by and coolies bearing their everlasting loads: itinerant sellers, selling almost anything that anyone can want to buy, jostle you as you pass.

The shops are wide open to the street, without windows or doors, and they are crowded too. They are like an exhibition of arts and crafts, and you may see what a street looked like in mediæval England when each town made all that was necessary to its needs. The various industries are huddled together so that you will pass through a street of butchers where carcasses and entrails hang bloody on each side of you, with flies buzzing about them and mangy dogs prowling hungrily below; you will pass through a street where in each house there is a hand-loom and they are busily weaving cloth or silk. There are innumerable eating houses from which come heavy odours, and here at all hours people are eating. Then, generally at a corner, you will see tea-houses, and here all day long again the tables are packed with men of all sorts drinking tea and smoking. The barbers ply their trade in the public view and you will see men leaning patiently on their crossed arms while their heads are being shaved; others are having their ears cleaned, and some, a revolting spectacle, the inside of their eyelids scraped.

It is a city of a thousand noises. There are the peddlers who announce their presence by a wooden gong; the clappers of the blind musician or of the masseuse; the shrill falsetto of a man singing in a tavern; the loud beating of a gong from a house where a wedding or a funeral is being celebrated. There are the raucous shouts of the coolies and chair-bearers; the menacing whines of the beggars, caricatures of humanity, their emaciated limbs barely covered by filthy tatters and revolting with disease; the cracked melancholy of the bugler who incessantly practises a call he can never get; and then, like a bass to which all these are a barbaric melody, the insistent sound of conversation, of people laughing, quarrelling, joking, shouting, arguing, gossiping. It is a ceaseless din. It is extraordinary at first, then confusing, exasperating, and at last maddening. You long for a moment's utter silence. It seems to you that it would be a voluptuous delight.

And then combining with the irksome throng and the din that exhausts your ears is a stench which time and experience enable you to distinguish into a thousand separate stenches. Your nostrils grow cunning. Foul odours beat upon your harassed nerves like the sound of uncouth instruments playing a horrible symphony.

You cannot tell what are the lives of these thousands who surge about you. Upon your own people sympathy and knowledge give you a hold; you can enter into their lives, at least imaginatively, and in a way really possess them. By the effort of your fancy you can make them after a fashion part of yourself. But these are as strange to you as you are strange to them. You have no clue to their mystery. For their likeness to yourself in so much does not help you; it serves rather to emphasize their difference. Someone attracts your attention, a pale youth with great horn spectacles and a book under his arm, whose studious look is pleasant, or an old man, wearing a hood, with a grey sparse beard and tired eyes: he looks like one of those sages that the Chinese artists painted in a rocky landscape or under Kang-hsi modelled

in porcelain; but you might as well look at a brick wall. You have
nothing to go upon, you do not know the first thing about them,
and your imagination is baffled.

But when, reaching the top of the hill, you come once more
to the crenellated walls that surround the city and go out through
the frowning gate, you come to the graves. They stretch over the
country, one mile, two miles, three, four, five, interminable
green mounds, up and down the hills, with grey stones to which
the people once a year come to offer libation and to tell the dead
how fare the living whom they left behind; and they are as thickly
crowded, the dead, as are the living in the city; and they seem to
press upon the living as though they would force them into the
turbid, swirling river. There is something menacing about those
serried ranks. It is as though they were laying siege to the city,
with a sullen ruthlessness, biding their time; and as though in
the end, encroaching irresistibly as fate, they would drive those
seething throngs before them till the houses and the streets were
covered by them, and the green mounds came down to the water
gate. Then at last silence, silence would dwell there undisturbed.

They are uncanny, those green graves, they are terrifying.
They seem to wait.

ACROSS SOUTHEAST ASIA

from *The Gentleman in the Parlour*

PAGAN

THE CIRCUIT HOUSE stood on the river bank, quite close to the water, and all round it were great trees, tamarinds, banyans, and wild gooseberries. A flight of wooden steps led to a broad veranda, which served as a living room, and behind this were a couple of bedrooms, each with a bathroom. I found that one of these was occupied by another traveller, and I had but just examined the accommodation and talked to the Madrassi in charge about meals and taken stock of what pickles and canned goods and liquor he had on the premises when a little man appeared in a mackintosh and a topee dripping with rain. He took off his soaking things, and presently we sat down to the meal known in this country as brunch. It appeared that he was a Czecho-Slovak, employed by a firm of exporters in Calcutta, and was spending his holiday seeing the sights of Burma. He was a short man with wild black hair, a large face, a bold hooked nose, and gold-rimmed spectacles. His *stengah-shifter* fitted tightly over a corpulent figure. He was evidently an active and an energetic sightseer, for the rain had not prevented him from going out in the morning, and he told me that he had visited no less than seven pagodas. But the rain stopped while we were eating, and soon the sun shone brightly. We had no sooner finished than he set out again. I do not know how many pagodas there are at Pagan; when you stand on an eminence they surround you as far as the eye can reach. They are almost as thickly strewn as the tombstones in a cemetery. They are of all sizes and in all states of preservation. Their solidity and size and magnificence are the more striking by reason of their surroundings, for they alone remain to show that here a vast and populous city once flourished. Today there is only a straggling village with broad untidy roads lined with great trees, a pleasant enough little place with matting houses, neat and trim, in which live the workers in lacquer; for this is the industry on which Pagan, forgetful of its ancient greatness, now modestly thrives.

But of all these pagodas only one, the Ananda, is still a place of pilgrimage. Here are four huge gilded Buddhas standing against a gilded wall in a lofty gilded chamber. You look at them one by one through a gilded archway. In that glowing dimness they are inscrutable. In front of one a mendicant in his yellow robe chants in a high-pitched voice some litany that you do not understand. But the other pagodas are deserted. Grass grows in the chinks of the pavement, and young trees have taken root in the crannies. They are the refuge of birds. Hawks wheel about their summits, and little green parrots chatter in the eaves. They are like bizarre and monstrous flowers turned to stone. There is one in which the architect has taken as his model the lotus, as the architect of St. John's, Smith Square, took Queen Anne's footstool, and it has a baroque extravagance that makes the Jesuit churches in Spain seem severe and classical. It is preposterous, so that it makes you smile to look at it, but its exuberance is captivating. It is quite unreal, shoddy but strange, and you are staggered at the fantasy that could ever have devised it. It looks like the fabric of a single night made by the swarming hands of one of those wayward gods of the Indian mythology. Within the pagodas images of the Buddha sit in meditation. The gold leaf has long since worn away from the colossal figures, and the figures are crumbling to dust. The fantastic lions that guard the entrance ways are rotting on their pedestals.

A strange and melancholy spot. But my curiosity was satisfied with a visit to half a dozen of the pagodas, and I would not let the vigour of my Czecho-Slovak be a reproach to my indolence. He divided them into various types and marked them down in his notebook according to their peculiarities. He had theories about them, and in his mind they were neatly ticketed to support a theory or clinch an argument. None was so ruined that he did not think it worth while to give it his close and enthusiastic attention, and to examine the make and shape of tiles he climbed up broken places like a mountain goat. I preferred to sit idly on the veranda of the circuit house and watch the scene before me. In the full tide of noon the sun burned all the colour from the landscape, so that the trees and the dwarf scrub that grew wildly where in time past were the busy haunts of men were pale and grey; but with the declining day the colour crept back, like an emotion that tempers the character and has been submerged for a while by the affairs of the world, and trees and scrub were again a sumptuous and living green. The sun set on the other side of the river, and a red cloud in the west was reflected on the tranquil bosom of the Irrawaddy. There was not a ripple on the water. The river seemed no longer to flow. In the distance a solitary fisherman in a dugout plied his craft. A little to one side but in full view was one of the loveliest of the pagodas. In the setting sun its colours, cream and fawn-grey, were soft like the silk of old dresses in a museum. It had a symmetry that was grateful to the eye; the turrets at one corner were repeated by the turrets at every other; and the flamboyant windows repeated the flamboyant doors below. The decoration had a sort of bold violence, as though it sought to scale fantastic pinnacles of the spirit and in the desperate struggle, with life and soul engaged, could not concern itself with reticence or good taste. But withal it had at that moment a kind of majesty, and there was majesty in the solitude in which it stood. It seemed to weigh upon the earth with too great a burden. It was impressive to reflect that it had stood for so many centuries and looked down impassively upon the smiling bend of the Irrawaddy. The birds were singing noisily in the trees; the crickets chirped and the frogs croaked, croaked, croaked. Somewhere a boy was whistling a melancholy tune on a rude pipe, and in the compound the natives were chattering loudly. There is no silence in the East.

It was at this hour that the Czecho-Slovak returned to the circuit house. He was very hot and dusty, tired but happy, for he had missed nothing. He was a mine of information. The night began gradually to enfold the pagoda, and it looked now unsubstantial, as though it were built of lath and plaster, so that you would not have been surprised to see it at the Paris exhibition housing a display of colonial produce. It was a strangely sophisticated building in that exquisitely rural scene. But the Czecho-Slovak told me when it was built and under what king, and then, gathering way, began to tell me something of the history of Pagan. He had a retentive memory. He marshalled his facts with precision and delivered them with the fluency of a lecturer delivering a lecture he has repeated too often. But I did not want to know the facts he gave me. What did it matter to me what kings had reigned there, what battles they had fought and what lands they had conquered? I was content to see them as a low relief on a temple wall in a long procession, with their hieratic attitudes, seated on a throne and receiving gifts from the envoys of subjugated nations, or else, with a confusion of spears, in the hurry and skelter of chariots, in the turmoil of battle. I asked the Czecho-Slovak what he was going to do with all the information he had acquired.

"Do? Nothing," he replied. "I like facts. I want to know things. Whenever I go anywhere I read everything about it that has been written. I study its history, the fauna and flora, the manners and customs of the people, I make myself thoroughly acquainted with its art and literature. I could write a standard book on every country I have visited. I am a mine of information."

"That is just what I was saying to myself. But what is the good of information that means nothing to you? Information for its own sake is like a flight of steps that leads to a blank wall."

"I do not agree with you. Information for its own sake is like a pin you pick up and put in the lapel of your coat or the piece of string that you untie instead of cutting and put away in a drawer. You never know when it will be useful."

And to show me that he did not choose his metaphors at random the Czecho-Slovak turned up the bottom of his *stengah-shifter* (which has no lapel) and showed me four pins in a neat row.

MANDALAY

FIRST OF ALL Mandalay is a name. For there are places whose names from some accident of history or happy association have an independent magic, and perhaps the wise man would never visit them, for the expectations they arouse can hardly be realized. Names have a life of their own, and though Trebizond may be nothing but a poverty-stricken village the glamour of its name must invest it for all right-thinking minds with the trappings of Empire. And Samarkand: can anyone write the word without a quickening of the pulse and at his heart the pain of unsatisfied desire? The very name of the Irrawaddy informs the sensitive fancy with its vast and turbid flow. The streets of Mandalay, dusty, crowded, and drenched with a garish sun, are broad and straight. Tramcars lumber down them with a rout of passengers; they fill the seats and gangways and cling thickly to the footboard like flies clustered upon an overripe mango. The houses, with their balconies and verandas, have the slatternly look of the houses in the Main Street of a Western town that has fallen upon evil days. Here are no narrow alleys or devious ways down which the imagination may wander in search of the unimaginable. It does not matter: Mandalay has its name; the falling cadence of the lovely word has gathered about itself the chiaroscuro of romance.

But Mandalay has also its fort. The fort is surrounded by a high wall, and the high wall by a moat. In the fort stands the palace, and stood, before they were torn down, the offices of King Thebaw's government and the dwelling places of his ministers. At intervals in the wall are gateways washed white with lime, and each is surmounted by a sort of belvedere, like a summerhouse in a Chinese garden; and on the bastions are teak pavilions too fanciful to allow you to think they could ever have served a war-like purpose. The wall is made of huge sun-baked bricks, and the colour of it is old rose. At its foot is a broad stretch of sward planted quite thickly with tamarind, cassia, and acacia; a flock of brown sheep, advancing with tenacity, slowly but intently grazes the luscious grass; and here in the evening you see the Burmese in their coloured skirts and bright headkerchiefs wander in twos and threes. They are little brown men of a solid and sturdy build, with something a trifle Mongolian in their faces. They walk deliberately as though they were owners and tillers of the soil. They have none of the sidelong grace, the deprecating elegance, of the Indian who passes them; they have not his refinement of features, nor his languorous, effeminate distinction. They smile easily. They are happy, cheerful, and amiable.

In the broad water of the moat the rosy wall and the thick foliage of the trees and the Burmese in their bright clothes are sharply reflected. The water is still but not stagnant, and peace rests upon it like a swan with a golden crown. Its colours, in the early morning and towards sunset, have the soft, fatigued tenderness of pastel; they have the translucency, without the stubborn definiteness, of oils. It is as though light were a prestidigitator and in play laid on colours that he had just created and were about with a careless hand to wash them out again. You hold your breath, for you cannot believe that such an effect can be anything but evanescent. You watch it with the same expectancy with which you read a poem in some complicated metre when your ear awaits the long delayed rhyme that will fulfil the harmony. But at sunset, when the clouds in the west are red and splendid so that the wall, the trees, and the moat are drenched in radiance, and at night under the full moon when the white gateways drip with silver and the belvederes above them are shot with silhouetted glimpses of the sky, the assault on your senses is shattering. You try to guard yourself by saying it is not real. This is not a beauty that steals upon you unawares, that flatters and soothes your bruised spirit; this is not a beauty that you can hold in your hand and call your own and put in its place among familiar beauties that you know: it is a beauty that batters you and stuns you and leaves you breathless; there is no calmness in it nor control; it is like a fire that on a sudden consumes you, and you are left shaken and bare and yet by a strange miracle alive.

THE NUNS AT MENGON

THEN I WENT to see the great bell at Mengon. Here is a Buddhist convent, and as I stood looking a group of nuns surrounded me. They wore robes of the same shape and size as the monks', but instead of the monks' fine yellow, of a grimy dun. Little old toothless women, their heads shaven but covered with an inch of thin grey stubble, and their little old faces deeply lined and wrinkled. They held out skinny hands for money and gabbled with bare, pale gums. Their dark eyes were alert with covetousness, and their smiles were mischievous. They were very old, and they had no human ties or affections. They seemed to look upon the world with a humorous cynicism. They had lived through every kind of illusion and held existence in a malicious and laughing contempt. They had no tolerance for the follies of men and no indulgence for their weakness. There was something vaguely frightening in their entire lack of attachment to human things. They had done with love, they had finished with the anguish of separation, death had no terrors for them, they had nothing left now but laughter. They struck the great bell so that I might hear its tone: boom, boom, it went, a long low note that travelled in slow reverberations down the river, a solemn sound that seemed to call the soul from its tenement of clay and reminded it that though all created things were illusion, in the illusion was also beauty; and the nuns, following the sound, burst into ribald cackles of laughter, hi, hi, hi, that mocked the call of the great bell. Dupes their laughter said, dupes and fools. Laughter is the only reality.

ON THE TRAIL

BUT EVEN WHEN I had learned by experience that if I wanted a quiet ride I must give the mules an hour's start of me, I found it impossible to concentrate my thoughts on any of the subjects that I had selected for meditation. Though nothing of the least consequence happened, my attention was distracted by a hundred trifling incidents of the wayside. Two big butterflies in black and white fluttered along in front of me, and they were like young war widows bearing the loss they had sustained for their country's sake with cheerful resignation: so long as there were dances at Claridge's and dressmakers in the Place Vendôme they were ready to swear that all was well with the world. A little cheeky bird hopped down the road, turning round every now and then jauntily as though to call my attention to her smart suit of silver grey. She looked like a neat typist tripping along from the station to her office in Cheapside. A swarm of saffron butterflies upon the droppings of an ass reminded me of pretty girls in evening frocks hovering round an obese financier. At the roadside grew a flower that was like the sweet William that I remembered in the cottage gardens of my childhood, and another had the look of a more leggy white heather. I wish, as many writers do, I could give distinction to these pages by the enumeration of the birds and flowers that I saw as I ambled along on my little Shan pony. It has a scientific air, and though the reader skips the passage it gives him a slight thrill of self-esteem to know that he is reading a book with solid fact in it. It puts you on strangely familiar terms with your reader when you tell him that you came across *P. Johnsonii*. It has a significance that is almost cabalistic; you and he (writer and reader) share a knowledge that is not common to all and sundry, and there is the sympathy between you that there is between men who wear masonic aprons or Old Etonian ties. You communicate with one another in a secret language. I should be proud to read in a

footnote of a learned work on the botany or ornithology of
Upper Burma, "Maugham, however, states that he observed
F. Jonesia in the Southern Shan States." But I know nothing of
botany and ornithology. I could, indeed, fill a page with the
names of all the sciences of which I am completely ignorant.
A yellow primrose to me, alas! is not *Primula vulgaris*, but just a
small yellow flower, ever so faintly scented with the rain, and
grey balmy mornings in February when you have a funny little
flutter in your heart, and the smell of the rich wet Kentish earth,
and kind dead faces, and the statue of Lord Beaconsfield in his
bronze robes in Parliament Square, and the yellow hair of a girl
with a sweet smile, hair now grey and shingled.

I passed a party of Shans cooking their dinner under a tree.
Their wagons were placed in a circle round them, making a kind
of laager, and the bullocks were grazing a little way off. I went
on a mile or two and came upon a respectable Burman sitting
at the side of the road and smoking a cheroot. Round him were
his servants, with their loads on the ground beside them, for he
had no mules, and they were carrying his luggage themselves.
They had made a little fire of sticks and were cooking the rice
for his midday meal. I stopped while my interpreter had a chat
with the respectable Burman. He was a clerk from Keng Tung
on his way to Taunggyi to look for a situation in a government
office. He had been on the road for eighteen days and with only
four more to go looked upon his journey as nearly at an end.
Then a Shan on horesback threw confusion among the thoughts
I tried to marshal. He rode a shaggy pony, and his feet were bare
in his stirrups. He wore a white jacket, and his coloured skirt
was tucked up so that it looked like gay riding breeches. He had
a yellow handkerchief bound round his head. He was a romantic
figure cantering through that wide upland, but not so romantic as Rembrandt's Polish Rider, who rides through space and
time with so gallant a bearing. No living horseman has ever
achieved that effect of mystery so that when you look at him
you feel that you stand on the threshold of an unknown that
lures you on and yet closes the way to you. Nor is it strange, for
nature and the beauty of nature are dead and senseless things
and it is only art that can give them significance.

But with so much to distract me I could not but suspect that
I should reach my journey's end without after all having made

up my mind upon a single one of the important subjects that I had promised myself to consider.

THE SALWEEN

WHEN I SET out in the early morning the dew was so heavy that I could see it falling, and the sky was grey; but in a little while the sun pierced through, and in the sky, blue now, the cumulus clouds were like white sea monsters gambolling sedately round the North Pole. The country was thinly peopled, and on each side of the road was the jungle. For some days we went through pleasant uplands by a broad track, unmetalled but hard, its surface deeply furrowed by the passage of bullock carts. Now and then I saw a pigeon and now and then a crow, but there were few birds. Then, leaving the open spaces, we passed through secluded hills and forests of bamboo. A bamboo forest is a graceful thing. It has the air of an enchanted wood, and you can imagine that in its green shade the princess, heroine of an Eastern story, and the prince, her lover, might very properly undergo their incredible and fantastic adventures. When the sun shines through and a tenuous breeze flutters its elegant leaves, the effect is charmingly unreal: it has a beauty not of nature, but of the theatre.

At last we arrived at the Salween. This is one of the great rivers that rise far up in the Tibetan steppes, the Bramahputra, the Irrawaddy, the Salween, and the Mekhong, and roll southwards in parallel courses to pour their mighty waters into the Indian Ocean. Being very ignorant, I had never heard of it till I went to Burma, and even then it was nothing to me but a name. It had none of the associations that are forever attached to such rivers as the Ganges, the Tiber, and the Guadalquivir. It was only as I went along that it gained a meaning to me, and with a meaning, mystery. It was a measure of distance, we were seven days from the Salween, then six; it seemed very remote; and at Mandalay I had heard people say:

"Don't the Rogerses live on the Salween? You must go and stay with them when you cross."

"Oh, my dear fellow," someone expostulated, "they live right down on the Siamese frontier; he won't be going within three weeks' journey of them."

And when we passed some rare traveller on the road perhaps my interpreter after talking to him would come and tell me that he had crossed the Salween three days before. The water was high but was going down; in bad weather it was no joke crossing. "Beyond the Salween" had a stirring sound, and the country seemed dim and aloof. I added one little impression to another, a detached fact, a word, an epithet, the recollection of an engraving in an old book, enriching the name with associations as the lover in Stendhal's book decks his beloved with the jewels of his fancy, and soon the thought of the Salween intoxicated my imagination. It became the Oriental river of my dreams, a broad stream, deep and secret, flowing through wooded hills, and it had romance, and a dark mystery so that you could scarcely believe that it rose here and there poured itself into the ocean, but that, like a symbol of eternity, it flowed from an unknown source to lose itself at last in an unknown sea.

We were two days from the Salween; then one. We left the high road and took a rocky path that wound through the jungle in and out of the hills. There was a heavy fog, and the bamboos on each side were ghostly. They were like the pale wraiths of giant armies that had fought desperate wars in the beginning of the world's long history, and now, lowering, waited in ominous silence, waited and watched for one knew not what. But every now and then, straight and imposing, rose dimly the shadow of a tall, an immensely tall tree. An unseen brook babbled noisily, but for the rest silence surrounded one. No birds sang, and the crickets were still. One seemed to go stealthily, as though one had no business there, and dangers encompassed one all about. Spectral eyes seemed to watch one. Once when a branch broke and fell to the ground, it was with so sharp and unexpected a sound that it startled one like a pistol shot.

But at last we came out into the sunshine and soon passed through a bedraggled village. Suddenly I saw the Salween shining silvery in front of me. I was prepared to feel like stout Cortez on his peak and was more than ready to look upon that sheet of water with a wild surmise, but I had already exhausted the emotion it had to offer me. It was a more ordinary and less imposing stream than I had expected; indeed, then and there, it was no wider than the Thames at Chelsea Bridge. It flowed without turbulence, swiftly and silently.

The raft (two dugouts on which was built a platform of bamboos) was at the water's edge, and we set about unloading the mules. One of them, seized with a sudden panic, bolted for the river and before anyone could stop him plunged in. He was carried away on the current. I would never have thought that that turbid, sluggish stream had such a power. He was swept along the beach swiftly, swiftly, and the muleteers shouted and waved their arms. We would see the poor brute struggling desperately, but it was inevitable that he would be drowned, and I was thankful when a bend of the river robbed me of the sight of him. When with my pony and my personal effects I was ferried across the stream I looked at it with more respect, and since the raft seemed to me none too secure I was not sorry when I reached the other side.

The bungalow was on the top of the bank. It was surrounded by lawns and flowers. Poinsettias enriched it with their brilliant hues. It had a little less than the austerity common to the bungalows of the P.W.D., and I was glad that I had chosen this place to linger at for a day or two in order to rest the mules and my own weary limbs. From the windows the river, shut in by the hills, looked like an ornamental water. I watched the raft going backwards and forwards, bringing over the mules and their loads. The muleteers were cheerful because they were to get their rest and I had given the headman a trifling sum so that they could have a treat.

Then, their duties accomplished and the servants having unpacked my things, peace descended upon the scene, and the river, empty as though man had never adventured up its winding defiles, regained its dim remoteness. There was not a sound. The day waned, and the peace of the water, the peace of the tree-clad hills, and the peace of the evening were three exquisite things. There is a moment just before sundown when the trees seem to detach themselves from the dark mass of the jungle and become individuals. Then you cannot see the wood for the trees. In the magic of the hour they seem to acquire a life of a new kind, so that it is not hard to imagine that spirits inhabit them and with dusk they will have the power to change their places. You feel that at some uncertain moment some strange thing will happen to them and they will be wondrously transfigured. You hold your breath waiting for a marvel the thought of which stirs your heart

with a kind of terrified eagerness. But the night falls; the moment
has passed, and once more the jungle takes them back. It takes
them back as the world takes young people who, feeling in themselves the genius which is youth, hesitate for an instant on the
brink of a great adventure of the spirit, and then, engulfed by
their surroundings, sink back into the vast anonymity of human
kind. The trees again become part of the wood; they are still and,
if not lifeless, alive only with the sullen and stubborn life of the
jungle.

The spot was so lovely, and the bungalow with its lawns and
trees so homelike and peaceful, that for a moment I toyed with
the notion of staying there not a day but a year, not a year but all
my life. Ten days from a railhead and my only communication
with the outside world the trains of mules that passed occasionally between Taunggyi and Keng Tung, my only intercourse the
villagers from the bedraggled village on the other side of the
river, and so to spend the years away from the turmoil, the envy
and bitterness and malice of the world, with my thoughts, my
books, my dog and my gun and all about me the vast, mysterious,
and luxuriant jungle. But alas, life does not consist only of years,
but of hours, the day has twenty-four, and it is no paradox that
they are harder to get through than a year; and I knew that in a
week my restless spirit would drive me on, to no envisaged goal,
it is true, but on as dead leaves are blown hither and thither to
no purpose by a gusty wind. But being a writer (no poet, alas!
but merely a writer of stories) I was able to lead for others a life
I could not lead for myself. This was a fit scene for an idyll of
young lovers, and I let my fancy wander as I devised a story to
fit the tranquil and lovely scene. But, I do not know why, unless
it is that in beauty is always something tragic, my invention threw
itself into a perverse mould and disaster fell upon the thin wraiths
of my imagination.

THE MARKET

IN THE MARKET was to be found everything to eat, to wear, and
to furnish his house that was necessary to the needs of the simple
Shan. There were silks from China, and the Chinese hucksters,
sedately smoking their water pipes, were dressed in blue trousers,

tight-fitting black coats, and black silk caps. They were not lacking in elegance. The Chinese are the aristocracy of the East. There were Indians in white trousers, a white tunic that fitted closely to their thin bodies, and round caps of black velvet. They sold soap and buttons, and flimsy Indian silks, rolls of Manchester cotton, alarm clocks, looking glasses, and knives from Sheffield. The Shans retailed the goods brought down by the tribesmen from the surrounding hills and the simple products of their own industry. Here and there a little band of musicians occupied a booth, and a crowd stood round, idly listening. In one three men beat on gongs, one played the cymbals, and another thumped a drum as long as himself. My uneducated ear could discern no pattern in that welter of sound, but only a direct and not unexhilarating appeal to crude emotion; but a little farther on I came across another band, not of Shans this time but of hillmen, who played on long wind instruments of bamboo, and their music was melancholy and tremulous. Every now and then I seemed in its vague monotony to catch a few notes of a wistful melody. It gave you an impression of something immensely old. Every violence of statement had been worn away from it and every challenge to an energetic reaction, and there remained but subdued suggestions on which the imagination might work and references, as it were, to desires and hopes and despairs deep buried in the heart. You had the feeling of a music recollected at night by the camp fires of nomad tribes on their wanderings from the grass lands of their ancient homes and begotten of the scattered sounds of the jungle and the silence of flowing rivers; and to my fancy (worked up now, as is the writer's way, by the power of the words, so difficultly controlled, that throng upon his imagination) it suggested the perplexity in the midst of strange and hostile surroundings of men who came they knew not whence and went they knew not whither, a plaintive, questioning cry and a song sung together (as men at sea in a storm tell one another lewd stories to drive away the uneasiness of the battering waves and the howling wind) to reassure themselves by the blessed solace of human companionship against the loneliness of the world.

But there was nothing doleful or forlorn in the throng that crowded the streets of the market. They were gay, voluble, and blithe. They had come not only to buy and sell, but to gossip and pass the time of day with their friends. It was the meeting place not only of Keng Tung but of the whole countryside for fifty miles around. Here they got the news and heard the latest stories. It was as good as a play and doubtless much better than most. Among the Shans, who were in the majority, wandered in their distinctive costumes members of many tribes. They held together in little groups as though, feeling shy in this foreign environment, they were afraid of being parted from one another. To them it must have seemed a vast and populous city, and they kept themselves to themselves with the countryman's odd mingling of awe and contempt for the inhabitants of a city. There were Tais, Laos, Kaws, Palaungs, Was, and heaven knows what else. The Was are divided by people wise in these matters into wild and tame, but the wild ones do not leave their mountain fastnesses. They are head hunters, not from vainglory like the Dyaks, nor for aesthetic reasons like the people of the Mambwe country, but for the purely utilitarian purpose of protecting their crops. A fresh skull will guard and strengthen the growing grain, and so at the approach of a spring from each village a small party of men goes out to look for a likely stranger. A stranger is sought since he does not know his way about the country and his spirit will not wander away from his earthly remains. But it is said that travel in those parts is far from popular during the hunting season. But the tame Was have the air of amiable and kindly people, and certainly their appearance, though wild enough, is picturesque. The Kaws stand out from among the others by reason of their fine physique and swarthy colour. The authorities, however, state that the darkness of their complexion is due for the most part to their dislike of the use of water. The women wear a headdress covered with silver beads so that it looks like a helmet; their hair is parted in the middle and comes down over the ears as one sees it in the portraits of the Empress Eugenie, and in middle age they have funny little wrinkled faces full of humour. They wear a short coat, a kilt, and leggings; and there is quite an interval between the coat and the kilt: I could not fail to notice how much character it gives a woman's face to display her navel. The men are dressed in dingy blue, with turbans, and in these the young lads put marigolds as a sign that they are bachelors and want to marry. I wondered indeed if they kept them there or only put them in when the urge was strong upon them. For presumably no one feels inclined to marry on a cold and frosty morning. I saw one with half a dozen flowers in his turban. He was not going to leave his intentions in doubt. He cut a gay and jaunty figure, but the girls seemed to take no more notice of him than he, I am bound to confess, took of them. Perhaps they thought his eagerness was exaggerated, and he, I suppose, having put his advertisement in the paper, as it were, was willing to leave it at that. He was a pleasant creature, of a dusky complexion, with large dark eyes, bold and shining, and he stood, with his back a trifle arched, as though all his muscles quivered with strength. There were peasants threading their way among the throng with pigeons on a perch tied by the leg with a string, which you might either buy to release and so acquire merit or add to the next day's curry. One of these men passing him, the young Kaw, evidently a careless fellow with his money, on a sudden impulse (and you saw on his mobile face how unexpectedly it came into his head) bought a pigeon, and when it was given to him he held it for a moment in both his hands, a grey wood pigeon with a pink breast, and then throwing up his arms with the gesture of the bronze boy from Herculaneum flung it high into the air. He watched it fly rapidly away, fly back to its native woods, and there was a boyish smile on his handsome face.

KENG TUNG

I SPENT THE best part of a week in Keng Tung. The days were warm and sunny and the circuit house neat, clean, and roomy. After so many strenuous days on the road it was pleasant to have nothing much to do. It was pleasant not to get up till one felt inclined and to breakfast in pajamas. It was pleasant to lounge through the morning with a book. For it is an error to think that because you have no train to catch and no appointments to keep your movements on the road are free. Your times for doing this and that are as definite as if you lived in a city and had to go to business every morning. Your movements are settled not by your own whim, but by the length of the stages and the endurance of the mules. Though you would not think it mattered if you arrived half an hour sooner or later at your day's destination there is always a rush to get up in the morning, a bustle of preparation, and an urgent compulsion to get off without delay.

I kept the emotion with which Keng Tung filled me well under control. It was a village, larger than those I had passed on the way, but a village notwithstanding, of wooden houses, spacious, with wide dirt streets, and I was put to it to find objects of interest to visit. On other than market days it was empty. In the main street you saw nothing but a few gaunt pariah dogs. In one or two shops a woman, smoking a cheroot, sat idly on the floor; she had no thought that on such a day there would ever be a customer; in another four Chinamen, crouched on their heels, were gambling. Silence. The dusty road had great ruts in it, and the sun beat down on it from a clear blue sky. Three little women suddenly appeared in monstrous, diverting hats and passed along in single file; they had a couple of baskets suspended by a bamboo over the shoulder, and they walked with bent knees, speedily, as though if they went more slowly they would sink under their burdens. And against the emptiness of the street they made a quick and evanescent pattern.

And there was silence too in the monasteries. There are per-haps a dozen of them in Keng Tung, and their high roofs stand out when you look at the town from the little hill on which is the circuit house. Each one stands in its compound, and in the compound are a number of crumbling pagodas. The great hall in which the Buddha, enormous, sits in his hieratic attitude, sur-rounded by others, eight or ten, hardly smaller, is like a barn, but its roof is supported by huge columns of teak, gilt or lacquered, and the wooden walls and the rafters are gilt or lacquered too. Rude paintings of scenes in the Master's life hang from the eaves. It is dark and solemn, but the Buddhas sit on their great lotus leaves in the gloaming like gods who have had their day, and now neglected, but indifferent to neglect, in their decaying grandeur of gilt and mosaic continue to reflect on suffering and the end of suffering, transitoriness and the eightfold path. Their aloofness is almost terrifying. You tread on tiptoe in order not to disturb their meditations, and when you close behind you the carved and gilded doors and come out once more into the friendly day it is with a sigh of relief. You feel like a man who has gone by accident to a party at the wrong house and on realizing his mistake makes his escape quickly and hopes that no one has noticed him.

THE SOLITARY

MUSING UPON THE odd chance that had brought me to that
distant spot, my idle thoughts gathered about the tall, aloof figure
of the casual acquaintance whose words spoken at random had
tempted me to make the journey. I tried from the impression she
had left upon me to construct the living man. For when we meet
people we see them only in the flat, they offer us but one side of
themselves, and they remain shadowy: we have to give them our
flesh and our bones before they exist in the round. That is why
the characters of fiction are more real than the characters of life.
He was a soldier and for five years had been in command of the
Military Police Post at Loimwe, which is a few miles southeast
of Keng Tung. Loimwe signifies the Hill of Dreams.

I do not think he was a great hunter, for I have noticed that
most men who live in places where game is plentiful acquire a
distaste for killing the wild creatures of the jungle. When on their
arrival they have shot this animal or that, the tiger, the buffalo,
or the deer, for the satisfaction of their self-esteem, they lose
interest. It suggests itself to them that the graceful creatures,
whose habits they have studied, have as much right to life as they;
they get a sort of affection for them, and it is only unwillingly
that they take their guns to kill a tiger that is frightening the
villagers, or woodcock or snipe for the pot.

Five years is a big slice out of a man's life. He spoke of Keng
Tung as a lover might speak of his bride. It had been an experience so poignant that it had set him apart forever from his fellows.
He was reticent and as is the English way could tell but in clumsy
words what he had found there. I do not know whether even to
himself he was able to put into plain language the vague emotions
that touched his heart when in a secluded village at night he
sat and talked with the elders and whether he asked himself the
questions, so new and strange to one of his circumstances and
profession, that stood in silence (like homeless men in winter
outside a refuge for the destitute) waiting to be answered. He
loved the wild wooded hills and the starry nights. The days were
interminable and monotonous and on them he embroidered a
vague and misty pattern. I do not know what it was. I can only
guess that it made the world he went back to, the world of clubs
and mess tables, of steam engines and motor cars, dances and

tennis parties, politics, intrigue, bustle, excitement, the world of
the newspapers, strangely without meaning. Though he lived in
it, though he even enjoyed it, it remained utterly remote. I think
it had lost its sense for him. In his heart was the reflection of a
lovely dream that he could never quite recall.

We are gregarious, most of us, and we resent the man who
does not seek the society of his fellows. We do not content ourselves with saying that he is odd, but we ascribe to him unworthy
motives. Our pride is wounded that he should have no use for
us, and we nod to one another and wink and say that if he lives
in this strange way it must be to practise some secret vice, and if
he does not inhabit his own country it can only be because his
own country is too hot to hold him. But there are people who
do not feel at home in the world, the companionship of others
is not necessary to them, and they are ill at ease amid the exuberance of their fellows. They have an invincible shyness. Shared
emotions abash them. The thought of community singing, even
though it be but *God Save the King*, fills them with embarrassment, and if they sing it is plaintively in their baths. They are
self-sufficient, and they shrug a resigned and sometimes, it must
be admitted, a scornful shoulder because the world uses that
adjective in a depreciatory sense. Wherever they are they feel
themselves "out of it." They are to be found all over the service
of this earth, members of a great monastic order bound by no
vows and cloistered though not by walls of stone. If you wander
up and down the world you will meet them in all sorts of unexpected places. You are not surprised when you hear that an
elderly English lady is living in a villa on a hill outside a small
Italian town that you have happened on by an accident to the car
in which you were driving, for Italy has always been the preferred
refuge of these staid nuns. They have generally adequate means
and an extensive knowledge of the *cinque cento*. You take it as a
matter of course when a lonely *hacienda is* pointed out to you in
Andalusia and you are told that there has dwelt for many years
an English lady of a certain age. She is usually a devout Catholic
and sometimes lives in sin with her coachman. But it is more
surprising when you hear that the only white person in a Chinese
city is an Englishwoman, not a missionary, who has lived there,
none knows why, for a quarter of a century; and there is another
who inhabits an islet in the South Seas, and a third who has a

bungalow on the outskirts of a large village in the centre of Java. They live solitary lives, without friends, and they do not welcome the stranger. Though they may not have seen one of their own race for months they will pass you on the road as though they did not see you, and if, presuming on your nationality, you call, the chances are that they will decline to receive you; but if they do they will give you a cup of tea from a silver teapot and on a plate of old Worcester you will be offered hot scones. They will talk to you politely, as though they were entertaining you in a drawing room overlooking a London square, but when you take your leave they express no desire ever to see you again.

The men are at once shyer and more friendly. At first they are tongue-tied, and you see the anxious look on their faces as they rack their brains for topics of conversation, but a glass of whisky loosens their minds (for sometimes they are inclined to tipple) and then they will talk freely. They are glad to see you, but you must be careful not to abuse your welcome; they get tired of company very soon and grow restless at the necessity of making an effort. They are more apt to run to seed than women, they live in a higgledy-piggledy manner, indifferent to their surroundings and their food. They have often an ostensible occupation. They keep a little shop but do not care whether they sell anything, and their goods are dusty and fly-blown, or they run, with lackadaisical incompetence, a coconut plantation. They are on the verge of bankruptcy. Sometimes they are engaged in metaphysical speculation, and I met one who had spent years in the study and annotation of the works of Immanuel Swedenborg. Sometimes they are students and take endless pains to translate classical works which have been already translated, like the dialogues of Plato, or of which translation is impossible, like Goethe's *Faust*. They may not be very useful members of society, but their lives are harmless and innocent. If the world despises them, they on their side despise the world. The thought of returning to its turmoil is a nightmare to them. They ask nothing but to be left in peace. Their satisfaction with their lot is sometimes a trifle irritating. It needs a good deal of philosophy not to be mortified by the thought of persons who have voluntarily abandoned everything that for the most of us makes life worth living and are devoid of envy of what they have missed. I have never made up my mind whether they are fools or wise men.

They have given up everything for a dream, a dream of peace or happiness or freedom, and their dream is so intense that they make it true.

SIAM

I TRAVELLED LEISURELY down Siam. The country was pleasant, open and smiling, scattered with neat little villages, each surrounded with a fence, and fruit trees and areca palms growing in the compounds gave them an attractive air of modest prosperity. There was a good deal of traffic on the road, but it was carried on not, as in the little inhabited Shan States by mules, but by bullock carts. Where the country was flat rice was cultivated, but where it undulated teak forests grew. The teak is a handsome tree, with a large smooth leaf; it does not make a very dense jungle, and the sun shines through. To ride in a teak forest, so light, graceful, and airy, is to feel yourself a cavalier in an old romance. The rest houses were clean and trim. During this part of my journey I came across but one white man, and this was a Frenchman on his way north who came into the bungalow in which I had settled myself for the night. It belonged to a French teak company, of which he was a servant, and he seemed to look upon it as very natural that I, a stranger, should have made myself at home in it. He was cordial; there are few French in this business and the men, out in the jungle constantly to superintend the native labourer, live lives even more lonely than the English forest men, so that he was glad to have someone to talk to. We shared our dinner. He was a man of robust build, with a large, fleshy red face and a warm voice that seemed to wrap his fluent words in a soft, rich fabric of sound. He had just come from short leave in Bangkok, and with the Frenchman's ingenuous belief that you are any more impressed by the number of his amours than by the number of his hats talked much of the sexual experiences he had had there. He was a coarse fellow, ill bred and stupid. But he caught sight of a torn paper-bound book that was lying on the table.

"*Tiens*, where did you get hold of this?"

I told him that I had found it in the bungalow and had been glancing through it. It was that selection of Verlaine's poems which has for a frontispiece Carrière's misty but not uninteresting portrait of him.

"I wonder who the devil can have left it here," he said.

He took up the volume and, idly fingering the pages, told me various gross stories about the unhappy poet. They were not new to me. Then his eyes caught a line that he knew, and he began to read.

> "*Voici des fruits, des fleurs, des feuilles et des branches*
> *Et puis voici mon cœur qui ne bat que pour vous.*"

And as he read his voice broke and tears came into his eyes and ran down his face.

"*Ah, merde*," he said, "*ça me fait pleurer comme un veau.*"

He flung the book down and laughed and gave a little sob. I poured him out a drink of whisky, for there is nothing better than alcohol to still, or at least to enable one to endure, that particular heartache from which at the moment he was suffering. Then we played piquet. He went to bed early, since he had a long day before him and was starting at dawn, and by the time I got up he was gone. I did not see him again.

But as I rode along in the sunshine, bustling and quick like women gossiping at their spinning wheels, I thought of him. I reflected that men are more interesting than books but have this defect, that you cannot skip them; you have at least to skim the whole volume in order to find the good page. And you cannot put them on a shelf and take them down when you feel inclined; you must read them when the chance offers, like a book in a circulating library that is in such demand that you must take your turn and keep it no more than four and twenty hours. You may not be in the mood for them then or it may be that in your hurry you miss the only thing they had to give you.

And now the plain spread out with a noble spaciousness. The rice fields were no longer little patches laboriously wrested from the jungle, but broad acres. The days followed one another with a monotony in which there was withal something impressive. In the life of cities we are conscious but of fragments of days; they have no meaning of their own but are merely parts of time in which we conduct such and such affairs; we begin them when they are already well on their way and continue them without regard to their natural end. But here they had completeness, and one watched them unroll themselves with stately majesty from dawn to dusk; each day was like a flower, a rose that buds and blooms and, without regret but accepting the course of nature, dies. And this vast sun-drenched plain was a fit scene for the pageant of that ever-recurring drama. The stars were like the curious who wander upon the scene of some great event, a battle or an earthquake, that has just occurred, first one by one timidly and then in bands, and stand about gaping or looking for traces of what has passed.

The road became straight and level. Though here and there deep with ruts, and when a stream crossed it, muddy, great stretches could have been traversed by car. Now it is all very well to ride a pony at the rate of twelve or fifteen miles a day when you go along mountain paths, but when the road is broad and flat this mode of travel sorely tries your patience. It was six weeks now that I had been on the way. It seemed endless. Then on a sudden I found myself in the tropics. I suppose that little by little, as one uneventful day followed another, the character of the scene had been changing, but it had been so gradual that I had scarcely noticed it, and I drew a deep breath of delight when, riding into a village one noon, I was met, as by an unexpected friend, with the savour of the harsh, the impetuous, the flamboyant South. The depth of colour, the hot touch of the air on one's cheek, the dazzling yet strangely veiled light, the different walk of the people, the lazy breadth of their gestures, the silence, the solemnity, the dust – this was the real thing, and my jaded spirits rose. The village street was bordered by tamarinds, and they were like the sentences of Sir Thomas Browne, opulent, stately, and self-possessed. In the compounds grew plantains, regal and bedraggled, and the crotons flaunted the riches of their sepulchral hues. The coconut trees with their dishevelled heads were like long lean old men suddenly risen from sleep. In the monastery was a grove of areca palms, and they stood, immensely tall and slender, with the gaunt precision and the bare, precise, and intellectual nakedness of a collection of apothegms. It was the South.

BANGKOK

A FEW HOURS later I was in Bangkok.

It is impossible to consider these populous modern cities of the East without a certain malaise. They are all alike, with their straight streets, their arcades, their tramways, their dust, their blinding sun, their teeming Chinese, their dense traffic, their ceaseless din. They have no history and no traditions. Painters have not painted them. No poets, transfiguring dead bricks and mortar with their divine nostalgia, have given them a tremulous melancholy not their own. They live their own lives, without associations, like a man without imagination. They are hard and glittering and as unreal as a backcloth in a musical comedy. They give you nothing. But when you leave them it is with a feeling that you have missed something, and you cannot help thinking that they have some secret that they have kept from you. And though you have been a trifle bored you look back upon them wistfully; you are certain that they have after all something to give you which, had you stayed longer or under other conditions, you would have been capable of receiving. For it is useless to offer a gift to him who cannot stretch out a hand to take it. But if you go back the secret still evades you and you ask yourself whether after all their only secret is not that the glamour of the East enwraps them. Because they are called Rangoon, Bangkok, or Saigon, because they are situated on the Irrawaddy, the Menam, or the Mehkong, those great turbid rivers, they are invested with the magic spell that the ancient storied East has cast upon the imaginative West. A hundred travellers may seek in them the answer to a question they cannot put and that yet torments them; only to be disappointed, a hundred travellers more will continue to press.

And who can so describe a city as to give a significant picture of it? It is a different place to everyone who lives in it. No one can tell what it really is. Nor does it matter. The only thing of importance – to me – is what it means to me; and when the money lender said, "You can 'ave Rome," he said all there was to be said, by him, about the Eternal City.

I put my impressions on the table, as a gardener puts the varied flowers he has cut in a great heap, leaving them for you to arrange, and I ask myself what sort of pattern I can make out of them. For my impressions are like a long frieze, a vague tapestry, and my business is to find in it an elegant and at the same time moving decoration. But the materials that are given me are dust and heat and noise and whiteness and more dust.

The New Road is the main artery of the city, five miles long, and it is lined with houses, low and sordid, and shops, and the goods they sell, European and Japanese for the most part, look shop-soiled and dingy. A leisurely tram, crowded with passengers, passes down the whole length of the street, and the conductor never ceases to blow his horn. Gharries and rickshaws go up and down ringing their bells, and motors sounding their klaxons. The pavements are crowded, and there is a ceaseless clatter of the clogs the people wear. Clopperty-clop, they go, and it makes a sound as insistent and monotonous as the sawing of the cicadas in the jungle.

There are Siamese. The Siamese, with short bristly hair, wearing the *panaung*, a wide piece of stuff which they tuck in to make baggy and comfortable breeches, are not a comely race, but old age gives them distinction; they grow thin, emaciated even, rather than fat, and grey rather than bald, and then their dark eyes peer brightly out of a ravaged, yellow, and wrinkled face; they walk well and uprightly, not from the knees as do most Europeans, but from the hips. There are Chinese, in trousers white, blue, or black, that come to just above the ankle, and they are innumerable. There are Arabs, tall and heavily bearded, with white hats and a hawklike look, who walk with assurance, leisurely, and in their bold eyes you discern contempt for the race they exploit and pride in their own astuteness. There are turbaned natives of India with dark skins and the clean, sensitive features of their Aryan blood; as in all the East outside India they seem deliberately alien and thread their way through the host as though they walked a lonely jungle path: their faces are the most inscrutable of all those inscrutable faces. The sun beats down, and the road is white, and the houses are white, and the sky is white; there is no colour but the colour of dust and heat.

But if you turn out of the main road you will find yourself in a network of small streets, dark, shaded, and squalid, and tortuous alleys paved with cobble-stones. In numberless shops, open to the street, with their gay signs, the industrious Chinese ply the various crafts of an Oriental city. Here are druggists and coffin shops, money changers and tea houses. Along the streets, uttering the raucous cry of China, coolies lollop swiftly, bearing loads, and the peddling cook carries his little kitchen to sell you the hot dinner you are too busy to eat at home. You might be in Canton. Here the Chinese live their lives apart and indifferent to the Western capital that the rulers of Siam have sought to make out of this strange, flat, confused city. What they have aimed at you see in the broad avenues, straight dusty roads, sometimes running by the side of a canal, with which they have surrounded this conglomeration of sordid streets. They are handsome, spacious, and stately, shaded by trees, the deliberate adornment of a great city devised by a king ambitious to have an imposing seat; but they have no reality. There is something stagey about them so that you feel they are more apt for court pageants than for the use of every day. No one walks in them. They seem to await ceremonies and processions. They are like the deserted avenues in the park of a fallen monarch.

It appears that there are three hundred and ninety wats in Bangkok. A wat is a collection of buildings used as a Buddhist monastery, and it is surrounded by a wall, often crenellated so as to make a charming pattern, like the walled enclosure of a city. Each building has its own use. The main one is called a *bote*, it is a great and lofty hall, with a central nave, generally, and two aisles, and here the Buddha stands on his gilded platform. There is another building, very like the *bote*, called the *vihara* and distinguished from it by the fact that it is not surrounded by the sacred stones; which is used for feasts and ceremonies and assemblies of the common folk. The *bote*, and sometimes the *vihara*, is surrounded by a cloister. Then there are shelters, libraries, bell towers, and the priests' dwellings. Round the main buildings in due order are pagodas, large and small; (they have their names, Phra Prang and Phra Chedi;) some contain the ashes of royal or pious persons (it may be even of royal *and* pious persons), and some, merely decorative, serve only to acquire merit for those that built them.

But not by this list of facts (which I found in a book on the architecture of Siam) can I hope to give an impression of the surprise, the stupefaction almost, which assailed me when I saw these incredible buildings. They are unlike anything in the world, so that you are taken aback, and you cannot fit them into the scheme of the things you know. It makes you laugh with delight to think that anything so fantastic could exist on this sombre earth. They are gorgeous; they glitter with gold and whitewash, yet are not garish; against that vivid sky, in that dazzling sunlight, they hold their own, defying the brilliancy of nature and supplementing it with the ingenuity and the playful boldness of man. The artists who developed them step by step from the buildings of the ancient Khmers had the courage to pursue their fantasy to the limit; I fancy that art meant little to them, they desired to express a symbol; they knew no reticence, they cared nothing for good taste; and if they achieved art it is as men achieve happiness, not by pursuing it, but by doing with all their heart whatever in the day's work needs doing. I do not know that in fact they achieved art; I do not know that these Siamese wats have beauty, which they say is reserved and aloof and very refined; all I know is that they are strange and gay and odd, their lines are infinitely distinguished, like the lines of a proposition in a schoolboy's Euclid, their colours are flaunting and crude, like the colours of vegetables in the greengrocer's stall at an open-air market, and, like a place where seven ways meet, they open roads down which the imagination can make many a careless and unexpected journey.

The royal wat is not a wat but a city of wats; it is a gay, coloured confusion of halls and pagodas, some of them in ruins, some with the appearance of being brand new; there are buildings, brilliant of hue though somewhat run to seed, that look like monstrous vegetables in the kitchen-gardens of the djinn; there are structures made of tiles and encrusted with strange tile flowers, three of them enormous, but many small ones, rows of them, that look like the prizes in a shooting gallery at a village fair in the country of the gods. It is like a page of *Euphues*, and you are tickled to death at the sesquipedalian fancy that invented so many sonorous, absurd, grandiloquent terms. It is a labyrinth in which you cannot find your way. Roof rises upon roof, and the roofs in Siamese architecture are its chief glory. They are arranged in three tiers, the upper one steeply pitched, and the lower ones decreasing in angle as they descend. They are covered with glazed tiles, and their red and yellow and green are a feast to the eye. The gables are framed with Narga, the sacred snake, its head at the lower eaves and its undulating body climbing up the slope of the roof to end in a horn at the apex; and the gables are decorated with reliefs in carved wood of Indra on the Elephant or Vishnu on the Garuda; for the temples of Buddha extend without misgiving shelter to the gods of other faiths. It is all incredibly rich with the gilding and the glass mosaic of the architraves and door jambs and the black and gold lacquer of the doors and shutters. It is huge, it is crowded, it dazzles the eyes and takes the breath away, it is empty, it is dead; you wander about a trifle disconsolate, for after all it means nothing to you, the "oh" of surprise is extorted from you, but never the "ah" of emotion wrung; it makes no sense; it is an intricacy of odd, archaic, and polysyllabic words in a crossword puzzle. And when in the course of your rambles you step up to look over a tall balustrade and see a rockery it is with relief that you enter. It is made about a small piece of artificial water, with little rustic bridges built over it here and there; it looks like the stony desert in which an ancient sage in a Chinese picture has his hermitage, and on the artificial rocks by the water's edge are monkeys and wild cats in stone and little dwarfish men. A magnolia grows there and a Chinese willow and shrubs with fat, shining leaves. It is a pleasantly fantastic retreat where an Oriental king might fitly meditate, in comfort and peace, on the transitoriness of compound things.

But there is another wat, Suthat by name, that gives you no such impression of pell-mell confusion. It is clean and well swept and empty and quiet, and the space and the silence make a significant decoration. In the cloisters, all round, sitting cheek by jowl are gilded Buddhas, and as night falls and they are left to undistracted meditation, they are mysterious and vaguely sinister. Here and there in the court shrubs grow and stumpy gnarled trees. There is a multitude of rooks, and they caw loudly as they fly. The *bote* stands high on a double platform, and its whitewash is stained by the rain and burned by the sun to a mottled ivory. The square columns, fluted at the corners, slope slightly inwards, and their capitals are strange upspringing flowers like flowers in an enchanted garden. They give the effect of a fantastic filigree of gold and silver and precious gems, emeralds, rubies, and zircons. And the carving on the gable, intricate and elaborate, droops down like maidenhair in a grotto, and the climbing snake is like the waves of the sea in a Chinese painting.

The doorways, three at each end and very tall, are of wood heavily carved and dully gilt, and the windows, close together and high, have shutters of faded gilt that faintly shines. With the evening, when the blue sky turns pink, the roof, the tall steep roof with its projecting eaves, gains all kinds of opalescent hues, so that you can no longer believe it was made by human craftsmen, for it seems made of passing fancies and memories and fond hopes. The silence and the solitude seem about to take shape and appear before your eyes. And now the wat is very tall and very slender and of an incredible elegance. But, alas, its spiritual significance escapes you.

BUDDHA

IT SEEMED TO me that there was more of this in the humble little monasteries that I had passed on the road hither. With their wooden walls and thatched roofs and their small tawdry images there was a homeliness about them, but withal an austerity, that seemed to suit better the homely and yet austere religion that Gautama preached. It is, to my fancy, a religion of the countryside rather than of the cities, and there lingers about it always the green shade of the wild fig tree under which the Blessed One found enlightenment. Legend has made him out to be the son of a king, so that when he renounced the world he might seem to have abandoned power and great riches and glory; but in truth he was no more than the scion of a good family of country gentlemen, and when he renounced the world I do not suppose he abandoned more than a number of buffaloes and some rice fields. His life was as simple as that of the headman of any of the villages I had passed through in the Shan States. He lived in a world that had a passion for metaphysical disquisition, but he did not take kindly to metaphysics, and when he was forced by the subtle Hindu sages into argument he grew somewhat impatient. He would have nothing to do with speculations upon the origin, significance, and purpose of the Universe. "Verily," he said, "within this mortal body, some six feet high, but conscious and endowed with mind, is the world and its origin and its passing away." His followers were forced by the Brahman doctors to defend their positions with metaphysical arguments and in course of time elaborated a theory of their faith that would satisfy the keen intelligence of a philosophic people, but Gautama, like all the founders of religion, had in point of fact but one thing to say: "Come unto me all ye that are weary and heavy laden and I will give you rest."

Most of the gods that the world has seen have made a somewhat frantic claim that men should have faith in them, and have threatened with dreadful penalties such as could not (whatever their good will) believe. There is something pathetic in the violence with which they denounce those who thwart them in the bestowal of the great gifts they have to offer. They seem deep in their hearts to have felt that it was the faith of others that gave them divinity (as though, their godhead standing on an insecure foundation, every believer was as it were a stone to buttress it) and that the message they so ardently craved to deliver could only have its efficacy if they became god. And god they could only become if men believed in them. But Gautama made only the claim of the physician that you should give him a trial and judge him by results. He was more like the artist who does his work as best he can because to produce art is his function, and having offered his gift to all that are willing and able to take it, passes on to other work, shrugging his shoulders tolerantly if his gift is declined.

Buddhism is a way of life rather than a religion. It is terribly austere. It is like an unknown sea when the day breaks as though it had never broken before and the colours of the morning steal over the earth as though for the first time and you, your bearings lost, with none to point the way, look with dismay upon the water's desert wastes. "All is passing," said the Blessed One, "all is sorrow, all is unreal"; and he never ceased to insist on the transitoriness that embittered life.

But is it true that because things pass they are evil? For innumerable centuries moralists, divines, and poets have repined because of the transitoriness of created things. But is it not the better part of wisdom to see that change in itself is good? There is a story that Monet, the founder of the impressionists, being troubled with his eyes, went to an oculist, and trying on some spectacles cried, "Good heavens, with these I see the world just like Bouguereau." It is an instructive little anecdote. It is out of their limitations that men create beauty, and the new and lovely things that have been given to the world have been very often but the result of the conflict of the artist with his short-comings. I hazard the suggestion that Richard Wagner would never have written the Ring if he had been able to compose as neat a tune as Verdi and that Cézanne would never have painted his exquisite pictures if he had been able to draw as well as the academic Ingres. And so with life. Everything changes, nothing remains in one stay, the rose that poured out its perfume on the air this morning is scattered this eve; and it is but good sense not to bewail this, the necessity of life, nor even to accept it with resignation, but to welcome it; it is the chief of the colours we have to work with, nay, it is the canvas on which we paint, and shall we ignore it, shall we deplore it, shall we complain that it makes it impossible to complete our picture? Does the rose smell less sweet because in an hour it dies? Is love less precious because it passes? Is a song less lovely because we tire of it? If all things are transitory, let us find delight in their transitoriness.

And that on the whole is what we of the West are at last learning to do. We welcome change for its own sake, and because of the joy we take in it we have added a value to life. I think it is America that has taught us this lesson, and if that is so it is a greater benefit which that country has conferred upon the world than ragtime, cocktails, the phonograph, and the Pullman car.

But I do not suppose that anyone can wander through these Buddhist countries, Burma, the Shan States, and Siam, without being intrigued by the doctrine of Karma which is so inextricably interwoven with the habits, thoughts and affections of the peoples with whom he is thrown in contact. It is commonly thought that it was invented by the Blessed One, but in fact it was current in India in his time, and he did no more than adopt it with such modifications as were rendered necessary by his disbelief in the soul. For, as everyone knows, the most important point of the Buddha's teachings was that there was no such thing as a soul or a self. Every person is a putting together of qualities, material and mental; there can be no putting together without a becoming different, and there can be no becoming different without a passing away. Whatever has a beginning also has an end. The thought is exhilarating like a brisk winter morning when the sun shines and the road over the Downs is springy under the feet. Karma (I venture to remind the reader) is the theory that a man's actions in one existence determine his fate in the next. At death, under the influence of the desire of life, the impermanent aggregation of qualities which was a man re-assembles to form another aggregation as impermanent. He is merely the present and temporary link in a long chain of cause and effect. The law of Karma prescribes that every act must have its result. It is the only explanation of the evil of this world that does not outrage the heart.

On a previous page I informed the kindly reader that it was my habit to start the day with a perusal of a few pages of a metaphysical work. It is a practice as healthy to the soul as the morning bath is healthy to the body. Though I have not the kind of intelligence that moves easily among abstractions and I often do not altogether understand what I read (this does not too greatly distract me since I find that professional dialecticians often complain that they cannot understand one another) I read on and sometimes come upon a passage that has a particular meaning for me. My way is lighted now and then by a happy phrase, for the philosophers of the past often wrote more than ordinarily well, and since in the long run a philosopher only describes himself, with his prejudices, his personal hopes, and his idiosyncrasies, and they were for the most part men of robust character, I have often the amusement of making acquaintance with a curious personality. In this desultory way I have read most of the great philosophers that the world has seen, trying to learn a little here and there or to get some enlightenment on matters that must puzzle everyone who makes his tentative way through the labyrinthine jungle of this life: nothing has interested me more than the way they treat the problem of evil. I cannot say that I have been greatly enlightened. The best of them have no more to say than in the long run evil will be found to be good and that we who suffer must accept our suffering with an equal mind. In my perplexity I have read what the theologians had to say on the subject. After all, sin is their province, and so far as they are concerned the question is simple: if God is good and all powerful why does he permit evil? Their answers are many and confused; they satisfy neither the heart nor the head, and for my part – I speak of these things humbly because I am ignorant, and it may be that though the plain man must ask the question the answer can only be understood by the expert – I cannot accept them.

Now it happened that one of the books I had brought to read on the way was Bradley's *Appearance and Reality*. I had read it before, but had found it difficult and wanted to read it again, but since it was an unwieldy volume I tore off the binding and divided it into sections that I could conveniently put in my pocket when, having read enough, I mounted my pony and rode off from the bungalow in which I had passed the night. It is good reading, and though it scarcely convinces you it is often caustic, and the author has a pleasant gift of irony. He is never pompous. He handles the abstract with a light touch. But it is like one of those cubist houses in an exhibition, very light and trim and airy, but so severe in line and furnished with such austere taste that you cannot imagine yourself toasting your toes by the fire and lounging in an easy chair with a comfortable book. But when I came upon his treatment of the problem of evil I found myself as honestly scandalized as the Pope at the sight of a young woman's shapely calves. The Absolute, I read, is perfect, and evil, being but an appearance, cannot but subserve to the perfection of the whole. Error contributes to greater energy of life. Evil plays a part in a higher end, and in this sense unknowingly is good. The Absolute is the richer for every discord. And my memory brought back to me, I know not why, a scene at the beginning of the war.

It was in October, and our sensibilities were not yet blunted. A cold raw night. There had been what those who took part in it thought a battle, but which was so insignificant a skirmish that the papers did not so much as refer to it, and about a thousand men had been killed and wounded. They lay on straw on the floor of a country church, and the only light came from the candles on the altar. The Germans were advancing, and it was necessary to evacuate them as quickly as possible. All through the night the ambulance cars, without lights, drove back and forth, and the wounded cried out to be taken, and some died as they were being lifted on to the stretchers and were thrown on the heap of dead outside the door, and they were dirty and gory, and the church stank of blood and the rankness of humanity. And there was one boy who was so shattered that it was not worth while to move him, and as he lay there, seeing men on either side of him being taken out, he screamed at the top of his voice: *Je ne veux pas mourir. Je suis trop jeune. Je ne veux pas mourir.* And he went on screaming that he did not want to die till he died. Of course this is no argument. It was but an inconsiderable incident the only significance of which was that I saw it with my own eyes, and in my ears for days afterwards rang that despairing cry, but a greater than I, a philosopher and a mathematician into the bargain, if you please, said that the heart had its reasons which the head did not know, and (in the grip of compound things, to use the Buddhist phrase, as I am) this scene is to me a sufficient refutation of the metaphysician's fine-spun theories. But my heart can accept the evils that befall me if they are the consequence of actions that I (the I that is not my soul, which perishes, but the result of my deeds in another state of existence) did in past time, and I am resigned to the evils that I see about me, the death of the young (the most bitter of all), the grief of the mothers that bore them in anguish, poverty, and sickness and frustrated hopes, if these evils are but the consequence of the sins which those that suffer them once committed. Here is an explanation that outrages neither the heart nor the head; there is only one fault that I can find in it: it is incredible.

THE FEVER

THE HOTEL FACED the river. My room was dark, one of a long line, with a veranda on each side of it; the breeze blew through, but it was stifling. The dining room was large and dim, and for coolness' sake the windows were shuttered. One was waited on by silent Chinese boys. I did not know why, the insipid Eastern food sickened me. The heat of Bangkok was overwhelming. The wats oppressed me by their garish magnificence, making my head ache, and their fantastic ornaments filled me with malaise. All I saw looked too bright, the crowds in the street tired me, and the incessant din jangled my nerves. I felt very unwell, but I was not sure whether my trouble was bodily or spiritual (I am suspicious of the sensibility of the artist, and I have often dissipated a whole train of exquisite and sombre thoughts by administering to myself a little liver pill), so to settle the matter I took my temperature. I was startled to see that it was a hundred and five.

I could not believe it, so I took it again; it was still a hundred and five. No travail of the soul can cause anything like that. I went to bed and sent for a doctor. He told me that I had probably got malaria and took some of my blood to test; when he came back it was to say that there was no doubt about it and to give me quinine. I remembered then that towards the end of my journey down Siam the officer in command of the post had insisted that I should stay in his own house. He gave me his best bedroom and was so anxious that I should sleep in his grand European bed, of varnished pitch pine and all the way from Bangkok, that I had not the heart to say that I preferred my own little camp bed, which had a mosquito net, to his, which had not. The Anopheles snatched at the golden opportunity.

It was apparently a bad attack, since for some days the quinine had no effect on me: my temperature soared to those vertiginous heights that are common in malaria, and neither wet sheets nor ice packs brought it down. I lay there, panting and sleepless, and shapes of monstrous pagodas thronged my brain, and great gilded Buddhas bore down on me. Those wooden rooms with their verandas made every sound frightfully audible to my tortured ears, and one morning I heard the manageress of the hotel, an amiable creature but a good woman of business, in her guttural German voice say to the doctor: "I can't have him die here, you know. You must take him to the hospital." And the doctor replied: "All right. But we'll wait a day or two yet." "Well, don't leave it too long," she replied.

Then the crisis came. The sweat poured from me so that soon my bed was soaking, as though I had had a bath in it, and well-being descended upon me. I could breathe easily. My head ached no longer. And then, when they carried me on to a long chair and I was free from pain, I felt extraordinarily happy. My brain seemed wonderfully clear. I was as weak as a newborn child and for some days could do nothing but lie on the terrace at the back of the hotel and look at the river. Motor launches bustled to and fro. The sampans were innumerable. Large steamers and sailing vessels came up the river, so that it had quite the air of a busy port; and if you have a passion for travel it is impossible to look at the smallest, shabbiest, dirtiest sea-going tramp without a thrill of emotion and a hankering to be on it and on the way to some unknown haven. In the early morning, before the heat of the day, the scene was gay and lively; and then again towards sundown it was rich with colour and vaguely sinister with the laden shadows of the approaching night. I watched the steamers plod slowly up and with a noisy rattling of chains drop their anchors, and I watched the three-masted barques drop silently down with the tide.

For some reason that I forget I had not been able to see the palace, but I did not regret it, since it thus retained for me the faint air of mystery which of all the emotions is that which you can least find in Bangkok. It is surrounded by a great white wall, strangely crenellated, and the crenellations have the effect of a row of lotus buds. At intervals are gateways at which stand guards in odd Napoleonic costumes, and they have a pleasantly operatic air, so that you expect them at any minute to break into florid song. Towards evening the white wall becomes pink and trans-lucent, and then above it, the dusk shrouding their garishness with its own soft glamour, you see, higgledy-piggledy, the gay, fantastic, and multi-coloured roofs of the palace and the wats and the bright-hued tapering of the pagodas. You divine wide courtyards, with lovely gateways intricately decorated, in which officials of the court, in their sober but distinguished dress, are intent upon secret affairs; and you imagine walks lined with trim, clipped trees and temples sombre and magnificent, throne halls rich with gold and precious stones, and apartments, vaguely scented, dark, and cool, in which lie in careless profusion the storied treasures of the East.

And because I had nothing to do except look at the river and enjoy the weakness that held me blissfully to my chair I invented a fairy story.

ANGKOR

ONE THING THAT makes a visit to Angkor an event of unusual significance − preparing you to enter into the state of mind proper to such an experience − is the immense difficulty of getting there. For once you have reached Phnom-Penh − itself a place sufficiently off the beaten track − you must take a steamer and go a long way up a dull and sluggish river, a tributary of the Mehkong, till you reach a wide lake; you change into another steamer, flat bottomed, for there is no great depth, and in this you travel all night; then you pass through a narrow defile and come to another great stretch of placid water. It is night again when you reach the end of it. Then you get into a sampan and are rowed among clumps of mangroves up a tortuous channel. The moon is full, and the trees on the banks are sharply outlined against the night, and you seem to traverse not a real country but the fantastic land of the silhouettist. At last you come to a bedraggled little village of watermen, whose dwellings are houseboats, and landing you drive down by the riverside through plantations of coconut, betel, and plantain, and the river is now a shallow little stream (like the country stream in which on Sundays in your childhood you used to catch minnows and put them in a jam pot), till at length, looming gigantic and black in the moonshine, you see the great towers of Angkor Wat.

But now that I come to this part of my book I am seized with dismay. I have never seen anything in the world more wonderful than the temples of Angkor, but I do not know how on earth I am going to set down in black and white such an account of them as will give even the most sensitive reader more than a confused and shadowy impression of their grandeur. Of course, to the artist in words, who takes pleasure in the sound of them and their look on the page, it would be an opportunity in a thousand. What a chance for prose, pompous and sensual, varied, solemn, and harmonious; and what a delight to such a one it would be to reproduce in his long phrases the long lines of the buildings, in the balance of his paragraphs to express their symmetry, and in the opulence of his vocabulary their rich decoration! It would be enchanting to find the apt word and by putting it in its right place give the same rhythm to the sentence as he had seen in the massed grey stones; and it would be a triumph to hit upon the unusual, the revealing epithet that translated into another beauty the colour, the form, and the strangeness of what he alone had had the gift to see.

Alas, I have not the smallest talent for this sort of thing, and — doubtless because I cannot do it myself — I do not very much like it in others. A little of it goes a long way with me. I can read a page of Ruskin with enjoyment, but ten only with weariness; and when I have finished an essay by Walter Pater I know how a trout feels when you have taken him off the hook and he lies on the bank flapping his tail in the grass. I admire the ingenuity with which, little piece of glass by little piece of glass, Pater fitted together the mosaic of his style, but it bores me. His prose is like one of those period houses, all Genoese velvet and carved wood, that they used to have in America twenty years ago, and you looked round desperately for a corner on which to put down your empty glass. I can bear it better when this kind of stately writing is done by our forefathers. The grand style became them. I am awed by the magnificence of Sir Thomas Browne, it is like staying in a great Palladian palace with frescoes by Veronese on the ceilings and tapestries on the walls. It is impressive rather than homely. You cannot see yourself doing your daily dozen in those august surroundings.

When I was young I took much trouble to acquire a style; I used to go to the British Museum and note down the names of rare jewels so that I might give my prose magnificence, and I used to go to the Zoo and observe the way an eagle looked, or linger on a cab rank to see how a horse champed so that I might on occasion use a nice metaphor; I made lists of unusual adjectives so that I might put them in unexpected places. But it was not a bit of good. I found I had no bent for anything of the kind, we do not write as we want to but as we can; and though I have the greatest respect for those authors who are blessed with a happy gift of phrase I have long resigned myself to writing as plainly as I can. I have a very small vocabulary, and I manage to make do with it, I am afraid, only because I see things with no great subtlety. I think perhaps I see them with a certain passion, and it interests me to translate into words not the look of them but the emotion they have given me. But I am content if I can put this down as briefly and baldly as if I were writing a telegram.

A LAST DAY IN ANGKOR

I CAME TO the last day I could spend at Angkor. I was leaving it with a wrench, but I knew by now that it was the sort of place that, however long one stayed, it would always be a wrench to leave. I saw things that day that I had seen a dozen times, but never with such poignancy; and as I sauntered down those long grey passages and now and then caught sight of the forest through a doorway, all I saw had a new beauty. The still courtyards had a mystery that made me wish to linger in them a little longer, for I had a notion that I was on the verge of discovering some strange and subtle secret; it was as though a melody trembled in the air, but so low that the ears could just not catch it. Silence seemed to dwell in these courts like a presence that you could see if you turned round, and my last impression of Angkor was like my first, that of a great silence. And it gave me I know not what strange feeling to look at the living forest that surrounded this great grey pile so closely, the jungle luxuriant and gay in the sunlight, a sea of different greens; and to know that there all round me had once stood a multitudinous city.

That night a troup of Cambodian dancers were dancing on the terrace of the temple. We were escorted along the causeway by boys carrying a hundred lighted torches. The resin of which they were made charged the air with an acrid, pleasant perfume. They formed a great circle of flame, flickering and uncertain, on the terrace, and in the middle of it the dancers trod their strange measure. Musicians, hidden by the darkness, played on pipes and drums and gongs, a vague and rhythmical music that troubled the nerves. My ears awaited with a sort of tremor the resolution of harmonies strange to me, but never attained it. The dancers wore tight-fitting dresses of richly glowing colours and on their heads high golden crowns. By day no doubt they would have looked trumpery, but in that unexpected light they had a gorgeousness and a mystery that you find with difficulty in the East. Their impassive faces were dead white with powder so that they looked like masks. No emotion, no fleeting thought was permitted to disturb the immobility of their expression. Their hands were beautiful, with small and tapering fingers, and in the progress of the dance their gestures, elaborate and complicated, pointed their elegance and emphasized their grace. Their hands were like rare and fantastic orchids. There was no abandon in their dance. Their attitudes were hieratic and their movements formal. They were like idols that had come to life but still were impregnated with divinity.

And those gestures, those attitudes, were the same as those of the bayadères that the old sculptors had graven on the stone walls of the temples. They had not changed in a thousand years.

Repeated endlessly on every wall in every temple, you will see the self-same elegant writhing of the delicate fingers, the self-same arching of the slender body, as delights your eye in the living dancer before you. No wonder they are grave under their gold crowns when they bear the weight of so long an ancestry.

The dance ended, the torches were extinguished, and the little crowd shuffled away pell-mell into the night. I sat on a parapet taking a last look at the five towers of Angkor Wat.

My thoughts went back to a temple that I had visited a day or two before. It is called Bayon. It surprised me because it had not the uniformity of the other temples I had seen. It consists of a multitude of towers one above the other, symmetrically arranged, and each tower is a four-faced, gigantic head of Siva the Destroyer. They stand in circles one within the other and the four faces of the god are surmounted by a decorated crown. In the middle is a great tower with face rising above face till the apex is reached. It is all battered by time and weather, creepers and parasitic shrubs grow all about, so that at a first glance you see only a shapeless mass and it is only when you look a little more closely that these silent, heavy, impassive faces loom out at you from the rugged stone. Then they are all round you. They face you, they are at your side, they are behind you, and you are watched by a thousand unseeing eyes. They seem to look at you from the remote distance of primeval time, and all about you the jungle grows fiercely. You cannot wonder that the peasants when they pass should break into loud song in order to frighten away the spirits; for towards evening the silence is unearthly, and the effect of all those serene and yet malevolent faces is eerie. When the night falls the faces sink away into the stones and you have nothing but a strange, shrouded collection of oddly shaped turrets.

But it is not on account of the temple itself that I have described it – I have, albeit with a halting pen, already described more than enough – it is for the sake of the bas-reliefs that line one of its corridors. They are not very well done, and the sculptors had but too obviously little sense of form or line, but they have notwithstanding an interest which at this moment called them up vividly to my memory. For they represent scenes in the common life of the day in which they were done: the preparation of rice for the pot, the cooking of food, the catching

of fish and the snaring of birds, the buying and selling at the
village shop, the visit to the doctor: in short, the various activities
of a simple people. It was startling to discover how little in a
thousand years this life of theirs had changed. They still do the
same things with the same utensils. The rice is pounded or
husked in the self-same way, and the village shopkeeper offers
for sale the same bananas and the same sugar cane on the same
tray. These patient, industrious folk carry on the same yokes the
same burdens as their ancestors carried so many generations
back. The centuries have passed leaving no trace upon them, and
some sleeper of the Tenth Century, awakening now in one of
these Cambodian villages, would find himself at home in the
artless round of daily life.

Then it seemed to me that in these countries of the East the
most impressive, the most awe-inspiring monument of antiquity is neither temple, nor citadel, nor great wall, but man. The
peasant with his immemorial usages belongs to an age far more
ancient than Angkor Wat, the Great Wall of China, or the
Pyramids of Egypt.

SAIGON AND TOURANE

AT THE MOUTH of the little river I got once more into the flat-
bottomed steamer and crossed the wide, shallow lake, changed
into another boat, and went down another river. Finally I
reached Saigon.

Notwithstanding the Chinese city that has grown up since the
French occupied the country, and notwithstanding the natives
who saunter along the pavements or, in wide straw hats like
extinguishers, pull rickshaws, Saigon has all the air of a little provincial town in the South of France. It is laid out with broad
streets, shaded with handsome trees, and there is a bustle in them
that is quite unlike the bustle of an Eastern town in an English
colony. It is a blithe and smiling little place. It has an opera house,
white and shining, built in the flamboyant style of the Third
Republic, which faces a broad avenue; and it has a Hôtel de Ville
which is very grand, new, and ornate. Outside the hotels are
terraces, and at the hour of the *apéritif* they are crowded with
bearded, gesticulating Frenchmen, drinking the sweet and sickly

beverages, Vermouth Casis, Byrrh, and Quinquina Dubonnet, which they drink in France, and they talk nineteen to the dozen in the rolling accent of the Midi. Gay little ladies who have something to do with the local theatre are dressed in smart clothes and with their pencilled eyebrows and rouged cheeks bring a cheerful air of sophistication to this far distant spot. In the shops you will find Paris dresses from Marseilles and London hats from Lille. Victorias drawn by two little ponies gallop past, and motor cars toot their horns. The sun beats down from a cloudless sky, and the shade is heavy with the heat and solid.

Saigon is a pleasant enough place to idle in for a few days; life is made easy for the casual traveller; and it is very agreeable to sit under the awning on the terrace of the Hôtel Continental, an electric fan just above your head, and with an innocent drink before you to read in the local paper heated controversies upon the affairs of the Colony and the *faits divers* of the neighbourhood. It is charming to be able to read steadily through the advertisements without an uneasy feeling that you are wasting your time and it must be a dull mind that in such a perusal does not find here and there occasion for a pleasant gallop on a hobby horse through the realms of time and space. But I only stayed long enough to catch my boat for Huë.

Huë is the capital of Annam, and I was bound there in order to see the festivities for the Chinese New Year which were to be held at the Emperor's court. But Huë is situated on a river, and the port for it is Tourane. It was there then that the Messageries boat – a clean white comfortable craft, properly arranged for travel in hot latitudes with plenty of space and plenty of air and cold drinks – set me down at two one morning. She anchored in the bay, seven or eight kilometres from the wharf, and I got into a sampan. The crew consisted of two women, a man, and a small boy. The bay was calm, and the stars were shining thick overhead. We rowed out into the night, and the lights on the quay seemed immensely far away. The boat was heavy with water, and every now and then one of the women stopped rowing and baled it out with an empty kerosene tin. There was the shadow of a breeze, and presently they put up a great square sail of bamboo matting, but it was too light a wind to help us much, and the journey looked as though it would last till daybreak. So far as I was concerned it might have lasted forever; I lay on bamboo mats, smoking a pipe and now and then falling into a light doze, and when I awoke and relighted my pipe the match showed me for a moment the brown fat faces of the two women squatting by the mast. The man at the tiller made a short remark and one of the women answered him. Then again the silence was complete but for the faint swish of the water under the boards on which I lay. The night was so warm that with nothing on but a shirt and a pair of khaki trousers I did not feel cold, and the air was as soft as the feel of flowers. We made a long tack into the night and then going about found our slow way to the mouth of the river. We passed fishing boats lying at anchor and others silently creeping out into the stream. The banks of the river were dark and mysterious. On a word from the man the two women lowered the clumsy sail and began once more to row. We came to the quay, and the water was so shallow that I had to be carried ashore on the back of a coolie. It is a proceeding that has always seemed to me both terrifying and undignified, and I clung to the coolie's neck in a manner that I well knew ill became me. The hotel was just across the road, and coolies shouldered my luggage. But it was barely five and still very dark and no one was awake in the hotel. The coolies hammered on the door, and at last a sleepy servant opened it. The rest of them were lying about, fast asleep, on the billiard table and on the floor. I asked for a room and coffee. The fresh bread was just ready, and my *café au lait* with rolls hot from the oven, very welcome after that long journey across the bay, made a meal such as I have not often had the good luck to eat. I was shown a dirty, sordid little room, with a mosquito net grimy and torn, and I do not know how many commercial travellers and officials of the French government had passed through the sheets on the bed since last they were washed. I did not care. It seemed to me that I had never arrived anywhere in such romantic style, and I could not but think that this must be the preface to an experience that would be memorable.

But there are places of which the only point is the arrival; they promise the most fantastic adventures of the spirit and give you no more than three meals a day and last year's films. They are like a face, full of character that intrigues and excites you, but that on close acquaintance you discover is merely the mask of a vulgar soul. Such is Tourane.

I spent one morning there in order to visit the museum in

which there is a collection of Khmer sculpture. The reader may possibly remember that when I wrote of Phnom-Penh I became strangely eloquent (for a person who does not much like others to gush and is shy of superlatives) about a statue to be seen there. This was a Khmer work, and now I may remind him (or tell him if, like me till I went to Indo-China, he never knew that Khmers or their sculpture existed) that this was a mighty nation, the off-spring of the aboriginal tribes of Indo-China and an invading race from the plateaux of Central Asia, who founded a far-flung and powerful empire. Immigrants from Eastern India brought them the Sanskrit language, Brahmanism, and the culture of their native land; but the Khmers were vigorous people, and they had a creative instinct that enabled them to make their own use of the knowledge the strangers brought them. They built magnificent temples and adorned them with sculptures, founded, it is true, on the art of India, but which have at their best an energy, a boldness of execution, a fertility, and a brilliant fancy to be found nowhere else in the East. The statue of Harihara* at Phnom-Penh testifies to the greatness of their genius. It is a miracle of grace. It calls to mind the archaic statuary of Greece and the Mayan sculpture of Mexico; but it has a character all its own. Those early Greek works have the dewy freshness of the morn-ing, but their beauty is a trifle vacant; the Mayan statues have something primeval in them, they excite awe rather than admira-tion, for they have in them still the touch of early man who drew in the dark recesses of his caverns magic pictures to cast a spell on the beasts he feared or hunted; but in the Harihara you have a singular and enigmatic union of the archaic and the sophis-ticated. It has the candour of the primitive quickened by the complexity of the civilized. The Khmer brought a long inherit-ance of thought to the craft which had so suddenly captivated his fancy. It is as though to the England of the Elizabethan age had come, a bolt from the blue, the art of painting in oil; and the artists, their souls charged with the plays of Shakespeare, the

---

* I am somewhat puzzled by the name given by the French authorities to the deity represented in this statue. I always thought that Hari and Hara were the names under which were commonly known Siva and Vishnu, and to call a god Harihara looks very much like calling a single respectable person Crosseandblackwell. But since I suppose the experts know better than I, I have referred to this statue throughout by the name they give it.

conflict of religions at the Reformation, and the Armada, had begun to paint with the hand of Cimabue. Something like this must have been the state of mind of the sculptor who made the statue in Phnom-Penh. It has power and simplicity and an exquisite line, but it has also a spiritual quality that is infinitely moving. It has not only beauty, but intelligence.

These great works of the Khmers gain a peculiar poignancy when you reflect that a few ruined temples strewn about the jungle and a few mutilated statues scattered here and there in museums are all that remains of this mighty empire and this restless people. Their power was broken, they were dispersed, becoming drawers of water and hewers of wood, they died out; and now, the rest of them assimilated by their conquerors, their name endures only in the art they so lavishly produced.

HUË

HUË IS A pleasant little town with something of the leisurely air of a cathedral city in the West of England, and though the capital of an empire it is not imposing. It is built on both sides of a wide river, crossed by a bridge, and the hotel is one of the worst in the world. It is extremely dirty, and the food is dreadful; but it is also a general store in which everything is provided that the colonist may want from camp equipment and guns, women's hats and men's reach-me-downs, to sardines, *pâté de foie gras*, and Worcester sauce; so that the hungry traveller can make up with tinned goods for the inadequacy of the bill of fare. Here the inhabitants of the town come to drink their coffee and *fine* in the evening and the soldiers of the garrison to play billiards. The French have built themselves solid, rather showy houses without much regard for the climate or the environment; they look like the villas of retired grocers in the suburbs of Paris.

The French carry France to their colonies just as the English carry England to theirs, and the English, reproached for their insularity, can justly reply that in this matter they are no more singular than their neighbours. But not even the most superficial observer can fail to notice that there is a great difference in the manner in which these two nations behave towards the natives of the countries of which they have gained possession. The

Frenchman has deep down in him a persuasion that all men are equal and that mankind is a brotherhood. He is slightly ashamed of it, and in case you should laugh at him makes haste to laugh at himself, but there it is, he cannot help it, he cannot prevent himself from feeling that the native, black, brown, or yellow, is of the same clay as himself, with the same loves, hates, pleasures and pains, and he cannot bring himself to treat him as though he belonged to a different species. Though he will brook no encroachment on his authority and deals firmly with any attempt the native may make to lighten his yoke, in the ordinary affairs of life he is friendly with him without condescension and benevolent without superiority. He inculcates in him his peculiar prejudices; Paris is the centre of the world, and the ambition of every young Annamite is to see it at least once in his life; you will hardly meet one who is not convinced that outside France there is neither art, literature, nor science. But the Frenchman will sit with the Annamite, eat with him, drink with him, and play with him. In the market place you will see the thrifty Frenchwoman with her basket on her arm jostling the Annamite housekeeper and bargaining just as fiercely. No one likes having another take possession of his house, even though he conducts it more efficiently and keeps it in better repair that ever he could himself; he does not want to live in the attics even though his master has installed a lift for him to reach them; and I do not suppose the Annamites like it any more than the Burmese that strangers hold their country. But I should say that whereas the Burmese only respect the English, the Annamites admire the French. When in course of time these peoples inevitably regain their freedom it will be curious to see which of these emotions has borne the better fruit.

The Annamites are a pleasant people to look at, very small, with yellow flat faces and bright dark eyes, and they look very spruce in their clothes. The poor wear brown of the colour of rich earth, a long tunic slit up the sides, and trousers, with a girdle of apple green or orange round their waists; and on their heads a large flat straw hat or a small black turban with very regular folds. The well-to-do wear the same neat turban, with white trousers, a black silk tunic, and over this sometimes a black lace coat. It is a costume of great elegance.

But though in all these lands the clothes the people wear attract our eyes because they are peculiar, in each everyone is dressed very much alike; it is a uniform they wear, picturesque often and always suitable to the climate, but it allows little opportunity for individual taste; and I could not but think it must amaze the native of an Eastern country visiting Europe to observe the bewildering and vivid variety of costume that surrounds him. An Oriental crowd is like a bed of daffodils at a market gardener's, brilliant but monotonous; but an English crowd, for instance that which you see through a faint veil of smoke when you look down from above on the floor of a promenade concert, is like a nosegay of every kind of flower. Nowhere in the East will you see costumes so gay and multifarious as on a fine day in Piccadilly. The diversity is prodigious. Soldiers, sailors, policemen, postmen, messenger boys; men in tail coats and top hats, in lounge suits and bowlers, men in plus fours and caps, women in silk and cloth and velvet, in all the colours, and in hats of this shape and that. And besides this there are the clothes worn on different occasions and to pursue different sports, the clothes servants wear, and workmen, jockeys, huntsmen, and courtiers. I fancy the Annamite will return to Huë and think his fellow countrymen dress very dully.

A NIGHT ON THE RIVER

IT WAS LATE now, and I was setting out at dawn by car for Hanoi. It seemed hardly worth while to go to bed, and as I drove in my rickshaw to the hotel I asked myself why I should not spend the rest of the night on the river. It would do if I got back in time to change, bathe myself, and have a cup of coffee before starting. I explained to my rickshaw boy what I wanted, and he took me down to the river. There was a landing stage just below the bridge, and here we found half a dozen sampans moored to the side. Their owners were sleeping in them, but at least one of them was sleeping lightly, for he awoke as he heard me walk down the stone steps, and put his head out of the blanket in which he was wrapped. The rickshaw boy spoke to him and he got up. He called to a woman asleep in the boat. I stepped in. The woman untied, and we slipped out into the stream. These boats have a low round awning of bamboo matting, just high enough to sit upright under, and bamboo matting on the boards.

You can shut them up with shutters, but I told the man to leave the front open so that I could look at the night. In the heights of heaven the stars shone very bright, as though up there too there were a party. The man brought me a pot of Chinese tea and a cup. I poured some out and lighted my pipe. We went along very slowly, and the sound of the paddle in the water was the only sound that broke the silence. It was delightful to think that I had all those hours before me to enjoy that sense of well-being, and I thought to myself how when I was once in Europe, imprisoned in stony cities, I would remember that perfect night and the enchanting solitude. It would be the most imperishable of my memories. It was a unique occasion, and I said to myself that I must hoard the moments as they passed. I could not afford to waste one of them. I was laying up treasure for myself. And I thought of all the things I would reflect upon, and of the melancholy that I would subtly savour as you savour the first scented strawberries of the year; and I would think of love, and invent stories, and meditate upon beautiful things like art and death. The paddle hit the water very gently, and I could just feel the boat glide on. I made up my mind to watch and cherish every exquisite sensation that came to me.

Suddenly I felt a bump. What was it? I looked out and it was broad day. The bump was the bump of the boat against the landing stage, and there was the bridge just above me.

"Good God!" I cried, "I've been asleep."

I had slept right through the night, and there was my cup of tea cold by my side. My pipe had fallen out of my mouth. I had lost all those priceless moments and had slept solidly through the hours. I was furious. I might never have the opportunity again to spend a night in a sampan on an Eastern river, and now I should never have those wonderful thoughts and matchless emotions that I had promised myself. I paid for the boat and, still in evening clothes, ran up the steps and went to the hotel. My hired car was waiting for me at the door.

A CLASSMATE IN HAIPHONG

HERE I HAD the intention of finishing this book, for at Hanoi I found nothing much to interest me. It is the capital of Tonkin, and the French tell you it is the most attractive town in the East, but when you ask them why, answer that it is exactly like a town, Montpellier or Grenoble, in France. And Haiphong to which I went in order to get a boat to Hong Kong is a commercial town and dull. It is true that from it you can visit the Bay of Along, which is one of the *sehenswürdigkeiten* of Indo-China, but I was tired of sights. I contented myself with sitting in the café (for here it was none too warm, and I was glad to get out of tropical clothes) and reading back numbers of *L'Illustration* or, for the sake of exercise, taking a brisk walk along straight, wide streets. Haiphong is traversed by canals, and sometimes I caught a glimpse of a scene which in its varied life, with all the native craft on the water, was multicoloured and charming. There was one canal, with tall Chinese houses on each side of it, that had a pleasant curve. The houses were whitewashed, but the white-wash was discoloured and stained; with their grey roofs they made an agreeable composition against the pale sky. The picture had the faded elegance of an old water colour. There was nowhere an emphatic note. It was soft and a little weary and inspired one with a faint melancholy. I was reminded, I scarcely know why, of an old maid I knew in my youth, a relic of the Victorian age, who wore black silk mittens and made crochet shawls for the poor, black for widows and white for married women. She had suffered in her youth, but whether from ill health or unrequited love, no one exactly knew.

But there was a local paper at Haiphong, a small dingy sheet with stubby type the ink of which came off on your fingers, and it gave you a political article, the wireless news, advertisements, and local intelligence. The editor, doubtless hard pressed for matter, printed the names of the persons, Europeans, natives of the country, or Chinese, who had arrived each day at Haiphong or left it, and mine was put in with the rest. On the morning of the day before that on which my boat was to sail for Hong Kong I was sitting in the café of the hotel drinking a Dubonnet before luncheon when the boy came in and said that a gentleman wished to see me. I did not know a soul in Haiphong and asked who it was. The boy said he was an Englishman and lived there, but he could not tell me his name. The boy spoke very little French, and it was hard for me to understand what he said. I was mystified, but told him to show the visitor in. A moment later he came back followed by a white man and pointed me out to him. The man gave me a look and walked towards me. He was a very tall fellow, well over six feet high, rather fat and bloated, with a red, clean-shaven face and extremely pale blue eyes. He wore very shabby khaki shorts, and a *stengah-shifter* unbuttoned at the neck, and a battered helmet. I concluded at once that he was a stranded beach comber who was going to touch me for a loan and wondered how little I could hope to get off for.

He came up to me and held out a large red hand with broken, dirty nails.

"I don't suppose you remember me," he said. "My name's Grosely. I was at St. Thomas's Hospital with you. I recognized your name as soon as I saw it in the papers, and I thought I'd look you up."

I had not the smallest recollection of him, but I asked him to sit down and offered him a drink. By his appearance I had first thought he would ask me for ten piastres, and I might have given him five, but now it looked more likely that he would ask for a hundred, and I should have to think myself lucky if I could content him with fifty. The habitual borrower always asks twice what he expects to get, and it only dissatisfies him to give him what he has asked, since then he is vexed with himself for not having asked more. He feels you have cheated him.

"Are you a doctor?" I asked.

"No, I was only at the bloody place a year."

He took off his sun helmet and showed me a mop of grey hair which needed a brush. His face was curiously mottled, and he did not look healthy. His teeth were badly decayed, and at the corners of his mouth were empty spaces. When the boy came to take the orders he asked for brandy.

"Bring the bottle," he said. "*La bouteille.* Savvy?" He turned to me. "I've been living here for the last five years, but I can't get along with French somehow. I talk Tonkinese." He leaned his chair back and looked at me. "I remember you, you know. You used to go about with those twins. What was their name? I expect I've changed more than you have. I've spent the best part of my life in China. Rotten climate, you know. It plays hell with a man."

I still had not the smallest recollection of him. I thought it best to say so.

"Were you the same year as I was?" I asked.

"Yes, '92."

"It's a devil of a long time ago."

About sixty boys and young men entered the hospital every year; they were most of them shy and confused by the new life they were entering upon; many had never been in London before; and to me at least they were shadows that passed without any particular rhyme or reason across a white sheet. During the first year a certain number for one reason or another dropped out, and in the second year those that remained gained by degrees the beginnings of a personality. They were not only themselves, but the lectures one had attended with them, the scone and coffee one had eaten at the same table for luncheon, the dissection one had done at the same board in the same dissecting room, and *The Belle of New York* one had seen together from the pit of the Shaftesbury Theatre.

The boy brought the bottle of brandy, and Grosely, if that was really his name, pouring himself out a generous helping, drank it down at a gulp without water or soda.

"I couldn't stand doctoring," he said. "I chucked it. My people got fed up with me, and I went out to China. They gave me a hundred pounds and told me to shift for myself. I was damned glad to get out, I can tell you. I guess I was just about as much fed up with them as they were with me. I haven't troubled them much since."

Then from somewhere in the depths of my memory a faint hint crept into the rim, as it were, of consciousness, as on a rising tide the water slides up the sand and then withdraws, to advance with the next wave in a fuller volume. I had first an inkling of some shabby little scandal that had got into the papers. Then I saw a boy's face, and so gradually the facts recurred to me; I remembered him now. I didn't believe he was called Grosely then, I think he had a one syllabled name, but that I was uncertain of. He was a very tall lad (I began to see him quite well), thin, with a slight stoop, he was only eighteen and had grown too fast for his strength; he had curly, shining brown hair, rather large features (they did not look so large now, perhaps because his face was fat and puffy) and a peculiarly fresh complexion, very pink and white, like a girl's. I imagine people, women especially, would have thought him a very handsome boy, but to us he was only a clumsy, shuffling lout. Then I remembered that he did not often come to lectures – no, it wasn't that I remembered; there were too many students in the theatre to recollect who was there and who wasn't. I remembered the dissecting room. He had a leg at the next table to the one I was working at, and he hardly ever touched it. I forget why the men who had other parts of the body complained of his neglecting the work; I suppose somehow it interfered with them. In those days a good deal of gossip went on over the dissection of a "part," and out of the distance of thirty years some of it came back to me. Someone started the story that Grosely was a very gay dog. He drank like a fish and was an awful womanizer. Most of those boys were very simple, and they had brought to the hospital the notions they had acquired at home and at school. Some were prudish and they were shocked; others, those who worked hard, sneered at him and asked how he could hope to pass his exams; but a good many were excited and impressed, he was doing what they would have liked to do if they had had the courage. Grosely had his admirers, and you could often see him surrounded by a little band listening open-mouthed to stories of his adventures. Recollections now were crowding upon me. In a very little while he lost his shyness and assumed the airs of a man of the world. They must have looked absurd on this smooth-cheeked boy with his pink and white skin. Men (so they called themselves) used to tell one another of his escapades. He became quite a hero. He would make caustic remarks as he passed the museum and saw a pair of earnest students going over their anatomy together. He was at home in the public houses of the neighbourhood and was on familiar terms with the barmaids. Looking back, I imagine that, newly arrived from the country and the tutelage of parents and schoolmasters, he was captivated by his freedom and the thrill of London. His dissipations were harmless enough. They were due only to the urge of youth. He lost his head.

But we were all very poor, and we did not know how Grosely managed to pay for his garish amusements. We knew his father was a country doctor, and I think we knew exactly how much he gave his son a month. It was not enough to pay for the harlots he picked up on the promenade at the Pavilion and for the drinks he stood his friends in the Criterion Bar. We told one another in awestruck tones that he must be getting fearfully into debt. Of course, he could pawn things, but we knew by experience that you could not get more than three pounds for a microscope and thirty shillings for a skeleton. We said he must be spending at least ten pounds a week. Our ideas were not very grand, and this seemed to us the wildest pitch of extravagance. At last one of his friends disclosed the mystery: Grosley had discovered a wonderful system for making money. It amused and impressed us. None of us would have thought of anything so ingenious or have had the nerve to attempt it if he had. Grosely went to auctions, not Christie's, of course, but auctions in the Strand and Oxford Street and in private houses, and bought anything portable that was going cheap. Then he took his purchase to a pawnbrokers and pawned it for ten shillings or a pound more than he had paid. He was making money, four or five pounds a week, and he said he was going to give up medicine and make a regular business of it. Not one of us had ever made a penny in his life, and we regarded Grosley with admiration.

"By Jove, he's clever," we said.

"He's just about as sharp as they make them."

"That's the sort that ends up as a millionaire."

We were all very worldly wise, and what we didn't know about life at eighteen we were pretty sure wasn't worth knowing. It was a pity that when an examiner asked us a question we were so nervous that the answer often flew straight out of our head and when a nurse asked us to post a letter we blushed scarlet. It became known that the dean had sent for Grosely and hauled him over the coals. He had threatened him with sundry penalties if he continued systematically to neglect his work. Grosely was indignant. He'd had enough of that sort of thing at school, he said, he wasn't going to let a horse-faced eunuch treat him like a boy. Damn it all, he was getting on for nineteen, and there wasn't much you could teach him. The dean had said he heard he was drinking more than was good for him. Damned cheek. He could carry his liquor as well as any man of his age; he'd been blind last Saturday, and he meant to get blind next Saturday, and if anyone didn't like it he could do the other thing. Grosely's friends quite agreed with him that a man couldn't let himself be insulted like that.

But the blow fell at last, and now I remembered quite well the shock it gave us all. I suppose we had not seen Grosely for two or three days, but he had been in the habit of coming to the hospital more and more irregularly, so if we thought anything about it, I imagine we merely said that he was off on one of his bats. He would turn up again in a day or so, rather pale, but with a wonderful story of some girl he had picked up and the time he had had with her. The anatomy lecture was at nine in the morning, and it was a rush to get there in time. On this particular day little attention was paid to the lecturer who, with a visible pleasure in his limpid English and admirable elocution, was describing I know not what part of the human skeleton, for there was much excited whispering along the benches and a newspaper was surreptitiously passed from hand to hand. Suddenly the lecturer stopped. He had a pedagogic sarcasm. He affected not to know the names of his students.

"I am afraid I am disturbing the gentleman who is reading the paper. Anatomy is a very tedious science, and I regret that the regulations of the Royal College of Surgeons oblige me to ask you to give it enough of your attention to pass an examination in it. Any gentleman, however, who finds this impossible is at liberty to continue his perusal of the paper outside."

The wretched boy to whom this reproof was addressed reddened to the roots of his hair and in his embarrassment tried to stuff the newspaper in his pocket. The professor of anatomy observed him coldly.

"I am afraid, sir, that the paper is a little too large to go into your pocket," he remarked. "Perhaps you would be good enough to hand it down to me."

The newspaper was passed from row to row to the well of the theatre, and, not content with the confusion to which he had put the poor lad, the eminent surgeon, taking it, asked:

"May I inquire what it is in the paper that the gentleman in question found of such absorbing interest?"

The student who gave it to him without a word pointed out the paragraph that we had all been reading. The professor read it, and we watched him in silence. He put the paper down and went on with his lecture. The headline ran: "ARREST OF A MEDICAL STUDENT." Grosely had been brought before the police court magistrate for getting goods on credit and pawning them. It appears that this is an indictable offence, and the magistrate had remanded him for a week. Bail was refused. It looked as though his method of making money by buying things at auctions and pawning them had not in the long run proved as steady a source of income as he expected, and he had found it more profitable to pawn things that he was not at the expense of paying for. We talked the matter over excitedly as soon as the lecture was over, and I am bound to say that, having no property ourselves, so deficient was our sense of its sanctity we could none of us look upon his crime as a very serious one; but with the natural love of the young for the terrible there were few who did not think he would get anything from two years hard labour to seven years penal servitude.

I do not know why, but I did not seem to have any recollection of what happened to Grosely. I think he may have been arrested towards the end of a session, and his case may have come on again when we had all separated for holidays. I did not know if it was disposed of by the police court magistrate or whether it went up for trial. I had a sort of feeling that he was sentenced to a short term of imprisonment, six weeks perhaps, for his operations had been pretty extensive; but I knew that he had vanished from our midst and in a little while was thought of no more. It was strange to me that after all these years I should recollect so much of the incident so clearly. It was as though, turning over an album of old snapshots, I saw all at once the photographs of a scene I had quite forgotten.

But of course in that gross elderly man with grey hair and mottled red face I should never have recognized the lanky pink-cheeked boy. He looked sixty, but I knew he must be much less than that. I wondered what he had done with himself in the intervening time. It did not look as though he had excessively prospered.

"What were you doing in China?" I asked him.

"I was a tide waiter."

"Oh, were you?"

It is not a position of great importance, and I took care to keep out of my tone any note of surprise. The tide waiters are employees of the Chinese customs whose duty it is to board the ships and junks at the various treaty ports, and I think their chief business is to prevent opium smuggling. They are mostly retired A.B.'s from the Royal Navy and noncommissioned officers who have finished their time. I have seen them come on board at various places up the Yangtze. They hobnob with the pilot and the engineer, but the skipper is a trifle curt with them. They learn to speak Chinese more fluently than most Europeans and often marry Chinese women.

"When I left England I swore I wouldn't go back till I'd made my pile. And I never did. They were glad enough to get anyone to be a tide waiter in those days, any white man, I mean, and they didn't ask questions. They didn't care who you were. I was damned glad to get the job, I can tell you; I was about broke to the wide when they took me on. I only took it till I could get something better, but I stayed on; it suited me. I wanted to make money, and I found out that a tide waiter could make a packet if he knew the right way to go about. I was with the Chinese customs for the best part of twenty-five years, and when I came away I wouldn't mind betting that lots of commissioners would have been glad to have the money I had."

He gave me a sly, mean look. I had an inkling of what he meant. But there was a point on which I was willing to be reassured; if he was going to ask me for a hundred piastres (I was resigned to that sum now) I thought I might just as well take the blow at once.

"I hope you kept it," I said.

"You bet I did. I invested all my money in Shanghai, and when I left China I put it all in American railway bonds. Safety first is my motto. I know too much about crooks to take any risks myself."

I liked that remark, so I asked him if he wouldn't stay and have luncheon with me.

"No, I don't think I will. I don't eat much tiffin, and, anyway, my chow's waiting for me at home. I think I'll be getting along." He got up and he towered over me. "But look here, why don't you come along this evening and see my place? I've married a Haiphong girl. Got a baby too. It's not often I get a chance of talking to anyone about London. You'd better not come to dinner. We only eat native food, and I don't suppose you'd care for that. Come along about nine, will you?"

"All right," I said.

I had already told him that I was leaving Haiphong next day. He asked the boy to bring him a piece of paper so that he might write down his address. He wrote laboriously in the hand of a boy of fourteen.

"Tell the porter to explain to your rickshaw boy where it is. I'm on the second floor. There's no bell. Just knock. Well, see you later."

He walked out, and I went in to luncheon.

After dinner I called a rickshaw and with the porter's help made the boy understand where I wanted to go. I found presently that he was taking me along the curved canal the houses of which had looked to me so like a faded Victorian water colour. He stopped at one of them and pointed to the door. It looked so shabby and the neighbourhood was so squalid that I hesitated, thinking he had made a mistake. It seemed unlikely that Grosely could live so far in the native quarter and in a house so bedraggled. I told the rickshaw boy to wait and pushing open the door saw a dark staircase in front of me. There was no one about, and the street was empty. It might have been the small hours of the morning. I struck a match and fumbled my way upstairs. On the second floor I struck another match and saw a large brown door in front of me. I knocked, and in a moment it was opened by a little Tonkinese woman holding a candle. She was dressed in the earth brown of the poorer classes, with a tight little black turban on her head; her lips and the skin round them were stained red with betel, and when she opened her mouth to speak I saw that she had the black teeth and black gums that so disfigure these people. She said something in her native language, and then I heard Grosely's voice.

"Come along in. I was beginning to think you weren't going to turn up."

I passed through a little dark antechamber and entered a large room that evidently looked on the canal. Grosely was lying on a long chair, and he raised his length from it as I came in. He was reading the Hong Kong papers by the light of a paraffin lamp that stood on a table by his side.

"Sit down," he said, "and put your feet up."

"There's no reason I should take your chair."

"Go on. I'll sit on this."

He took a kitchen chair and, sitting on it, put his feet on the end of mine.

"That's my wife," he said, pointing with his thumb at the

Tonkinese woman who had followed me into the room. "And over there in the corner's the kid."

I followed his eyes, and against the wall, lying on bamboo mats and covered with a blanket, I saw a child sleeping.

"Lively little beggar when he's awake. I wish you could have seen him. She's going to have another soon."

I glanced at her, and the truth of what he said was apparent. She was very small, with tiny hands and feet, but her face was flat and the skin muddy. She looked sullen but may only have been shy. She went out of the room and presently came back with a bottle of whisky, two glasses, and a siphon. I looked round. There was a partition at the back of dark unpainted wood which I suppose shut off another room, and pinned against the middle of this was a portrait cut out of an illustrated paper of John Galsworthy. He looked austere, mild, and gentlemanly, and I wondered what he did there. The other walls were whitewashed, but the whitewash was dingy and stained. Pinned on to them were pages of pictures from *The Graphic* or *The Illustrated London News*.

"I put them up," said Grosely, "I thought they made the place look homelike."

"What made you put up Galsworthy? Do you read his books?"

"No, I didn't know he wrote books. I liked his face."

There were one or two torn and shabby rattan mats on the floor and in a corner a great pile of *The Hong Kong Times*. The only furniture consisted of a washstand, two or three kitchen chairs, a table or two, and a large teak native bed. It was cheerless and sordid.

"Not a bad little place, is it?" said Grosely. "Suits me all right. Sometimes I've thought of moving, but I don't suppose I ever shall now." He gave a little chuckle. "I came to Haiphong for forty-eight hours and I've been here five years. I was on my way to Shanghai really."

He was silent. Having nothing to say I said nothing. Then the little Tonkinese woman made a remark to him, which I could not of course understand, and he answered her. He was silent again for a minute or two, but I thought he looked at me as though he wanted to ask me something. I did not know why he hesitated.

"Have you ever tried smoking opium on your travels in the East?" he inquired at last casually.

"Yes, I did once, at Singapore. I thought I'd like to see what it was like."

"What happened?"

"Nothing very thrilling to tell you the truth. I thought I was going to have the most exquisite emotions. I expected visions, like De Quincey's, you know. The only thing I felt was a kind of physical well-being, the same sort of feeling that you get when you've had a Turkish bath and are lying in the cooling room, and then a peculiar activity of mind so that everything I thought of seemed extremely clear."

"I know."

"I really felt that two and two are four and there could not be the smallest doubt about it. But next morning – oh, God! My head reeled. I was as sick as a dog, I was sick all day, I vomited my soul out, and as I vomited I said to myself miserably: 'And there are people who call this fun.' "

Grosley leaned back in his chair and gave a low, mirthless laugh.

"I expect it was bad stuff. Or you went at it too hard. They saw you were a mug and gave you dregs that had been smoked already. They're enough to turn anybody up. Would you like to have another try now? I've got some stuff here that I know's good."

"No, I think once was enough for me."

"D'you mind if I have a pipe or two? You want it in a climate like this. It keeps you from getting dysentery. And I generally have a bit of a smoke about this time."

"Go ahead," I said.

He spoke again to the woman, and she, raising her voice, called out something in a raucous tone. An answer came from the room behind the wooden partition, and after a minute or two an old woman came out carrying a little round tray. She was shrivelled and old and when she entered gave me an ingratiating smile of her stained mouth. Grosely got up and crossed over to the bed and lay on it. The old woman set the tray down on the bed; on it was a spirit lamp, a pipe, a long needle, and a little round box of opium. She squatted on the bed, and Grosely's wife got on it too and sat, her feet tucked up under her with her back against the wall. Grosely watched the old woman while she put a little pellet of the drug on the needle, held it over the flame till it sizzled, and then plugged it into the pipe. She handed it to him, and with a great breath he inhaled it. He held the smoke for a little while and then blew it out in a thick grey cloud. He handed her back the pipe, and she started to make another. Nobody spoke. He smoked three pipes in succession and then sank back.

"By George, I feel better now. I was feeling all in. She makes a wonderful pipe, this old hag. Are you sure you won't have one?"

"Quite."

"Please yourself. Have some tea, then."

He spoke to his wife, who scrambled off the bed and went out of the room. Presently she came back with a little china pot of tea and a couple of Chinese bowls.

"A lot of people smoke here, you know. It does you no harm if you don't do it to excess. I never smoke more than twenty to twenty-five pipes a day. You can go on for years if you limit yourself to that. Some of the Frenchmen smoke as many as forty or fifty a day. That's too much. I never do that, except now and then when I feel I want a binge. I'm bound to say it's never done me any harm."

We drank our tea, pale and vaguely scented and clean on the palate. Then the old woman made him another pipe and then another. His wife had got back on to the bed and soon, curling herself up at his feet, went to sleep. Grosely smoked two or three pipes at a time and while he was smoking seemed intent upon nothing else, but in the intervals he was loquacious. Several times I suggested going, but he would not let me. The hours wore on. Once or twice while he smoked I dozed. He told me all about himself. He went on and on. I spoke only to give him a cue. I cannot relate what he told me in his own words. He repeated himself. He was very long-winded, and he told me his story confusedly, first a late bit, then an early bit, so that I had to arrange the sequence for myself; sometimes I saw that, afraid he had said too much, he held something back; sometimes he lied and I had to make a guess at the truth from the smile he gave me or the look in his eyes. He had not the words to describe what he had felt, and I had to conjecture his meaning from slangy metaphors and hackneyed, vulgar phrases. I kept on asking myself what his real name was: it was on the tip of my tongue, and it irritated me not to be able to recall it, though why it should in the least matter to me I did not know. He was somewhat suspicious of me at first, and I saw that this escapade of his in London and his imprisonment had been all these years a tormenting secret. He had always been haunted by the fear that sooner or later someone would find out.

"It's funny that even now you shouldn't remember me at the hospital," he said, looking at me shrewdly. "You must have a rotten memory."

"Hang it all, it's nearly thirty years ago. Think of the thousands of people I've met since then. There's no reason why I should remember you any more than you remember me."

"That's right. I don't suppose there is."

It seemed to reassure him. At last he had smoked enough, and the old woman made herself a pipe and smoked it. Then she went over to the mat on which the child was lying and huddled down beside it. She lay so still that I supposed she had fallen directly asleep. When at last I went I found my boy curled up on the footboard of the rickshaw in so deep slumber that I had to shake him. I knew where I was, and I wanted air and exercise, so I gave him a couple of piastres and told him I would walk.

It was a strange story I carried away with me.

It was with a sort of horror that I had listened to Grosely telling me of those twenty years he had spent in China. He had made money, I do not know how much, but from the way he talked I should think something between fifteen and twenty thousand pounds, and for a tide waiter it was a fortune. He could not have come by it honestly, and little as I knew of the details of his trade, by his sudden reticences, by his leers and hints I guessed that there was no base transaction that, if it was made worth his while, he jibbed at. I suppose that nothing paid him better than smuggling opium, and his position gave him the opportunity to do this with safety and profit. I understood that his superior officers had often had their suspicions of him, but had never been able to get such proof of his malpractices as to justify them in taking any steps. They contented themselves with moving him from one port to another, but that did not disturb him; they watched him, but he was too clever for them. I saw that he was divided between the fear of telling me too much to his discredit and the desire to boast of his own astuteness. He prided himself on the confidence the Chinese had placed in him.

"They knew they could trust me," he said, "and it gave me a pull. I never double-crossed a Chinaman once."

The thought filled him with the complacency of the honest man. The Chinese discovered that he was keen on curios, and they got in the habit of giving him bits or bringing him things to buy; he never made inquiries how they had come by them, and he bought them cheap. When he had got a good lot he sent them to Peking and sold them at a handsome profit. I remembered how he had started his commercial career by buying things at auctions and pawning them. For twenty years, by shabby shift and petty dishonesty he added pound to pound, and everything he made he invested in Shanghai. He lived penuriously, saving half his pay; he never went on leave because he did not want to waste his money; he would not have anything to do with the Chinese women, he wanted to keep himself free from any entanglement; he did not drink. He was consumed by one ambition, to save enough to be able to go back to England and live the life from which he had been snatched as a boy. That was the only thing he wanted. He lived in China as though in a dream; he paid no attention to the life around him; its colour and strangeness, its possibilities of pleasure, meant nothing to him. There was always before him the mirage of London, the Criterion Bar, himself standing with his foot on the rail, the promenade at the Empire and the Pavilion, the picked-up harlot, the serio-comic at the music hall, and the musical comedy at the Gaiety. This was life and love and adventure. This was romance. This was what he yearned for with all his heart. There was surely something impressive in the way in which during all those years he had lived like an anchorite with that one end in view of leading again a life that was so vulgar. It showed character.

"You see," he said to me, "even if I'd been able to get back to England on leave I wouldn't have gone. I didn't want to go till I could go for good. And then I wanted to do the thing in style."

He saw himself putting on evening clothes every night and going out with a gardenia in his buttonhole, and he saw himself going to the Derby in a long coat and a brown hat and a pair of opera glasses slung over his shoulder. He saw himself giving the girls a look-over and picking out the one he fancied. He made up his mind that on the night he arrived in London he would get blind, he hadn't been drunk for twenty years; he couldn't afford to in his job, you had to keep your wits about you. He'd take care not to get drunk on the ship on the way home. He'd wait till he got to London. What a night he'd have! He thought of it for twenty years.

I do not know why Grosely left the Chinese customs, whether the place was getting too hot for him, whether he had reached the end of his service, or whether he had amassed the sum he had fixed. But at last he sailed. He went second class; he did not intend to start spending money till he reached London. He took rooms in Jermyn Street, he had always wanted to live there, and he went straight to a tailor's and ordered himself an outfit. Slap up. Then he had a look round the town. It was different from how he remembered it, there was much more traffic, and he felt confused and a little at sea. He went to the Criterion and found there was no longer a bar where he had been used to lounge and drink. There was a restaurant in Leicester Square where he had been in the habit of dining when he was in funds, but he could not find it; he supposed it had been torn down. He went to the Pavilion, but there were no women there. He was rather disgusted and went on to the Empire: he found they had done away with the Promenade. It was rather a blow. He could not quite make it out. Well, anyhow, he must be prepared for changes in twenty years, and if he couldn't do anything else he could get drunk. He had had fever several times in China, and the change of climate had brought it on again. He wasn't feeling any too well, and after four or five drinks he was glad to go to bed.

That first day was only a sample of many that followed it. Everything went wrong. Grosely's voice grew peevish and bitter as he told me how one thing and another had failed him. The old places were gone, the people were different, he found it hard to make friends, he was strangely lonely; he had never expected that in a great city like London. That's what was wrong with it, London had become too big; it wasn't the jolly, intimate place it had been in the early 'Nineties. It had gone to pieces. He picked up a few girls, but they weren't as nice as the girls he had known before; they weren't the fun they used to be, and he grew dimly conscious that they thought him a rum sort of cove. He was only just over forty, and they looked upon him as an old man. When he tried to cotton on to a lot of young fellows standing round a bar they gave him the cold shoulder. Anyway, these young fellows didn't know how to drink. He'd show them. He got soused every night, it was the only thing to do in that damned place, but, by jove, it made him feel rotten next day. He supposed it was the climate of China. When he was a medical student he could drink a bottle of whisky every night and be as fresh as a daisy in the morning. He began to think more about China. All sorts of things that he never knew he had noticed came back to him. It wasn't a bad life he'd led there. Perhaps he'd been a fool to keep away from those Chinese girls: they were pretty little things, some of them, and they didn't put on the airs these English girls did. One could have a damned good time in China if one had the money he had. One could keep a Chinese girl and get into the club, and there'd be a lot of nice fellows to drink with and play bridge with and billiards. He remembered the Chinese shops and all the row in the streets and the coolies carrying loads and the ports with the junks in them and the rivers with pagodas on the banks. It was funny, he never thought much of China while he was there, and now – well, he couldn't get it out of his mind. It obsessed him. He began to think that London was no place for a white man. It had just gone to the dogs, that was the long and short of it, and one day the thought came to him that perhaps it would be a good thing if he went back to China. Of course it was silly, he'd worked like a slave for twenty years to be able to have a good time in London, and it was absurd to go and live in China. With his money he ought to be able to have a good time anywhere. But somehow he couldn't think of anything else but China. One day he went to the pictures and saw a scene at Shanghai. That settled it. He was fed up with London. He hated it. He was going to get out, and this time he'd get out for good. He had been home a year and a half, and it seemed longer to him than all his twenty years in the East. He took a passage on a French boat sailing from Marseilles, and when he saw the coast of Europe sink into the sea he heaved a great sigh of relief. When they got to Suez and he felt the first touch of the East he knew he had done the right thing. Europe was finished. The East was the only place.

He went ashore at Djibouti and again at Colombo and Singapore, but though the ship stopped for two days at Saigon he remained on board there. He'd been drinking a good deal and he was feeling a bit under the weather. But when they reached

Haiphong where they were staying for forty-eight hours he thought he might just as well have a look at it. That was the last stopping place before they got to China. He was bound for Shanghai. When he got there he meant to go to a hotel and look around a bit and then get hold of a girl and a place of his own. He would buy a pony or two and race. He'd soon make friends. In the East they weren't so stiff and stand-offish as they were in London. Going ashore, he dined at the hotel, and after dinner he got into a rickshaw and told the boy he wanted a woman. The boy took him to the shabby tenement in which I had sat for so many hours, and there were the old woman and the girl who was now the mother of his child. After a while the old woman asked him if he wouldn't like to smoke. He had never tried opium, he had always been frightened of it, but now he didn't see why he shouldn't have a go. He was feeling good that night and the girl was a jolly, cuddlesome little thing; she was rather like a Chinese girl, small and pretty, like an idol. Well, he had a pipe or two, and he began to feel very happy and comfortable. He stayed all night. He didn't sleep. He just lay, feeling very restful, and thought about things.

"I stopped there till my ship went on to Hong Kong," he said. "And when she left I just stopped on."

"How about your luggage?" I asked.

For I am perhaps unworthily interested in the manner people combine practical details with the ideal aspects of life. When in a novel penniless lovers drive away in a long swift racing car over the distant hills I have always a desire to know how they managed to pay for it; and I have often asked myself how the characters of Henry James in the intervals of subtly examining their situation coped with the physiological necessities of their bodies.

"I only had a trunk full of clothes, I was never one to want much more than I stood up in, and I went down with the girl in a rickshaw to fetch it. I only meant to stay on till the next boat came through. You see, I was so near China here I thought I'd wait a bit and get used to things, if you understand what I mean, before I went on."

I did. Those last words of his revealed him to me. I knew that on the threshold of China his courage had failed him. England had been such a terrible disappointment that now he was afraid to put China to the test too. If that failed him he had nothing.

For years England had been like a mirage in the desert. But when he had yielded to the attraction, those shining pools and the palm trees and the green grass were nothing but the rolling sandy dunes. He had China, and so long as he never saw it again he kept it.

"Somehow I stayed on. You know, you'd be surprised how quickly the days pass. I don't seem to have time to do half the things I want to. After all, I'm comfortable here. The old woman makes a damned good pipe, and she's a jolly little girl, my girl, and then there's the kid. A lively young beggar. If you're happy somewhere what's the good of going somewhere else?"

"And are you happy here?" I asked him.

I looked round that large, bare, sordid room. There was no comfort in it, and not one of the little personal things that one would have thought might have given him the feeling of home. Grosely had taken on this equivocal little apartment which served as a house of assignation and as a place for Europeans to smoke opium in, with the old woman who kept it, just as it was, and he camped, rather than lived, there still as though next day he would pack his traps and go. After a little while he answered my question.

"I've never been so happy in my life. I often think I'll go on to Shanghai some day, but I don't suppose I ever shall. And God knows I never want to see England again."

"Aren't you awfully lonely sometimes for people to talk to?"

"No. Sometimes a Chinese tramp comes in with an English skipper or a Scotch engineer and then I go on board and we have a talk about old times. There's an old fellow here, a Frenchman who was in the customs, and he speaks English; I go and see him sometimes. But the fact is I don't want anybody very much. I think a lot. It gets on my nerves when people come between me and my thoughts. I'm not a big smoker, you know, I just have a pipe or two in the morning to settle my stomach, but I don't really smoke till night. Then I think."

"What d'you think about?"

"Oh, all sorts of things. Sometimes about London and what it was like when I was a boy. But mostly about China. I think of the good times I had and the way I made my money, and I remember the fellows I used to know, and the Chinese. I had some narrow squeaks now and then, but I always came through all right. And I wonder what the girls would have been like that I might have had. Pretty little things. I'm sorry now I didn't keep one or two. It's a great country, China; I love those shops with an old fellow sitting on his heels smoking a water pipe, and all the shop signs. And the temples. By George, that's the place for a man to live in. There's life."

The mirage shone before his eyes. The illusion held him. He was happy. I wondered what would be his end. Well, that was not yet. For the first time in his life perhaps he held the present in his hand.

I took a shabby little steamer from Haiphong to Hong Kong, which ran along the coast stopping at various French ports on the way to take on and discharge cargo. It was very old and dirty. There were but three passengers besides myself. Two were French missionaries bound for the island of Hainan. One was an elderly man with a large square grey beard, and the other was young, with a round red face on which his beard grew in little black patches. They spent most of the day reading their breviaries, and the younger one studied Chinese. Then there was an American Jew called Elfenbein who was travelling in hosiery. He was a tall fellow, powerfully built and strong, clumsy of gesture, with a long sallow face, a big straight nose, and dark eyes. His voice was loud and strident. He was aggressive and irascible. He abused the ship, he abused the steward, he abused the boys, he abused the food. Nothing satisfied him. All the time you heard his voice raised in anger because his boxes of show goods were not placed as they should be, because he couldn't get a hot bath, because the soda water wasn't cold enough. He was a man with a chip on his shoulder. Everyone seemed in a conspiracy to slight or injure him, and he kept threatening to give the captain or the steward a hit on the nose. Because I was the only person on board who spoke English he attached himself to me, and I could not settle down on deck for five minutes without his coming to sit by me and telling me his latest grievance. He forced drinks on me which I did not want and when I refused, cried, "Oh, come on, be a sport," and ordered them notwithstanding. To my confusion he addressed me constantly as brother. He was odious, but I must admit that he was often amusing; he would tell damaging stories about his fellow Jews in a racy idiom that made them very entertaining. He talked interminably. He hated to be alone for a minute, and it never occurred to him that you might not want his company; but when he was with you he was perpetually on the lookout for affronts. He trod heavily on your corns, and if you tucked your feet out of the way thought you insulted him. It made his society excessively fatiguing. He was the kind of Jew who made you understand the pogrom. I told him a little story about the Peace Conference. It appears that on one occasion Monsieur Paderewski was pressing upon Mr. Wilson, Mr. Lloyd George, and M. Clemenceau the Polish claims on Danzig.

"If the Poles do not get it," he said, "I warn you that their disappointment will be so great, there will be an outbreak and they will assassinate the Jews."

Mr. Wilson looked grave, Mr. Lloyd George shook his head, and M. Clemenceau frowned.

"But what will happen if the Poles get Danzig?" asked Mr. Wilson.

M. Paderewski brightened. He shook his leonine mane.

"Ah, that will be quite another thing," he replied. "Their enthusiasm will be so great, there will be an outbreak and they will assassinate the Jews."

Elfenbein saw nothing funny in it.

"Europe's no good," he said. "If I had my way I'd sink the whole of Europe under the sea."

Then I told him about Henri Deplis. He was by birth a native of the Grand Duchy of Luxembourg. On maturer reflection he became a commercial traveller. This did not amuse him either, so with a sigh for Saki's sake I desisted. We must accept with resignation the opinion of the hundred per cent. American that the English have no sense of humour.

At meal times the captain sat at the head of the table, the two priests on one side of him and Elfenbein and I on the other.

The captain, a jovial little grey-headed man from Bordeaux, was retiring at the end of the year to make his own wine in his own vineyard.

"*Je vous enverrai un fût, mon père,*" he promised the elderly priest.

Elfenbein spoke fluent and bad French. He seized the conversation and held it. Pep, that's what he'd got. The Frenchmen were polite to him, but it was not hard to see that they heartily disliked him. Many of his remarks were singularly tactless, and when he used obscene language in addressing the boy who was serving us the priests looked down their noses and pretended not to hear. But Elfenbein was argumentative and at one luncheon began to talk of religion. He made a number of observations upon the Catholic faith which were certainly not in good taste. The younger priest flushed and was about to make some observation when the elder said something to him in an undertone, and he held his tongue. But when Elfenbein addressed a direct question to him the old man answered him mildly.

"There is no compulsion in these matters. Everyone is at liberty to believe what he pleases."

Elfenbein made a long tirade, but it was received in silence. He was not abashed. He told me afterwards that they couldn't answer his arguments.

"I don't think they chose to," I said. "I imagine they merely thought you a very rude, vulgar, and ill-mannered fellow."

"Me?" he cried in astonishment.

"They are perfectly inoffensive, and they have devoted their lives to what they think is the service of God. Why should you gratuitously insult them?"

"I wasn't insultin' them. I was only puttin' my point of view as a rational man. I wanted to start an argument. D'you think I've hurt their feelings? Why, I wouldn't do that for the world, brother."

His surprise was so ingenuous that I laughed.

A LIFE IN RETROSPECT

from *The Partial View*

EARLY TRAVELS

I HAD MY full share of the intellectual's arrogance and if, as I hope, I have lost it, I must ascribe it not to my own virtue or wisdom but to the chance that made me more of a traveller than most writers. I am attached to England, but I have never felt myself very much at home there. I have always been shy with English people. To me England has been a country where I had obligations that I did not want to fulfil and responsibilities that irked me. I have never felt entirely myself till I had put at least the Channel between my native country and me. Some fortunate persons find freedom in their own minds; I, with less spiritual power than they, find it in travel. While still at Heidelberg I managed to visit a good many places in Germany (at Munich I saw Ibsen drinking a glass of beer at the Maximilianerhof and with a scowl on his face reading the paper) and I went to Switzerland; but the first real journey I made was to Italy. I went primed with much reading of Walter Pater, Ruskin and John Addington Symonds. I had the six weeks of the Easter vacation at my disposal and twenty pounds in my pocket. After going to Genoa and Pisa, where I trudged the interminable distance to sit for a while on the pine wood in which Shelley read Sophocles and wrote verses on a guitar, I settled down for the inside of a month in Florence in the house of a widow lady, with whose daughter I read the Purgatorio, and spent laborious days, Ruskin in hand, visiting the sights. I admired everything that Ruskin told me to admire (even that horrible tower of Giotto) and turned away in disgust from what he condemned. Never can he have had a more ardent disciple. After that I went to Venice, Verona and Milan. I returned to England very much pleased with myself and actively contemptuous of anyone who did not share my views (and Ruskin's) of Botticelli and Bellini. I was twenty.

A year later I went to Italy again, travelling as far down as Naples, and discovered Capri. It was the most enchanting spot I had ever seen and the following summer I spent the whole of my vacation there. Capri was then little known. There was no funicular from the beach to the town. Few people went there in summer and you could get board and lodging, with wine included, and from your bedroom window a view of Vesuvius, for four shillings a day. There was a poet there then, a Belgian composer, my friend from Heidelberg, Brown, a painter or two, a sculptor (Harvard Thomas) and an American colonel who had fought on the southern side in the Civil War. I listened with transport to conversations, up at Anacapri at the colonel's house, or at Morgano's, the wine shop just off the Piazza, when they talked of art and beauty, literature and Roman history. I saw two men fly at one anther's throats because they disagreed over the poetic merit of Heredia's sonnets. I thought it all grand. Art, art for art's sake, was the only thing that mattered in the world; and the artist alone gave this ridiculous world significance. Politics, commerce, the learned professors – what did they amount to from the standpoint of the Absolute? They might disagree, these friends of mine (dead, dead every jack one of them), about the value of a sonnet or the excellence of a Greek bas-relief (Greek, my eye! I tell you it's a Roman copy and if I tell you a thing it is so); but they were all agreed about this, that they burned with a hard, gem-like flame. I was too shy to tell them that I had written a novel and was half-way through another and it was a great mortification to me, burning as I was too with a hard, gem-like flame, to be treated as a philistine who cared for nothing but dissecting dead bodies and would seize an unguarded moment to give his best friend an enema.

Presently I was qualified. I had already published a novel and it had had an unexpected success. I thought my fortune was made, and, abandoning medicine to become a writer, I went to Spain. I was then twenty-three. I was much more ignorant than are, it seems to me, young men of that age at the present day. I settled down in Seville. I grew a moustache, smoked Filipino cigars, learnt the guitar, bought a broad-brimmed hat with a flat crown, in which I swaggered down the Sierpes, and hankered for a flow-ing cape, lined with green and red velvet. But on account of the expense I did not buy it. I rode about the countryside on a horse lent me by a friend. Life was too pleasant to allow me to give an undivided attention to literature. My plan was to spend a year there till I had learnt Spanish, then go to Rome which I knew only as a tripper and perfect my superficial knowledge of Italian, follow that up with a journey to Greece where I intended to learn the vernacular as an approach to ancient Greek, and finally go to Cairo and learn Arabic. It was an ambitious programme, but I am glad now that I did not carry it out. I duly went to Rome (where I wrote my first play) but then I went back to Spain; for something had occurred that I had not anticipated. I fell in love with Seville and the life one led there and incidentally with a young thing with green eyes and a gay smile (but I got over that) and I could not resist its lure. I returned year after year. I wandered through the white and silent streets and strolled along the Guadalquivir, I dawdled about the Cathedral, I went to bull-fights and made light love to pretty little creatures whose demands on me were no more than my exiguous means could satisfy. It was heavenly to live in Seville in the flower of one's youth. I postponed my education to a more convenient moment. The result is that I have never read the Odyssey but in English and I have never achieved my ambition to read *A Thousand Nights and a Night* in Arabic.

When the intelligentsia took up Russia I, remembering that Cato had begun to learn Greek when he was eighty, set about learning Russian, but I had by then lost my youthful enthusiasm; I never got farther than being able to read the plays of Chekov and have long since forgotten the little I knew. I think now that these schemes of mine were a trifle nonsensical. Words are not important, but their meanings, and it is of no spiritual advantage that I can see to know half a dozen languages. I have met polyglots; I have not noticed that they were wiser than the rest of us. It is convenient if you are travelling in a country to have a sufficient smattering of its speech to find your way about and get what you want to eat; and if it has a considerable literature it is pleasant to be able to read it. But such a knowledge as this can be acquired easily. To attempt to learn more is futile. Unless you devote your whole life to it, you will never learn to speak the language of another country to perfection; you will never know its people and its literature with complete intimacy. For they, and the literature which is their expression, are wrought, not only of the actions they perform and the words they use, neither of which offer great difficulty, but of ancestral instincts, shades of feeling that they have absorbed with their mothers' milk, and innate attitudes which the foreigner can never quite seize. It is hard enough for us to know our own people; we deceive ourselves, we English especially, if we think we can know those of other lands. For the sea-girt isle sets us apart and the link that a common religion gave, which once mitigated our insularity, was snapped with the Reformation. It seems hardly worth while to take much trouble to acquire a knowledge that can never be more than superficial. I think then it is merely waste of time to learn more than a smattering of foreign tongues. The only exception I would make to this is French. For French is the common language of educated men and it is certainly convenient to speak it well enough to be able to treat of any subject of discourse that may arise. It has a great literature; other countries, with the exception of England, have great writers rather than a great literature; and its influence on the rest of the world has, till the last twenty years, been profound. It is very well to be able to read French as easily as if it were your native tongue. There are limits, however, to the excellence with which you should allow yourself to speak it. As a matter of practice it is good to be on your guard against an Englishman who speaks French perfectly; he is very likely to be a card-sharper or an attaché in the diplomatic service.

MOBILITY

I HAD A FRIEND who was a cabinet minister and I wrote and asked him to help me to do something, whereupon I was invited to present myself at the War Office; but fearing that I should be set to clerical work in England and anxious to get out to France at once I joined a unit of ambulance cars. Though I do not think I was less patriotic than another my patriotism was mingled with the excitement the new experience offered me and I began keeping a notebook the moment I landed in France. I kept it till the work got heavy and then at the end of the day I was too tired to do anything but go to bed. I enjoyed the new life I was thrown into and the lack of responsibility. It was a pleasure to me who had never been ordered about since I was at school to be told to do this and that and when it was done to feel that my time was my own. As a writer I had never felt that; I had felt on the contrary that I had not a minute to lose. Now with a clear conscience I wasted long hours at *estaminets* in idle chatter. I liked meeting a host of people, and, though writing no longer, I treasured their peculiarities in my memory. I was never in any particular danger. I was anxious to see how I should feel when exposed to it; I have never thought myself very courageous nor did I think there was any necessity for me to be so. The only occasion upon which I might have examined myself was when in the Grande Place at Ypres a shell blew up a wall against which I had been standing just as I had moved over to get a view of the ruined Cloth Makers Hall from the other side; but I was too much surprised to observe my state of mind.

Later on I joined the Intelligence Department where it looked as though I could be more useful than in somewhat inadequately driving an ambulance. The work appealed both to my sense of romance and my sense of the ridiculous. The methods I was instructed to use in order to foil persons who were following me; the secret interviews with agents in unlikely places; the conveying of messages in a mysterious fashion; the reports smuggled over a frontier; it was all doubtless very necessary but so reminiscent of what was then known as the shilling shocker that for me it took most of its reality away from the war and I could not but look upon it as little more than material that might one day be of use to me. But it was so hackneyed that I doubted whether I should ever be able to profit by it. After a year in Switzerland my work there came to an end. It had entailed a good deal of exposure, the winter was bitter and I had to take journeys across the Lake of Geneva in all weathers. I was in very poor health. There seemed nothing much for me to do at the moment, so I went to America where two of my plays were about to be produced. I wanted to recover my peace of mind shattered through my own foolishness and vanity by occurrences upon which I need not dwell and so made up my mind to go to the South Seas. I had wanted to go ever since as a youth I had read *The Ebb-Tide* and *The Wrecker* and I wanted besides to get material for a novel I had long been thinking over based on the life of Paul Gauguin.

I went, looking for beauty and romance and glad to put a great ocean between me and the trouble that harassed me. I found beauty and romance, but I found also something I had never expected. I found a new self. Ever since I left St. Thomas's Hospital I had lived with people who attached value to culture. I had come to think that there was nothing in the world more important than art. I looked for a meaning in the universe and the only one I could find was the beauty that men here and there produced. On the surface my life was varied and exciting; but beneath it was narrow. Now I entered a new world, and all the instinct in me of a novelist went out with exhilaration to absorb the novelty. It was not only the beauty of the islands that took me, Herman Melville and Pierre Loti had prepared me for that, and though it is a different beauty it is not a greater beauty than that of Greece or Southern Italy; nor was it their ramshackle, slightly adventurous, easy life; what excited me was to meet one person after another who was new to me. I was like a naturalist who comes into a country where the fauna are of an unimaginable variety. Some I recognized; they were old types that I had read of and they gave me just the same feeling of delighted surprise that I had once in the Malayan Archipelago when I saw sitting on the branch of a tree a bird that I had never seen before but in a zoo. For the first moment I thought it must have escaped from a cage. Others were strange to me and they thrilled me as Wallace was thrilled when he came upon a new species. I found them easy to get on with. They were of all sorts; indeed, the variety would have been bewildering but that my powers of observation were by now well trained and I found it possible without conscious effort to pigeon-hole each one in my awareness. Few of them had culture. They had learnt life in a different school from mine and had come to different conclusions. They led it on a different plane; I could not, with my sense of humour, go on thinking mine a higher one. It was different. Their lives too formed themselves to the discerning eye into a pattern that had order and finally coherence.

I stepped off my pedestal. It seemed to me that these men had more vitality than those I had known hitherto. They did not burn with a hard, gem-like flame, but with a hot, smoky, consuming fire. They had their own narrownesses. They had their prejudices. They were often dull and stupid. I did not care. They were different. In civilized communities men's idiosyncrasies are mitigated by the necessity of conforming to certain rules of behaviour. Culture is a mask that hides their faces. Here people showed themselves bare. These heterogeneous creatures thrown into a life that had preserved a great deal of its primitiveness had never felt the need to adapt themselves to conventional standards. Their peculiarities had been given opportunity to develop unchecked. In great cities men are like a lot of stones thrown together in a bag; their jagged corners are rubbed off till in the end they are as smooth as marbles. These men had never had their jagged corners rubbed away. They seemed to me nearer to the elementals of human nature than any of the people I had been living with for so long and my heart leapt towards them as it had done years before to the people who filed into the out-patients' room at St. Thomas's. I filled my notebook with brief descriptions of their appearance and their character, and presently, my imagination excited by these multitudinous impressions, from a hint or an incident or a happy invention, stories began to form themselves round certain of the most vivid of them.

I returned to America and shortly afterwards was sent on a mission to Petrograd. I was diffident of accepting the post, which seemed to demand capacities that I did not think I possessed; but there seemed to be no one more competent available at the moment and my being a writer was very good "cover" for what I was asked to do. I was not very well. I still knew enough medicine to guess the meaning of the haemorrhages I was having. An X-ray photograph showed clearly that I had tuberculosis of the lungs. But I could not miss the opportunity of spending certainly a considerable time in the country of Tolstoi, Dostoievski and Chekov; I had a notion that in the intervals of the work I was being sent to do I could get something for myself that would be of value; so I set my foot hard on the loud pedal of patriotism and persuaded the physician I consulted that under the tragic circumstances of the moment I was taking no undue risk. I set off in high spirits with unlimited money at my disposal and four devoted Czechs to act as liaison officers between me and Professor Masaryk who had under his control in various parts of Russia something like sixty thousand of his compatriots. I was exhilarated by the responsibility of my position. I went as a private agent, who could be disavowed if necessary, with instructions to get in touch with parties hostile to the government and devise a scheme that would keep Russia in the war and prevent the Bolsheviks, supported by the Central Powers, from seizing power. It is not necessary for me to inform the reader that in this I failed lamentably and I do not ask him to believe me when I state that it seems to me at least possible that if I had been sent six months before I might quite well have succeeded. Three months after my arrival in Petrograd the crash came and put an end to all my plans.

I returned to England. I had had some interesting experiences and had got to know fairly well one of the most extraordinary men I have ever met. This was Boris Savinkov, the terrorist who had assassinated Trepov and the Grand Duke Sergius. But I came away disillusioned. The endless talk when action was needed, the vacillations, the apathy when apathy could only result in destruction, the high-flown protestations, the insincerity and half-heartedness that I found everywhere sickened me with Russia and the Russians. I also came back very ill indeed, for in the position I was in I could not profit by the abundant supplies that made it possible for the embassies to serve their countries on a full stomach and I was (like the Russians themselves) reduced to a meagre diet. (When I arrived in Stockholm, where I had a day to wait for the destroyer that was to take me across the North Sea, I went into a confectioner's, bought a pound of chocolates and ate them in the street.) A scheme to send me to Rumania in connection with some Polish intrigue, the details of which I now forget, fell through. I was not sorry, for I was coughing my head off and constant fever made my nights very uncomfortable. I went to see the most eminent specialist I could find in London. He packed me off to a sanatorium in the North of Scotland, Davos and St. Moritz at that time being inconvenient to go to, and for the next two years I led an invalid life.

I had a grand time. I discovered for the first time in my life how very delightful it is to lie in bed. It is astonishing how varied life can be when you stay in bed all day and how much you find to do. I delighted in the privacy of my room with the immense window wide open to the starry winter night. It gave me a delicious sense of security, aloofness and freedom. The silence was enchanting. Infinite space seemed to enter it and my spirit, alone with the stars, seemed capable of any adventure. My imagination was never more nimble; it was like a barque under press of sail scudding before the breeze. The monotonous days, whose only excitement was the books I read and my reflections, passed with inconceivable rapidity. I left my bed with a pang.

It was a strange world that I entered when I grew well enough to mix during part of the day with my fellow-patients. In their different ways these people, some of whom had been in the sanatorium for years, were as singular as any of those I had met in the South Seas. Illness and the queer, sheltered life affected them strangely, twisting, strengthening, deteriorating their character just as in Samoa or Tahiti it was deteriorated, strengthened or twisted by the languorous climate and the alien environment. I think I learnt a good deal about human nature in that sanatorium that otherwise I should never have known.

When I recovered from my illness the war was over. I went to China. I went with the feelings of any traveller interested in art and curious to see what he could of the manners of a strange people whose civilization was of great antiquity; but I went also with the notion that I must surely run across men of various sorts whose acquaintance would enlarge my experience. I did. I filled notebooks with descriptions of places and persons and the stories they suggested. I became aware of the specific benefit I was capable of getting from travel; before, it had been only an instinctive feeling. This was freedom of the spirit on the one hand, and on the other, the collection of all manner of persons who might serve my purposes. After that I travelled to many countries. I journeyed over a dozen seas, in liners, in tramps, in schooners; I went by train, by car, by chair, on foot or on horseback. I kept my eyes open for character, oddness and personality. I learnt very quickly when a place promised me something and then I waited till I had got it. Otherwise I passed on. I accepted every experience that came my way. When I could I travelled as comfortably as my ample means allowed, for it seemed to me merely silly to rough it for the sake of roughing it; but I do not think I ever hesitated to do anything because it was uncomfortable or dangerous.

I have never been much of a sightseer. So much enthusiasm has been expended over the great sights of the world that I can summon up very little when I am confronted with them. I have preferred common things, a wooden house on piles nestling among fruit-trees, the bend of a little bay lined with coconuts, or a group of bamboos by the wayside. My interest has been in men and the lives they led. I am shy of making acquaintance with strangers, but I was fortunate enough to have on my journeys a companion who had an inestimable social gift. He had an amiability of disposition that enabled him in a very short time to make friends with people in ships, clubs, barrooms and hotels, so that through him I was able to get into easy contact with an immense number of persons whom otherwise I should have known only from a distance.

I made acquaintance with them with just the degree of intimacy that suited me. It was an intimacy born on their side of ennui or loneliness, that withheld few secrets, but one that separation irrevocably broke. It was close because its limits were settled in advance. Looking back on that long procession I cannot think of anyone who had not something to tell me that I was glad to know. I seemed to myself to develop the sensitiveness of a photographic plate. It did not matter to me if the picture I formed was true; what mattered was that with the help of my imagination I could make of each person I met a plausible harmony. It was the most entrancing game in which I had ever engaged.

One reads that no one exactly resembles anyone else, and that every man is unique, and in a way this is true, but it is a truth easy to exaggerate: in practice men are very much alike. They are divided into comparatively few types. The same circumstances mould them in the same way. Certain characteristics infer certain others. You can, like the palæontologist, reconstruct the animal from a single bone. The "characters" which have been a popular form of letters since Theophrastus, and the "humours" of the seventeenth century, prove that men sort themselves into a few marked categories. Indeed this is the foundation of realism, which depends for its attractiveness on recognition. The romantic method turns its attention to the exceptional; the realistic to the usual. The slightly abnormal circumstances in which men live in the countries where life is primitive or the environment alien to them, emphasize their ordinariness so that it gains a character of its own; and when they are in themselves extraordinary, which of course they sometimes are, the want of the usual restraints permits them to develop their kinks with a

freedom that in more civilized communities can be but hardly
won. Then you have creatures that realism can hardly cope with.
I used to stay away till my receptivity was exhausted and I found
that when I met people I had no longer the power to make the
imaginative effort to give them shape and coherence; then
I returned to England to sort out my impressions and rest till I felt
my powers of assimilation restored. At last, after seven, I think,
of these long journeys I found a certain sameness in people. I met
more and more often types that I had met before. They ceased
to interest me so much. I concluded that I had come to the end of
my capacity for seeing with passion and individuality the people
I went so far to find, for I had never doubted that it was I who
gave them the idiosyncrasy that I discovered in them, and so
I decided that there was no further profit for me in travel. I had
twice nearly died of fever, I had been nearly drowned, I had been
shot by bandits. I was glad to resume a more ordered way of life.

I came back from each of my journeys a little different. In my
youth I had read a great deal, not because I supposed that it would
benefit me, but from curiosity and the desire to learn; I travelled
because it amused me, and to get material that would be of use
to me: it never occurred to me that my new experiences were
having an effect on me, and it was not till long afterwards that
I saw how they had formed my character. In contact with all
these strange people I lost the smoothness that I had acquired
when, leading the humdrum life of a man of letters, I was one
of the stones in a bag. I got back my jagged edges. I was at last
myself. I ceased to travel because I felt that travel could give me
nothing more. I was capable of no new development. I had
sloughed the arrogance of culture. My mood was complete
acceptance. I asked from nobody more than he could give me.
I had learnt toleration. I was pleased with the goodness of my
fellows; I was not distressed by their badness. I had acquired independence of spirit. I had learnt to go my own way without
bothering with what others thought about it. I demanded freedom for myself and I was prepared to give freedom to others. It
is easy to laugh and shrug your shoulders when people act badly
to others; it is much more difficult when they act badly to you.
I have not found it impossible. The conclusion I came to about
men I put into the mouth of a man I met on board ship in the
China Seas. "I'll give you my opinion of the human race in a

nutshell, brother," I made him say. "Their heart's in the right place, but their head is a thoroughly inefficient organ."

CAPRI

CAPRI. I WANDER about alone, forever asking myself the same questions: What is the meaning of life? Has it any object or end? Is there such a thing as morality? How ought one to conduct oneself in life? What guide is there? Is there one road better than another? And a hundred more of the same sort. The other afternoon I was scrambling among the rocks and boulders up the hill behind the villa. Above me was the blue sky and all around the sea. Hazy in the distance was Vesuvius. I remember the brown earth, the ragged olive trees, and here and there a pine. And I stopped suddenly, in confusion, my head buzzing with all the thoughts that seethed in it. I could make nothing out of it all; it seemed to me one big tangle. In desperation, I cried out: I can't understand it. I don't know, I don't know.

AT WAR

I MET A CURIOUS man while I was having breakfast. He was a hussar and had ridden ahead of his regiment. While he breakfasted an orderly held his horse under the trees in the square. He told me he was a Cossack, born in Siberia, and for eleven years had been fighting Chinese brigands on the frontier. He was thin, with strongly marked features and large, very prominent blue eyes. He had been in Switzerland for the summer and three days before war broke out received orders to go to France at once. On the declaration he found himself unable to get back to Russia and was given a commission in a French cavalry regiment. He was talkative, vivacious and boastful. He told me that, having taken a German officer prisoner, he took him to his quarters. There he said to him: "Now I will show you how we treat prisoners and gentlemen," and gave him a cup of chocolate; when he had drunk it he said: "Now I will show you how you treat them." And he smacked his face. "What did he say?" I asked. "Nothing, he knew that if he had opened his mouth

I would have killed him." He talked to me about the Senegalese. They insist on cutting off the Germans' heads: "Then you're sure they're dead – *et ça fait une bonne soupe.*" He described the shells: "They go zzz, and until they fall you don't know if you're going to be killed or not."

Fighting is going on within twenty-five kilometres. While waiting for luncheon I talked to a sharp lad of thirteen. He told me that the other day two prisoners were brought through; the boy added that he had his cap full of hot chestnuts, and he threw them one by one in the wretched men's faces. When I told him that was very wrong he laughed and said: "Why? Everybody else was hitting them." Some Germans came in afterwards to get a car that they had requisitioned and drove with the mayor to the house where it was. The *gendarmes*, ten of them, heard of this and followed. When they arrived the officer was passing into the house with the mayor, and one of the Germans was under the car doing something to it. The officer stepped to one side to let the mayor precede him: "It showed that he had good manners," said the old lady with whom I am billeted; and as he did so the *gendarmes* shot him; then they shot the man who was under the car. The others held up their hands in surrender, but they shot them all.

I am billeted in a small, queer house with an elderly retired shopman and his wife; they have three sons mobilized; they are very cordial, glad to have an officer in their house, and anxious to do all they can for me. They offer me hot milk before I go to bed and say I shall be a son to them all the time I am there. It is a tiny room with a large wooden bed with a canopy, and looks out on a courtyard and a great sloping red roof.

All the morning I worked in a school turned into a hospital. There must have been between two and three hundred wounded. The whole place stank of pus, no windows were open, the floors were unswept, and it was incredibly dingy and melancholy. There seemed not to be more than two doctors in charge, and they were assisted by a couple of dressers and a number of women from the town who had no knowledge of nursing. There was one German prisoner with whom I talked a little. He had

had his leg cut off and was under the impression that it would not have been amputated if he had been French. The dresser asked me to explain to him that it was necessary to save his life, and with graphic detail explained to me in what a state the leg was. The prisoner was sullen and silent. He was suffering from home-sickness. He lay there, yellow, a straggly beard growing over his face, with wild, miserable eyes. In order to help him the doctor had put beside him a Frenchman whose leg had been amputated to show that this was done to the French too; and the Frenchman lay in his bed cheery and gay. I had done no work of this kind for many years and at first felt embarrassed and awkward, but soon I found I could do the little that it was possible to do – clean up the wounds, paint with iodine, and bandage. I have never seen such wounds. There are great wounds of the shoulder, the bone all shattered, running with pus, stinking; there are gaping wounds in the back; there are the wounds where a bullet has passed through the lungs; there are shattered feet so that you wonder if the limb can possibly be saved.

After luncheon we were asked to take a hundred wounded to the station because all efforts were being made to evacuate the temporary hospitals at Doullens in expectation of the large number of patients who must come when the great battle begins for which troops have been pouring along the road every day since we came here. Some could walk and some were carried out to the cars on stretchers. Just as the first stretchers were being brought out, there was a sound of chanting and the stretcher-bearers put down their burdens. A cracked bell began to tinkle with a melancholy sound. A priest, a big fat fellow, in a cassock and short surplice, came out preceded by a blind man, the beadle, I suppose, led by a little boy, and they chanted the beginning of the service for the dead. Then came, borne by four men, a coffin covered with poor black cloth, and lying on it was a little wooden cross of unstained deal tacked on to which was the indication tablet of the dead soldier. They were followed by four soldiers and a nurse. They went a few steps, then the priest stopped, looked round and peevishly shrugged his shoulders. They waited. At last another coffin came, then a third and a fourth; the procession started again, the cracked bell tinkled; they passed out of the courtyard into the road; the civilians took off their hats, the military saluted; and they went their way slowly to the cemetery. I wondered what the dying in the hospital felt each time they heard the ghastly tinkling of the little cracked bell.

It was in a château of white stone, a dignified building, with the date 1726 over the door, and it combined the solid grandeur of the age of Louis XIV with the beginnings of a lighter, daintier style. It had been hastily turned into a hospital. Wounded men were lying on straw mattresses on the floor in the hall and in the dining-room; the drawing-room had been made into a casualty ward – in the hurry the furniture had not been removed, but only pushed against the wall – and it was odd to see basins, dressings and drugs on the grand piano; the patient on his stretcher, waiting to be dressed, was placed on a Buhl writing-table. An attempt had been made the night before by the French to take the village of Andechy; the French had advanced before their artillery had properly prepared the way for them, one regiment had seized the enemy's trenches, but another regiment, territorials, had wavered and then fled, so that the regiment already in possession of the German trenches had to retreat, and in retreating was terribly cut up. There were three hundred dead and sixteen hundred wounded. We took our stretchers out of the ambulances and waited for them to be loaded with those whom it was possible to move. The circular bit of lawn in front of the house, which one could imagine under usual circumstances neat and trim, was muddy like a field after a football match in the rain, and cut up by the stretcher-bearers who had walked over it through the night, and the heavy wheels of motor ambulances. In an outhouse by the side were piled the dead, those who were found to be dead when they reached the hospital and those who had died in the night. They were packed close together in every kind of grotesque attitude, their uniforms filthy with mud and blood, some were strangely contorted as though they had died in agony, one had his arms outstretched as though he were playing the harp, some were flung down shapelessly like clothes without a body in them; but in death their bloodless hands, the rough, dirty hands of private soldiers, had acquired an extraordinary delicacy and distinction. We made two or three journeys to this hospital and then went to the church of the village. It stood, a bare, weather-beaten village church, on the crest of a steep little hill. The chairs had been piled up in one of the chapels and the floor covered with straw. On this lay the wounded all round the wall and in long rows, so that there was scarcely room to thread one's way between them. In the emergency there had been no time to take away any of the emblems of religion, and from the high altar looked down a Virgin in plaster, with staring eyes and painted cheeks: on each side were candlesticks and gilded jars containing paper flowers. Everyone who was not too ill smoked cigarettes. It was a singular scene. Round the doorway was a group of soldiers, smoking and chatting, while they glanced now and then gravely at the wounded; here and there others wandered around, looking for wounded comrades and stopping now and then to ask one about his wounds; hospital orderlies passed among the stricken with water or soup; stretcher-bearers stepped gingerly through the crowd, bearing their load to the ambulance. Conversation mingled with groans of pain and the cries of the dying; some, less wounded than their fellows, joked and laughed because they were glad to be alive. By a column a priest was giving the last sacrament to one who was dying. He muttered his prayers hurriedly in a low voice. Most of them seemed badly wounded, and they lay already in the shapeless confusion which I had seen in the dead. Propped up against the central door of the church, by an accident apart from the others, lay a man with an ashy face, bearded, thin and haggard; he made no sound or movement, but stared sullenly in front of him as though, realizing death was inevitable, he was filled only with anger. He had a horrible wound in the belly, and nothing could be done for him; he waited for death. I saw another, quite a boy, round-faced and ugly, with a yellow skin and narrow eyes, so that he had almost the look of a Japanese, who was desperately wounded; he knew he was dying too, but he was horribly afraid. Three soldiers were standing at his head, leaning over him, and he clung to the hands of one of them, crying out: "Oh God, I'm going to die." He sobbed heart-rendingly and heavy tears rolled over his dirty, ugly face, and he kept saying: "I'm so unhappy, oh God, I'm so unhappy." The soldiers tried to comfort him, and the one whose hand he held caressingly passed his other hand over the boy's face. "*Mais non, mon vieux, tu guériras.*" Another sat against the chancel steps smoking a cigarette and coolly watched; his cheeks were rosy, he did not look ill; he smiled gaily as I went up to him. I saw his arm was bandaged and I asked him if the wound was severe. He laughed a little. "Oh, that's nothing, if I had no more than that! I've got a bullet in my spine, my legs are paralysed."

A billet at Montdidier. I found my way into the library. The neighbouring gentry before the French Revolution had town houses at Montdidier, to which they used to come in winter for society, but their mansions have now been divided into two or three houses for the bourgeoisie who have taken their place; that in which I am billeted gives one the impression of having been part of a much larger one, and the library is a little room on the ground floor which you reach by what may once have been a back staircase. It is a panelled room and the whole of one side is taken up by a bookcase built into the wall, and the books are protected by a wire network; the doors are locked, and it is impossible to get a book, but I amused myself by looking at their titles. They seem for the most part to have been collected in the eighteenth century. They are bound in calf decorated with gold tooling. On the upper shelves are devotional works, but among them, tucked away modestly, I found the picaresque novel *Don Guzman de Alfarache* and immediately below the *Mémoires d'un Homme de Qualité*; then there are the complete works of Bossuet, the sermons of Massillon, and the works in a dozen volumes of a writer I have never heard of. I am curious to know who he was and how he deserved this splendid edition. I should like also to dip into the four quarto volumes which contain the *Histoire de Montdidier*. Rousseau is represented only by the *Confessions*. On a lower shelf I found the identical edition of Buffon's works which amused my own childhood. The collector of these books was of a serious turn of mind, for I found the works of Descartes and an imposing history of the world, a history of France in many volumes, and a translation of Hume's *History of England*. There was a large edition of Scott's novels, full octavo, bound in black leather and very depressing to look at; and there was an edition of the works of Lord Byron that looked most unsuitably solemn. Soon I did not want to read any of the books I saw; it seemed to me much more entertaining to look at their titles behind their prison of gilt wicker; they had a magic thus which was greater far than I should have found if I had been able to take hold of them and turn their musty pages.

Amiens. There are nearly as many English people here as in Boulogne, and great ladies drive about in huge motor-cars and visit the sick and conduct hospitals. I was told an agreeable story of one of them. A train-load of wounded had just come from the front and the wounded were placed temporarily in the hospital at the station. A lady went round giving them hot soup. Presently she came to a man who had been shot through the gullet and the lungs; she was just about to give him soup when the doctor in charge told her that if she did she would drown him. "What do you mean?" she said. "Of course he must have soup. It can't possibly do him any harm." "I've been in practice a great many years and through three campaigns," answered the doctor, "and my professional opinion is that if you give that man soup he'll die." The lady grew very impatient. "What nonsense," she said. "You give him soup on your own responsibility," said the doctor. She held a cup to the man's mouth, who tried to swallow, and promptly died. The lady was furious with the doctor: "You've killed that man," she said. "Pardon me," he answered, "you killed him. I told you what would happen."

The landlord of the hotel at Steenvoorde. He is quite a character, a Fleming, cautious, slow, heavy and stout, with round eyes, a round nose, and a round face, a man of forty-five perhaps; he does not welcome the arriving guest, but puts obstacles in the way of his taking a room or having dinner and has to be persuaded to provide him with what he wants; when he has overcome his instinctive mistrust of the stranger, he is friendly. He has a childlike sense of humour, heavy and slow as himself, with a feeling for the practical joke; and he has a fat, tardy laugh. Now that he has come to know me, though still a little suspicious, he is pleasant and affable. When I said to him: "*Votre café est bien bon, patron,*" he answered elliptically: "*C'est lui qui le boit qui l'est.*" He speaks in a broad accent, mixing up chaotically the second person singular and the second person plural. He reminds one of those donors of altar pieces that you see in old Flemish pictures; and his wife might be the donor's wife; she is a large woman, with a stern, unsmiling, lined face, a rather alarming creature; but now and then you feel that there is the Flemish humour behind her severity, and sometimes I have heard her laugh heartily at the discomfiture of some offending person. The first day I arrived here, when. I was persuading the patron to give me dinner, he went to ask his wife if it was possible. "*Il faut bien que je la demande,*" he said, "*puisque je couche avec.*"

I enjoyed myself at Steenvoorde. It was cold and uncomfortable. It was impossible to get a bath. The food was poor. The work was hard and tedious. But what a delight it was to have no responsibility! I had no decisions to make. I did what I was told, and having done it my time was my own. I could waste it with a clear conscience. Till then I had always thought it so precious that I could not afford uselessly to waste a minute. I was obsessed by the ideas that seethed in my head and the desire to express them. There was so much I wanted to learn, so many places I wanted to see, so many experiences I felt I couldn't afford to miss; but the years were passing and time was short. I was never without a sense of responsibility. To what? Well, I suppose to myself and to such gifts as I had, desiring to make the most both of them and of myself. And now I was free. I enjoyed my liberty. There was a sensual, almost voluptuous, quality in the pleasure of it. I could well understand it when I was told of certain men that they were having the time of their lives in the war. I don't know if there's such a word as hebetude in English, but if there is that's the state I so thoroughly enjoyed.

HAWAII

HONOLULU. THE UNION Saloon. You get to it by a narrow passage from King Street, and in the passage are offices so that thirsty souls may be supposed bound for one of these just as well as for the bar. It is a large square room with three entrances, and opposite the bar two corners have been partitioned off into little cubicles. Legend states that they were built so that King Kalakaua might go and drink without being seen by his subjects. In one of these he may have sat over his bottle, a bronze potentate, with R.L.S., discussing the misdeeds of missionaries and the inhibitions of Americans. The saloon is wainscoted with dark brown wood to about five feet from the floor, and above, the wall is papered with a varied assortment of pictures. They are an odd collection. Prints of Queen Victoria, a portrait in oils, in a rich gold frame, of King Kalakaua, old line engravings of the eighteenth century (there is one after a theatrical picture by Dewilde, heaven knows how it got there), oleographs from the Christmas supplements of the *Graphic* and *Illustrated London News* of twenty years ago, advertisements of whisky, gin, champagne and beer, photographs of baseball teams and of native orchestras. Behind the bar serve two large half-castes, in white, fat, clean-shaven, dark-skinned, with thick curly hair and large, bright eyes.

Here gather American men of business, sailors, not able seamen, but captains, engineers and first mates, storekeepers and Kanakas. Business of all sorts is done here. The place has a vaguely mysterious air and you can imagine that it would be a fit scene for shady transactions. In the daytime the light is dim and at night the electric light is cold and sinister.

The Chinese quarter. Streets of frame houses, one, two, three storeys high, painted in various colours, but time and weather have made the colours dingy. They have a dilapidated look as though the leases were running out and it was worth no tenant's while to make repairs. In the stores is every imaginable article of Western and Eastern commerce. The Chinese clerks sit impassive within the shops and stare idly at the passers-by. Sometimes, at night, you see a pair, yellow, lined, with slanting eyes, intent on a mysterious game which might be the Chinese equivalent of chess. They are surrounded by onlookers as intense as they, and they take an immense time between each move, calculating deeply.

The Red Light District. You go down side-streets by the harbour, in the darkness, across a rickety bridge, and you come to a road, all ruts and holes; a little farther, and there is parking room for motors on either side; there are saloons gaily lit and a barber's shop; there is a certain stir, an air of expectant agitation; you turn down a narrow alley, either to the right or to the left, and find yourself in the district. The street divides Iwelei into two parts, but each part is exactly like the other. Rows of little bungalows, painted green and very neat and tidy in appearance, even a trifle prim; and the road between them is broad and straight.

Iwelei is laid out like a garden city, and in its respectable regularity, its order and trimness, gives an impression of sardonic horror; for never can the search for love have been so planned and systematized. The pretty bungalows are divided into two lodgings; each is inhabited by a woman, and each consists of two rooms and a kitchenette. One is a bedroom in which there is a chest-of-drawers, a large bed with a canopy and curtains, and a chair or two. It has an overcrowded look. The parlour contains a large table, a gramophone, sometimes a piano, and half a dozen chairs. On the walls are pennants from the San Francisco exhibition and sometimes cheap prints, the favourite of which is *September Morn*, and photographs of San Francisco and Los Angeles. In the kitchenette is disorder. Here beer and gin are kept for visitors.

The women sit at their windows so that they may be clearly seen. Some are reading, some are sewing, and take no notice of the passer-by; others watch him approach and call out to him as he passes. They are of all ages and all nations. There are Japanese, Negro women, Germans, Americans, Spaniards. (It is strange and nostalgic as you pass to hear on a gramophone *coplas* or a *seguidilla*. Most of them have no trace of youth or beauty, and you wonder how, looking as they do, they can earn a living. Their cheeks are heavily rouged and they are dressed in cheap finery. When you go in the blinds are drawn down and if someone knocks the answer is: Busy. You are at once invited to drink beer and the woman tells you how many glasses she has had that day. She asks you where you come from. The gramophone is turned on. The price is a dollar.

The streets between are lit by a rare street lamp, but chiefly by the light that comes from the open windows of the bungalows. Men wander about, for the most part silently, looking at the women; now and then one makes up his mind and slinks up the three steps that lead into the parlour, is let in, and then the door and window are shut and the blind is pulled down. Most of the men are only there to look. They are of all nationalities. Sailors from the ships in port, sailors from the American gunboats, mostly drunk, Hawaiians, soldiers from the regiments, white and black, quartered on the island, Chinese, Japanese. They wander about in the night, and desire seems to throb in the air.

For some time the local papers had been writing articles about the scandal of Iwelei, the missionaries had been clamorous, but the police refused to stir. Their argument was that with the great preponderance of men in Oahu prostitution was inevitable, and to localize it made it easy to control and rendered medical examination more reliable. The papers attacked the police and at last they were forced to act. A raid was made, and fourteen ponces were arrested; oddly enough on the charge sheet most of them claimed French nationality. It suggests that the profession is peculiarly attractive to the citizens of France. A few days later all the women were summoned and sentenced to be on their good behaviour for a year on pain of being sent to prison. Most of them went straight back to San Francisco. I went to Iwelei the night of the raid. Most of the houses were closed, and there was hardly anyone in the streets. Here and there little groups of three or four women discussed the news in undertones. The place was dark and silent. Iwelei had ceased to exist.

Haula. A little hotel on the windward side of Oahu kept by a German Swiss and his Belgian wife. It is a wooden bungalow with a wide veranda and the doors are protected from mosquitoes by wire netting. In the garden bananas, papaias and coconut trees. The Swiss is a little man with a square German head, a head too large for his body, bald, with a long, untidy moustache. His wife is matronly, stout and red-faced, with brown hair severely brushed back. She gives you the impression of being competent and business-like. They like to talk of their homes which they haven't seen for seventeen years, he of Berne, she of the village near Namur where she was born. After dinner the hostess comes into the living-rooms and chats while she plays patience and presently the landlord, who is also the cook, comes in and sits down to gossip.

From here you visit the sacred waterfall, passing through fields of sugar-cane, and then along a narrow brook upwards towards the mountains. A track runs along it, now on one side, now on the other, so that every now and then you have to ford the stream. Wherever there is a large stone with a flattish top, you see numbers of leaves that have been placed on it and are held down by a pebble. They are offerings to propitiate the deity of the place. The water falls through a narrow gorge into a deep round pool, and you are surrounded by tangled scrub, green and immensely luxuriant. Beyond, above, is a valley which, it is said, no one has ever explored.

THE MISSIONARY AND MISS THOMPSON

THE MISSIONARY. He was a tall thin man, with long limbs loosely jointed, hollow cheeks and high cheek-bones; his fine, large dark eyes were deep in their sockets, and he had full sensual lips; he wore his hair rather long. He had a cadaverous look, and a look of suppressed fire. His hands were large, rather finely shaped, with long fingers, and his naturally pale skin was deeply burned by the Pacific sun.

Mrs. W., his wife, was a little woman with her hair very elaborately done, with prominent blue eyes behind gold-rimmed *pince-nez*; her face was long, like a sheep's, but she gave no impression of foolishness, rather of extreme alertness. She had the quick movements of a bird. The most noticeable thing about her was her voice, high, metallic and without inflection; it fell on the ear with a hard monotony, irritating the nerves like the clamour of a pneumatic drill. She was dressed in black, and wore round her neck a thin gold chain from which hung a small cross. She was a New Englander.

Mrs. W. told me that her husband was a medical missionary, and as his district (the Gilberts) consisted of widely separated islands, he frequently had to go long distances by canoe. The sea was often rough and his journeys were not without danger. During his absence she remained at their headquarters and managed the mission. She spoke of the depravity of the natives in a voice nothing could hush, but with a vehement, unctuous horror; she described their marriage customs as obscene beyond description. She said that when first they went to the Gilberts it was impossible to find a single "good" girl in any of the villages. She was very bitter about the dancing.

Miss Thompson. Plump, pretty in a coarse fashion, perhaps not more than twenty-seven: she wore a white dress and a large white hat, and long white boots from which her calves, in white cotton stockings, bulged. She had left Iwelei after the raid and was on her way to Apia, where she hoped to get a job in the bar of a hotel. She was brought to the house by the quartermaster, a little, very wrinkled man, indescribably dirty.

The lodging house. It is a two-storey frame house with verandas on both floors, and it is about five minutes' walk from the dock, on the Broad Road, and faces the sea. Below is a store in which are sold canned goods, pork and beans, beef, hamburger steak, canned asparagus, peaches and apricots; and cotton goods, lava-lavas, hats, raincoats and such like. The owner is a half-caste with a native wife surrounded by little brown children. The rooms are almost bare of furniture, a poor iron bed with a ragged mosquito-curtain, a rickety chair and a washstand. The rain rattles down on the corrugated iron roof. No meals are provided.

On these three notes I constructed a story called "Rain".

A CASTAWAY

WMS. AN IRISHMAN. When he was a boy of fifteen he took on the paternity of a child got from some girl by the son of the local clergyman. This young man, after promising to pay for the child's keep, did not do so, and Wms had to pay half a crown a week till the child was fourteen. Twenty years later, on going back to Ireland, he sought the man out, then married and the father of children, and fought him till he made him ask his pardon.

For some time he was in New Zealand. One day he was shooting with a friend, a bank clerk, who had no gun licence: suddenly they saw a policeman, the clerk was in dismay, thinking he would be arrested, so Wms told him to keep on calmly and himself started running. The policeman pursued and they ran back to Auckland. Once there Wms stopped, the policeman came up, asked for his licence, which Wms immediately produced. The policeman asked him why he had run away, whereupon he answered: "Well, you're an Irishman same as I am, if you promise to hold your tongue about it I'll tell you; the other fellow hadn't a licence." The policeman burst out laughing and said: "You're a sport, come and have a drink."

He is a gross, sensual man, and he loves to tell you about the women he's lived with. He's had ten children by Samoan women; one, a girl of fifteen, he keeps at school in New Zealand, but the rest he's handed over to the Mormon mission with a sum of money. He came out to the islands when he was twenty-six as a planter. He was one of the few white men settled in Savaii at the time of the German occupation and had already a certain influence with the natives. He loves them as much as it is in his selfish nature to love anybody. The Germans made him Amtmann, a position he occupied for sixteen years. On one occasion, having to call on Solf, the German minister for foreign affairs, Solf said to him: "Being governor of a German colony I suppose you speak German fluently." "No," he answered, "I only know one word, *prosit*, and I haven't heard that since my arrival in Berlin." The minister laughed heartily and sent for a bottle of beer.

TAHITI

PAPEETE. SHARKS SURROUNDED the ship as she entered the passage in the reef and followed her into the lagoon. The lagoon was very quiet and still and the water clear. A number of white schooners lay along the wharf. A crowd had assembled to see the ship come in, the women in bright colours, the men in white or khaki or blue. On the bright sunny quay the crowd, so brilliantly coloured, was a sight charmingly gay.

There are stores and office buildings along the beach and a long line of old trees, with heavy green foliage, and here and there, making the green more vivid, the rich scarlet of the *flamboyant*. The buildings, the post office, the offices of the Compagnie Navale de l'Océanie, haven't the severe, businesslike dullness of most such buildings in the Pacific; they have a florid tawdriness which is not altogether unpleasing. The beach with its fine trees has something French about it and reminds you of the ramparts of a provincial town in Touraine. And Papeete as a whole, notwithstanding its English and American stores, its Chinese shops, has a subtly French character. It has an engaging trimness, and it is leisurely. You feel that people live there, and the desire for gain is not quite so much in evidence as in the English islands. The roads are good, as good and as carefully kept as many roads in France, and trees, giving a grateful shade, have been planted along them. By the beach, shaded by a huge mango tree, with a vast bamboo by the side of it, is a brick washing-place of exactly the same pattern as those I saw near Arras in which soldiers, resting, were washing their shirts. The market place might be in any village of some size in France. And yet the whole has an exotic note which gives it character peculiar to itself.

Besides Tahitian, English and French are spoken indifferently. The natives speak French trailingly, with an accent that reminds you of that of the Russian students in Paris. Round each little house there is a garden, wild and uncared for; a tangled mass of trees and gaudy flowers.

The Tahitians wear trousers for the most part, shirts and huge straw hats. They seem lighter than most Polynesians. The women wear the Mother Hubbard, but great numbers wear black.

The Hotel Tiare. It is about five minutes walk from the Custom House at the end of the town, and when you step out of the gate you walk straight into the country. In front is a little garden full of flowers and surrounded by a hedge of coffee shrubs. At the back is a compound in which grow a breadfruit tree, an avocado pear, oleander and taro. When you want a pear for lunch you pick one off the tree. The hotel is a bungalow surrounded by a terrace, part of which serves as a dining-room. There is a small sitting-room with a waxed parquet floor, a piano and bentwood furniture covered with velvet. The bedrooms are small and dark. The kitchen is a little house by itself and here, all day long, sits Madame Lovaina superintending the Chinese cook. She is a very good cook herself and very hospitable. Everyone in the neighbourhood in want of a meal comes to the hotel and gets one. Lovaina is a half-caste, very white, a woman of fifty, perhaps, and of enormous proportions. She is not merely fat, she is huge and shapeless; and she wears a pink Mother Hubbard and a small straw hat. Her face has kept its small features, but she has a vast expanse of chin. Her brown eyes are large and liquid; her expression pleasant and candid. She has a ready smile and a hearty, fat laugh. She takes a motherly interest in all young people, and when the boyish purser of the *Moana* got very drunk I saw her stir her immense bulk and take the glass out of his hand to prevent him from drinking more, and she sent her son to see him safely back to his ship.

The tiare is the national flower of Tahiti, a little star-shaped white flower which grows on a bush of rich green leaves, and it has a peculiarly sweet and sensual perfume. It is used for making wreaths, for putting in the hair and behind the ear, and when placed in the black hair of native women it shines with a dazzling brightness.

Johnny. At first glance no one would suspect that he had native blood in him. He is twenty-five. He is a rather stout young man, with black crinkly hair beginning to recede and a clean-shaven fleshy face. He is excitable and gesticulates a great deal. He speaks very quickly, his voice continually breaking into falsetto, English and French, fluently but not very correctly and with a curious accent, and his natural tongue is Tahitian. When he strips to bathe and puts on a pareo the native appears at once, and then only his colour betrays his white blood. At heart he is a native. He loves the native food and the native ways. He is proud of his native blood and has none of the false shame of the half-caste.

Johnny's house. It is about five miles from Papeete, perched on a little hill overlooking the sea on three sides, with Murea straight ahead. The shore is crowded thick with coconuts, and behind are the mysterious hills. The house is the most ramshackle affair imaginable. There is a large lower room, something like a barn, raised from the ground and reached by steps; the frame walls are broken away here and there; and at the back are a couple of small sheds. One of them serves as a kitchen; fire is made in a hole in the ground and the cooking is done on it. Above are two attics. There is a table in each one and a mattress on the floor and nothing else. The barn is the living-room. The furniture consists of a deal table covered with a green oilcloth, a couple of deckchairs and two or three very old and battered bentwood chairs. It is decorated with coconut leaves, split at the top and nailed to the walls or woven round the supporting beams. Half a dozen Japanese lanterns hang from the ceiling, and a bunch of yellow hibiscus gives a note of bright colour.

The Chiefess. She lives in a two-storeyed frame house about thirty-five miles from Papeete. She is the widow of a chief who received the Legion of Honour for his services in the troubles at the time the French protectorate was changed into occupation; and on the walls of the parlour, filled with cheap French furniture, are the documents relating to this, signed photographs of various political celebrities, and the usual photographs of dusky marriage groups. The bedrooms are crowded with enormous beds. She is a large stout old woman, with grey hair, and one eye shut, which yet now and then opens and fixes you with a mysterious stare. She wears spectacles, a shabby black Mother Hubbard, and sits most comfortably on the floor smoking native cigarettes.

She told me there were pictures by Gauguin in a house not far from hers, and when I said I would like to see them called for a boy to show me the way. We drove along the road for a couple of miles and then, turning off it, went down a swampy grass path till we came to a very shabby frame house, grey and dilapidated. There was no furniture in it beyond a few mats, and the veranda was swarming with dirty children. A young man was lying on the veranda smoking cigarettes and a young woman was seated idly. The master of the house, a flat-nosed, smiling dark native came and talked to us. He asked us to go in, and the first thing I saw was the Gauguin painted on the door. It appears that Gauguin was ill for some time in that house and was looked after by the parents of the present owner, then a boy of ten. He was pleased with the way they treated him and when he grew better desired to leave some recollection of himself. In one of the two rooms of which the bungalow consisted there were three doors, the upper part of which was of glass divided into panels, and on each of them he painted a picture. The children had picked away two of them; on one hardly anything was left but a faint head in one corner, while on the other could still be seen the traces of a woman's torso thrown backwards in an attitude of passionate grace. The third was in tolerable preservation, but it was plain that in a very few years it would be in the same state as the other two. The man took no interest in the pictures as such, but merely as remembrances of the dead guest, and when I pointed out to him that he could still keep the other two he was not unwilling to sell the third. "But," he said, "I shall have to buy a new door." "How much will it cost?" I asked. "A hundred francs." "All right," I said, "I'll give you two hundred."

I thought I had better take the picture before he changed his mind, so we got the tools from the car in which I had come, unscrewed the hinges and carried the door away. When we arrived back at the chiefess's we sawed off the lower part of it in order to make it more portable, and so took it back to Papeete.

I went to Murea in a little open boat crowded with natives and Chinese. The skipper was a fair, red-faced native with blue eyes, tall and stout; he spoke a little English and perhaps his father was an English sailor. As soon as we got out of the reef it was clear that we were in for a bad passage. The sea was high and, sweeping over the boat, drenched us all. She rolled and pitched and tossed. Great squalls came suddenly and blinding sheets of rain. The waves seemed mountainous. It was an exciting (and to me alarming) experience to plunge through them. Through it all one old native woman sat on the deck, smoking the big native cigarettes one after the other. A Chinese boy was constantly and horribly sick. It was a relief to see Murea grow nearer, to discern the coconuts, and finally to enter the lagoon. The rain swept down in torrents. We were all soaked to the skin. We got into a whaleboat that came out from the shore and had to wade to land. Then followed a four-mile walk along a muddy road, through streams, the rain beating down continually, till we reached the house at which we were to stay. We took off our clothes and got into pareos.

It was a small frame house, consisting of a veranda and two rooms, in each of which was an enormous bed. Behind was a kitchen. It belonged to a New Zealander, then away, who lived there with a native woman. There was a little garden in front, filled with tiare, hibiscus and oleander. At the side rushed a stream, and a small pool in this served as a bathroom. The water was fresh and sparkling.

By the steps of the veranda was a large tin bowl of water with a small tin basin, so that one could wash one's feet before entering the house.

Murea. The native houses are oblong, covered with a rough thatch of great leaves, and made of thin bamboos placed close together which let in light and air. There are no windows, but generally two or three doors. Many of them have an iron bed and in almost all you see a sewing machine.

The meeting-house is built on the same plan, but is very large, and everyone sits on the floor. I went to a choir practice, led by a blind girl, in which hour after hour they sang long hymns. The voices were loud and raucous near-by, but when you listened from a distance, sitting in the soft night, the effect was beautiful.

Fish spearing. I walked along the road for a bit and then, guided by the sound of voices and laughter, struck through a swamp of reeds taller than a man, wading here and there through muddy water up to the waist, and presently came to a small rushing stream. Here were about a dozen men and women, clad only in pareos, with long spears, and on the ground beside them heaps of great silver fish, each one gory from the spear wound which had killed it. I waited for a time and then someone uttered a word of warning, everyone sprang to attention with poised spear, and all at once a shoal rushed down the stream towards the sea. There was an excitement and a shouting, a clashing of spears, a plunge into the water, and then the catch, a dozen big fish, was taken out and flung on the ground. The fish quivered and leapt and beat the earth with their tails.

Within the Reef. The water has all sorts of colours, from the deepest blue to pale emerald green. The reef is wide and the coral many-tinted. You can walk on the reef, and it is strange to see the great breakers so near at hand and the tumultuous sea, while inside, the water is as calm as a pond. All sorts of strange animals lurk among the coral, brightly coloured fish, sea snails, *bêches de mer*, urchins and wriggling things faintly pink.

The nets. The whole village turns out when the great net is cast; the owners of the net go out in a canoe and one or two of them plunge into the water; long strings of women, boys and men, seize each end of the rope and pull. Others sit on the beach to watch the fun. Gradually the net is drawn in and a boy leaps on to a silvery fish, putting it into his pareo, and the catch is landed. A hole is made in the sand and the fish are poured in. Then they are divided up among the assistants.

Christianity. A French admiral came to one of the islands in his flag-ship, and the native queen gave a formal luncheon in his honour. She proposed to put him on her right, but the mission-ary's wife insisted that he should sit on *her* right. As the wife of Christ's representative she ranked higher than the queen. The missionary agreed with her. When the natives protested they both flew into a rage; they threatened to get even with them if such a slight were put upon them, and the natives, frightened, at length yielded. The missionaries had their way.

Tetiaroa. We went over in a small cutter with a gasolene engine. We started at one in the morning so as to arrive at daybreak when the sea is supposed to be at its calmest and the passage over the reef less difficult. It was very lovely in the silence of the night. The air was balmy. The stars were reflected in the waters within the reef. There was not a breath of wind. We put a rug down on the deck and made ourselves comfortable. Outside the reef there was the inevitable swell of the Pacific. When dawn came we were still in the open sea, but presently we saw the island, a low line of coconut trees, some miles off. Then we came to the reef and got into a boat. The owner of the cutter was a man named Levy. He said he came from Paris, but he spoke French with a strong accent which suggested to me the Algerian Jew. He cast his anchor on the reef, we got into the dinghy and rowed to the opening. This is not an opening at all, but merely a slight dip in the reef and when something of a wave beats in there is just enough water for a boat to scrape over. Once over it is impossible to row, for the coral is thick, and the natives get out, up to their waists in water, and pull the boat through a narrow, tortuous passage to the shore. The beach is white sand, fragments of coral and the shells of innumerable crustacea; then there are the coconuts and you come upon the half-dozen huts which make up the tiny settlement. One is the hut of the headman; there are two huts for copra, and another for the workmen; then two pleasant grass huts, one serving as a parlour, the other as a bedroom, used by the owner of the island. There is a grove of old, enormous trees and it is among these the huts are built; they give coolness and shade. We unloaded our stores and bedding and proceeded to make ourselves at home. There were swarms of mosquitoes, more than I have ever seen anywhere, and it was impossible to sit down without being surrounded by them. We rigged up a mosquito-curtain on the veranda of the living hut and set a table and a couple of chairs beneath it. But the mosquitoes were ingenious to enter and before it was possible to settle down in anything like peace twenty at least had to be killed under the curtain. There was a little shed at the side which served as a kitchen, and here the Chinaman I had brought with me with a few sticks made a fire on which he did the cooking.

The island has evidently been raised from the sea at a comparatively recent date and much of the interior is barren, caked, almost swampy, so that you sink several inches as you walk, and it may be supposed that it was a brackish lake, now dried up; and in one part there is still a small lake which not so very long ago must have been much larger. Besides the coconuts nothing much seems to grow except rank grass and a shrub something like broom. In all these islands the mynah bird is seen everywhere; but here there are no more than two or three that have recently been brought. Bird life consists only in great seabirds, black in colour, with long sharp bills, which make a piercing sort of whistle.

The sand on the beach has really the silver whiteness that you read of in descriptions of South Sea islands, and when you walk along in the sunshine it is so dazzling that you can hardly bear to look at it. Here and there you see the white shells of dead crabs or the skeleton of a seabird. At night the beach seems to be all moving; it is at first quite strange, this perpetual, slight movement, weird and uncanny; but when you light your torch you see that it comes from the incessant activity of innumerable shelled things; they move hither and thither on the beach slowly, stealthily, but there are such vast numbers of them that the whole beach seems alive.

The Reef. It is a broad causeway along which you can walk all round the island, but it is so rough and uneven that it tears your feet to pieces. In the pools fish dart about and now and then an eel raises a vicious head. Lobster-catching: you go along the reef at night with hurricane lamps and walk, peering right and left, into every nook and cranny; fish slither away frightened by the light; and you have to walk carefully, since everywhere are great sea-hedgehogs capable of causing nasty wounds on the feet. There are great numbers of lobsters and you do not walk far before you see one. You put your foot on it and then a native comes, takes it up quickly and throws it in the old kerosene can which he has strapped on his shoulder. Walking thus in the night one loses all sense of direction, and on the way back it was not easy to find the boat. For a few minutes it looked as though we should have to stay on the reef till dawn. There was no moon, but the sky was unclouded and the stars were bright.

Fishing on the Reef. At one point, near the passage, the reef is abrupt, like a precipice, and you look down directly into I know not how many fathoms of water. The natives had spread a net among the coral rocks of the lagoon and we had a number of fish to use as bait. It was rather horrid to see the natives killing them. They hit them with their fists on the belly or banged them with a piece of coral. When we reached the fishing-place, the canoe was attached to a coral rock, and the headman proceeded to pound up a couple of fish and threw the fragments in the water. This soon attracted a lot of small fry, thin, worm-like, active little things, and then a number of large black fish. In a few minutes a couple of sharks' fins showed themselves on the surface and we saw the brown sharks circling round with a kind of horrible stealth. The rod was merely a bamboo, and to this a line was attached. The big black fish circled round the bait and took it voraciously, so that one pulled them out of the water one after the other. The sharks were greedy too and we had to snatch the bait away from them since the line was too thin to hold them. Once I got a shark on my hook and he snapped the line in a twinkling. We put down a couple of lines with the innards of fish on them and caught a tunny that must have weighed the best part of forty pounds.

Catching sharks. Towards evening you attach the lights of a large fish to a hook and then tie the line to a tree. Not long elapses before you hear a great splashing, and going down to the beach you find that a shark is caught. You drag him in and when you get him on the beach he struggles and beats about. The native takes his large knife, a descendant of the cutlass brought by the first discoverers of the islands, and strikes at the head to get to the brain. It is an ugly, malicious-looking beast with hideous jaws. When it is dead the hook is cut out. Then the Chinaman cuts off the fins to dry them in the sun and a kanaka hacks out the jaw with its terrible teeth. The dead fish is cast back into the sea.

The natives often tie the line to one of their legs before they go to sleep and are awakened by the tugging.

Fish. Their variety is indescribable. Bright yellow fish, fish black and yellow, fish black and white, fish striped, fish curiously patterned. One day the natives went fishing and when they raised their net I saw their catch in all its brilliance. I had a sudden thrill, for it reminded me of the casting of a net in one of the stories in the Arabian Nights and among that astonishing confusion of colour and strange shapes I half expected to find a bottle sealed with the seal of Suleyman, the prison of a powerful djin.

The colour of the sea. It is deep blue in the open sea, wine-coloured under the setting sun; but in the lagoon of an infinite variety, ranging from pale turquoise to the brightest, clearest green; and there the setting sun will turn it for a short moment to liquid gold. Then there is the colour of the coral, brown, white, pink, red, purple; and the shapes it takes are marvellous; it is like a magic garden, and the hurrying fish are like butterflies. It strangely lacks reality; it has the fantastic air of the product of some extravagant imagination. Among the coral are pools with a floor of white sand, and here the water is dazzling clear.

Varo. In the Pacific they call it the sea-centipede. It is like a small lobster, but pale cream in colour. Two of them live in each hole. The female is larger and stronger than the male and somewhat more brightly coloured. They are found only in very fine sand and to catch them we went over the lagoon, about a mile, I should think, to one of the islands of which the group of Tetiaroa is composed. The natives had prepared a singular instrument. It consisted of the strong fibre from the central stem of the coconut leaf, about two feet long, and pliable; to this was tied a circle of hooks, turned upwards, so that it had a sort of umbrella effect; and about this was tied a piece of fish as bait. We walked along looking into the shallow water of the beach for the small round holes which marked the varo's dwelling, and then let down the hooks. The native said an incantation, asking the varo to come up out of his hole, then flipped the water with his fingers; mostly nothing happened, but sometimes the fibre was pulled down and then we knew a varo had seized the bait and was entangled in the hooks. Very cautiously he was hauled up, and it was quite exciting to see the little beast emerge on the surface clinging to the fibre. He was released and put into a basket which the head-man rapidly made from a coconut leaf. However it was not quick work and in three hours we only caught eight.

Evening on the Lagoon. At sunset the sea turns to a bright purple; the sky is cloudless and the sun, burning red, sinks into the sea, rapidly, but not so rapidly as writers lead one to believe, and Venus shines. When evening comes, clear and silent, an ardent, frenzied life seems to break out. Countless shelled animals begin to crawl about at the edge of the water, and in the water every living thing seems to be in action. Fish leap, there are mysterious splashings, and a sudden swift turmoil as a shark frightens everything within sight of its cruel stealthiness. Small fry leap by hundreds into the air and sometimes a large coloured fish gleams above the surface with a momentary glitter. But the most impressive thing is that feeling of urgent, remorseless life. In the quiet of the lovely evening there is something mysterious about it and vaguely alarming.

The night is wonderfully silent. The stars shine with a fierce brilliancy, the Southern Cross and Canopus; there is not a breath of wind, but a wonderful balminess in the air. The coconut trees, silhouetted against the sky, seem to be listening. Now and then a seabird gives a mournful cry.

RUSSIA

IN THIS YEAR I was sent to Russia on a secret mission. That is how I came to make the following notes.

Russia. I have been led to an interest in Russia for pretty well the same reasons as most of my contemporaries. The obvious one was Russian fiction. Tolstoi and Turgenev, but chiefly Dostoievsky, offered an emotion that was different from any offered by the novels of other countries. They made the greatest novels of Western Europe look artificial. Their novelty made me unfair to Thackeray, Dickens and Trollope, with their conventional morality; and even the great writers of France, Balzac, Stendhal and Flaubert, in comparison seemed formal and a little

frigid. The life they portrayed, these English and French novel-
ists, was familiar; and I, like others of my generation, was tired
of it. They described a society that was policed. Its thoughts had
been thought too often. Its emotions, even when extravagant,
were extravagant within ordered limits. It was fiction fit for a
middle-class civilization, well-fed, well-clothed, well-housed,
and its readers were resolute to bear in mind that all they read
was make-believe.

The fantastic nineties stirred the intelligent from their apathy,
making them restless and discontented, but gave them nothing
satisfying. Old idols were shattered, but those set up in their place
were papier mâché. The nineties talked a great deal about art and
literature, but their works were like toy rabbits that hop about
for a while when you have wound them up and then suddenly
with a click stop dead.

Modern Poets. I should be content with less cleverness if only
they had more feeling. They make little songs not from great
sorrows but from the sober pleasures of a good education.

The Secret Agent. He was a man of scarcely middle height, but
very broad and sturdy; he walked on noiseless feet with quick
steps; he had a curious gait, somewhat like a gorilla's, and his
arms hung from his sides a little away from his body; he gave
you the impression of an almost simian creature prepared at any
moment to spring; and the feeling of enormous strength was
disquieting. He had a large square head on a short thick neck.
He was clean-shaven, with small shrewd eyes, and his face was
strangely flattened as though it had been bashed in by a blow. He
had a large, fleshy, flat nose and a big mouth, with small discoloured teeth. His thick pale hair was plastered down on his
head. He never laughed, but he chuckled often, and then his
eyes gleamed with a humour that was ferocious. He was decently
dressed in American reach-me-downs, and at first sight you
would have taken him for an immigrant of the middle class who
had established himself comfortably in a small way of business
in some thriving city of the Middle West. He spoke English
fluently, but without correctness. It was impossible to be with
him long without being impressed by his determination. His
physical strength corresponded to his strength of character. He

was ruthless, wise, prudent, and absolutely indifferent to the means by which he reached his ends. There was in the end something terrifying about him. His fertile brain teemed with ideas, and they were subtle and bold. He took an artist's delight in the tortuous ways of his service; when he told you a scheme he contemplated or a dodge that had succeeded his little blue eyes glistened and his face lit up with a satanic mirth. He had an heroic disregard for human life, and you felt that for the cause he would not have hesitated to sacrifice his friend or his son. None could doubt his courage, and with an equal mind he was capable of facing not only danger – that is not so difficult – but discomfort and boredom. He was a man of frugal habit and could go for an incredible time without food or sleep. Never sparing himself, he never thought of sparing others; his energy was amazing. Though ruthless, he was good-humoured, and he was capable of killing a fellow-creature without a trace of ill-feeling. He seemed to have but one passion in life, if you omit an extreme desire for good cigars, and that was patriotism. He had a great sense of discipline and obeyed as unquestioningly his leader as he exacted obedience from his subordinates.

The patriotism of the Russians is a singular thing; there is a great deal of conceit in it; they feel themselves different from other people and flatter themselves on their difference; they speak with self-satisfaction of the ignorance of their peasants; they vaunt their mysteriousness and complexity; they repeat that with one face they look to the west and with the other to the east; they are proud of their faults – like a boorish man who tells you he is as God made him – and will admit with complacency that they are besotted and ignorant, incoherent of purpose and vacillating in action; but in that complex feeling which is the patriotism one knows in other countries, they seem deficient. I have tried to analyse what this particular emotion in myself consists of. To me the very shape of England on the map is significant, and it brings to my mind pell-mell a hundred impressions, the white cliffs of Dover and the tawny sea, the pleasant winding roads of Kent and the Sussex downs, St. Paul's and the Pool of London; scraps of poetry, the noble ode of Collins and Matthew Arnold's *Scholar Gipsy* and Keats' *Nightingale*, stray lines of Shakespeare's and the pages out of English history, Drake with his ships, and Henry

VIII and Queen Elizabeth; Tom Jones and Dr. Johnson; and all my friends and the posters at Victoria Station; then some vague feeling of majesty and power and continuity; and then, heaven knows why, the thought of a barque in full sail going down the Channel – *Whither, O splendid ship, thy white sails crowding* – while the setting sun hangs redly on the edge of the horizon. These feelings and a hundred others make up an emotion which makes sacrifice easy, it is an emotion compact of pride and longing and love, but it is humble rather than conceited, and it does not preclude a sense of humour. Perhaps Russia is too large for sentiments so intimate, its past too barren of chivalry and high romance, its character too indefinite, its literature too poor, for the imagination to embrace the country, its history and culture, in a single emotion. Russians will tell you that the peasant loves his village. His outlook goes no further. And when you read histories of Russia you are amazed to find how little the feeling of nationality has meant to one age after another. It is a startling incident when a wave of patriotism has arisen to drive out an invader. The general attitude has been one of indifference to his presence on the part of those not actually afflicted by it. It is not by chance that Holy Russia bore so long and so submissively the yoke of the Tartar. Now it causes no indignation that the Central Powers may seize portions of Russian soil: the possibility is dismissed with a shrug and the words: "Russia is large enough anyway."

But my work throws me in close contact with the Czechs, and here I see a patriotism that fills me with amazement. It is a passion so single and so devouring that it leaves room for no others. I feel that awe rather than admiration is due to these men who have sacrificed everything for the cause, and not in twos and threes, fanatics among an apathetic herd, but in tens of thousands; they have given everything they had, their peace, their home, their fortune, their lives, to gain independence for their country. They are organized like a department store, disciplined like a Prussian regiment. Most of the patriots I have come across among my own countrymen, alas! too often have been eager to serve their country, but determined it should not be without profit to themselves (who will ever tell of the hunting for jobs, the intrigues, the exertion of influence, the personal jealousies, that have distracted the nation when its very existence was in peril?), but the

Czechs are completely disinterested. They think as little of pay-
ment as does a mother of reward for the care of her child. With
alacrity they accept drudgery when others are given the opportunity of adventure, mean offices when others are awarded posts
of responsibility. Like all men of political mind, they have parties
and programmes, but they submit them all to the common good.
Is it not a marvellous thing that in the great Czech organization
which has been formed in Russia, all, from the rich banker to
the artisan, have given a tenth part of their income to the cause
throughout the war? Even the prisoners of war — and heaven
knows how precious to these were their few poor kopecks —
found they could spare enough to amount to some thousands of
roubles.

THE NEVSKY PROSPEKT

NEVSKY PROSPEKT. Bond Street has the narrow tortuousness of
the medieval city, and it reminds one always of the town to which
great ladies came for the season; it was in Bond Street that the
last Duchess of Cleveland boxed her footman's ears. The rue de
la Paix has the flamboyance of the Second Empire; it is wide,
handsome, coldly stately and gay withal, as though the shadows
of Cora Pearl and Hortense Schneider still smiled brightly at
the gathered gems. Fifth Avenue is gay too, but with a different
gaiety, of high spirits, and it is splendid with the rich, unimagina-
tive splendour of youth in its buoyancy. Though each has its
character and could belong only to the city in which it is, these
great streets have in common a civilized opulence; they represent
fitly a society which is established and confident. But none of
them has more character than the Nevsky. It is dingy and sordid
and dilapidated. It is very wide and very straight. The houses on
either side are low, drab, with tarnished paint, and their architecture is commonplace. There is something haphazard about the
street, even though we know that it was built according to plan,
and it has an unfinished air; it reminds you of some street in a
town of the Western States of America which has been built in
the hurry of a boom, and, prosperity having departed from it,
has run to seed. The shop windows are crowded with vulgar
wares. They look like bankrupt stock from the suburbs of Vienna

or Berlin. The dense crowd flows ceaselessly to and fro. Perhaps
it is the crowd that gives the Nevsky its character. It does not, as
in those other streets, consist chiefly of one class of the population but of all; and the loiterer may there observe a great variety
of his fellow-creatures, soldiers, sailors and students, workmen
and bourgeoisie, peasants; they talk incessantly; in eager throngs
they surround the men who sell the latest edition of a paper. It
looks a good-natured crowd, easygoing and patient; I shouldn't
imagine that they had the quick temper of the crowd in Paris
which may so easily grow ugly and violent, and I can't believe
that they would ever behave like the crowd of the French Revolution. They give the impression of peaceable folk who want to
be amused and excited, but who look upon the events of life
chiefly as pleasant topics of conversation. Outside butchers' and
grocers' these days are the long food lines, women with kerchiefs
over their heads, boys and girls, grey-bearded men and pale
youths, waiting hour after hour, waiting patiently.

I think that the most astonishing thing in these crowds is the
diversity of appearance; these people have not the uniformity of
look which you find commonly in the crowds of other countries;
it is as though the passions of the soul were written more plainly
on their faces, and the faces were not a mask but an index, and
walking along the Nevsky you saw the whole gallery of the characters of the great Russian novels so that you could put a name
to one after the other. You see the thick-lipped, broad-faced
merchant with his exuberant beard, sensual, loud-voiced and
coarse; the pale-faced dreamer, with his pinched cheeks and
sallow skin; you see the stolid woman of the people with a face
so expressionless that it is like an instrument of music for wilful
hands to play on, and you divine the cruelty of her sex's tenderness. Lust walks abroad like the personified abstraction of an old
morality, and virtue and anger and meekness and gluttony. The
Russians say constantly that the world can as little understand
them as they understand themselves. There is a little vanity in
the mysteriousness upon which they dwell. I have no idea of
explaining what so many have claimed to be inexplicable, but
I ask myself whether the mystery does not lie in simplicity rather
than in complexity. They are strangely primitive in the completeness with which they surrender themselves to emotion.
With English people, for instance, there is a solid background of

character which emotion modifies, but which in turn reacts on emotion; with the Russians it looks as though each emotion took complete possession of the individual and swayed him wholly. They are like Aeolian harps upon which a hundred winds play a hundred melodies, and so it seems as though the instrument were of unimaginable complexity.

I often see brooding over the crowd on the Nevsky an extraordinary, a horrifying figure. It seems hardly human. It is a little misshapen dwarf, perched strangely on a tiny seat at the top of a stout pole high enough to bring him above the heads of the passers-by; and the pole is upheld by a sturdy peasant who collects the alms of the charitable. The dwarf sits on his perch like a monstrous bird and the effect is increased by something birdlike in his head, but the strange thing is that the head is fine shaped, the head of a young man, with a great hooked nose and a bold mouth. The eyes are large, rather close together, and they stare with an unwinking fixity. The temples are hollow, the cheeks wan and sunk. The strange beauty of the features is more than commonly striking because in Russia as a rule features are indistinct and flat. It is the head of a Roman of the Empire in a sculpture gallery. There is something sinister in the immobility of the creature, watching the crowd with the intentness of a bird of prey and yet seeing nothing, and that fierce bold mouth is curved into the shadow of a sardonic smile. There is something terrifying in the aloofness of the creature, contemptuous and yet indifferent, malicious and yet tolerant. It is like the spirit of irony watching the human race. The people pass to and fro and they put into the peasant's box kopecks and stamps and notes.

The Lavra of Alexander Nevsky. As you reach the end of the Nevsky Prospekt it grows shabbier and more dingy. The houses have the bedraggled look of those on the outskirts of a town, they suggest a sordid mystery, until the street ends abruptly in an oddly unfinished way and you come to the gateway of the monastery. You enter. There is a cemetery on each side of you and then you cross a narrow canal and come to the most unexpected scene in the world. It is a great quadrangle. Grass grows fresh and green as though you were in the country. On one side is a chapel and the cathedral and then, all around, the low white buildings of the monastery. There is something exquisitely strange in their architecture; the decoration is very simple and yet gives a sensation of being ornate; they remind you of a Dutch lady of the seventeenth century, soberly but affluently dressed in black. There is something prim about them, but not at all demure. In the birch trees rooks were cawing, and my recollection was carried back to the precincts of Canterbury; for there the rooks cawed too; it is a sound that never fails to excite my melancholy. I think of my boyhood, unhappy through the shyness which made me lonely among a crowd of boys, and yet rich with vague dreams of the future. The same grey clouds hung overhead. I felt homesick. I stood on the steps of the Greek church, looking at the long line of the monastery buildings, the leafless birches, but I saw the long nave of Canterbury cathedral with its flying buttresses and the central tower more imposing and lovely to my moved eyes than any tower in Europe.

OPIUM DREAM

SINGAPORE: OPIUM DREAM. I saw a road lined on each side with tall poplars, the sort of road that you see often in France, and it stretched in front of me, white and straight, immensely far; I saw farther than I had ever thought it possible to see, and still the white road continued with green poplars on either side. And then I seemed to go along it, rapidly, and the poplars fled past me more quickly, infinitely more quickly than the telegraph poles fly past when you are in an express train; and still they went and still they were ahead of me, the long rows of poplars. Then, on a sudden, there were no more poplars, but shady trees with large leaves, chestnuts and planes; and they were spaced out, and I went at no breakneck speed, but leisurely, and presently I came upon an open space and then, as I looked down, far below me, was the grey calm sea. Here and there a fishing-boat was sailing into harbour. Yonder, on the other side of the bay, stood a trim and tidy granite house with a flagstaff in the garden. It must have been the coastguard's.

THE SULTAN

THE SULTAN. It was arranged that we should be received by the Sultan in his audience chamber at ten, and as we walked along we saw him and his suite coming out of the place where he lives, which is above and at the side of the audience chamber, and we waited for a moment to allow him to enter. He was accompanied by two middle-aged men and a suite, all higgledy-piggledy, with a man holding an umbrella over his head. The audience chamber was a long low room with a gaudily-painted throne at one end. In front of this was a table with half a dozen dining-room chairs round it, and from this, on each side of the table, two rows of chairs ran down the hall. We were introduced to the Sultan and then to the two regents. The Sultan is a little boy of thirteen with a long face like a horse, a pale ivory skin, a large mouth which shows his long teeth and gums when he smiles, and very quick beady eyes. He was dressed in yellow silk, a coat, trousers and sarong, and on his head he wore a black fez decorated with an appliqué pattern of gold cloth enriched with imitation diamonds. Round his neck were a number of gold strings and chains and a large gold medal. The regents, who are his close relations, wore blueish-grey patterned silk handkerchiefs made into a kind of turban on their heads and dark trousers, bajus and sarongs. One of them had a very pronounced squint and wore spectacles of blue glass. The younger brother of the Sultan, a little pale-faced boy of eight, was carried in by an attendant on whose lap he sat throughout the audience. The Sultan looked every now and then at the cross-eyed regent to see what he was to do, but seemed to have self-assurance and to be not at all shy. He sat in an armchair at the head of the table, with the regents on one side of him and the British Resident and ourselves on the other. Behind him stood a group of officials in very shabby clothes. One of them bore a state sword of execution and there was another who bore a spear, a third with a cushion and a fourth with the apparatus for chewing betel-nut. Large native cigarettes were handed round, about the size of an ordinary candle, coarse Borneo tobacco wrapped in nipah palm leaves; but they smoked easily and coolly. The rest of the councillors sat on chairs on each side of the hall and appeared to be listening intently to the conversation that went on at the round table. At the side of the throne behind the Sultan stood two enormous burning candles in large brass candlesticks, and these were supposed to indicate the purity of the Sultan's sentiments towards us. The little boy, the Sultan's brother, stared with all his eyes. The regent on behalf of the Sultan paid us elaborate compliments, and then the Resident on my behalf made a long speech telling them all about me and who I was. After this there was a little desultory conversation, each side trying to think of something to say. Then after a final compliment from the regent and a graceful return from the Resident we took our leave.

A DREAM

AS I WALKED along I thought of a broad road which I see sometimes in a dream, a road winding over the hills just as this one did that I was on; it leads to a city which, I know not why, I am eager to reach. Men and women are hurrying along the road, and often I have awakened to find myself up and half across my room in my desire to be of their number. The city is plain to see, standing on the top of a hill, surrounded by battlemented walls, and the road, broad and white, can be seen winding up to its great gates. The air is fresh and sweet and the sky is blue. They press on, men, women and children, not talking with each other, for they are intent on their purpose, and their faces shine with expectancy. They look neither to the right nor to the left. They hurry and their eyes are eager and bright. I do not know what they await. I only know that they are impelled by some urgent hope. The city reminds one a little of those cities of El Greco which stand on the brow of a rocky hill, cities of the soul, seen tremulously in a flash of lightning that tears across the darkness of the night. But those are cities of narrow, tortuous streets, and the dark clouds encompass them round about. In the city which I see in my sleep the sun shines and the streets are broad and straight. I know vaguely what the men are in those cities of mystics, the manner of them and the peace they offer to the tortured heart; but what kind of men they are in this city of mine and why it is that all those others on the road so passionately seek it, I do not know. I only know that it imports me urgently to go there, and that when at last I slip through its gates, happiness awaits me.

INDIA

INDIA. MAJOR C. He was a tall, broad-built man, with close-cropped brown hair. It was hard to guess his age. He might not have been more than thirty-five and he might have been fifty. He had a clean-shaven face, rather large, but with small features and a short blunt nose. He had an expression of peaceful happiness. He spoke slowly, but fluently, in rather a loud voice. He smiled a great deal and laughed frequently. His manner was cheerful. He was very polite and anxious to do what he could to be pleasant. It was hard to tell if he was intelligent or a little stupid. He was certainly not widely read. There was something of the boy scout about him which was disconcerting; he was childishly pleased when the Yogi came into his room and sat on his chair, and he told me several times that he enjoyed privileges that no other inmate of the Ashrama was accorded. His attitude was a little like that of the schoolboy inclined to boast because he is in the headmaster's favour.

He has been living at the Ashrama for two years and by special favour has been allowed to build his own little shack with a kitchen behind it. He has his own cook. He does not eat meat or fish or eggs, but has a store of tinned goods from Madras to help out with the curry and curds that his cook prepares for him. He drinks nothing but tea.

In his one room is a pallet bed, a table, an armchair and another chair, a small bookcase in which are perhaps fifty books. They are translations of works on the Vedanta, the Upanishads and so forth, books by the Yogi and books about him. On the walls are a few small pictures, one of Leonardo's Christ, a few, hideous, of Vishnu, cheap coloured prints and a photograph of the Yogi. The walls are painted green. On the floor a rattan mat.

He wears a sort of Chinese coat and Chinese trousers of white cotton and goes barefoot.

He has an intense adoration for the Yogi and says that he looks upon him as the greatest spiritual figure that the world has known since Christ.

He is somewhat reticent about his past. He said he had no one close to him in England and had travelled a great deal in years gone by, but now, having arrived there, he had reached his goal and would travel no more. He said that he had found peace and (over and over again) that the presence and the sight of the Yogi gave him a spiritual serenity which was beyond all price. I asked him how he spent his day. In reading, he said, taking his exercise (he has a pushbike and cycles regularly eight miles a day), and in meditation. He spent many hours a day sitting in the hall with the Yogi, though often he did not speak more than a few words to him in a week. But he was a strong man in the prime of life, and I asked him whether his natural energy had sufficient outlet. He said that he was fortunate in that he was one of the few persons who had a real desire and liking for meditation; and that he had always practised it. He added that meditation was a strenuous exercise and after spending some hours in it one was physically exhausted and had to lie down and rest. But I could not get from him exactly what he meant by meditation. I could not understand if he was actively thinking of a certain subject. When I put before him the Jesuit contemplation of a particular theme, such as the Passion, he said it was not that at all. He said his effort was to realize the self in him in communion with the universal self, to separate the I that thinks from the self, for that, he said, is the infinite. When he had done that, and really seen, or felt, that the divine in himself was part of the infinite divine he would have reached enlightenment. He was of a mind to stay there till this happened or till the Yogi died.

It was hard to make up one's mind what sort of a man he was. He was certainly very happy. I had thought to discover something of the truth about him from what he looked like and from what he said, but I came away completely puzzled.

Hyderabad. Passing along the road by car to Hyderabad from Bida I saw a large crowd, the usual Indian crowd, women in bright saris, men in dhoties, ox wagons, cows – I thought it was a small market, but my bearer told me it was the place where a healer lived and all these people were gathered from the surrounding villages to have their ills cured and women, if they were sterile, to be made fertile. I asked if I could go and see him. The driver told me he was a well-to-do contractor in Hyderabad who had felt the call to live the life of a Sadhu and had given over his fortune to his family and settled in that spot. He lived under a peepul tree and tended a small wayside shrine to Siva. We made our way through the crowd. There must have been three or four hundred people. Sick men were lying on the ground. There were women with sick children in their arms. When we got near the shrine the healer came forward and greeted us by humbly doing obeisance to us. He was dressed in a grubby white turban, a shirt without a collar, the ends hanging over his grubby dhoty. He had silver earrings in his ears. He was clean-shaven, but for a short stubble of grey moustache. Small, perky, quick in his movements, gay, bustling and cheerful. He looked not at all like a saint but like any wideawake, active shop-keeper in the bazaar. You would have thought him an obvious fake, but for the fact that he had given up his house and belong-ings and accepted nothing for his ministrations. He lives on the rice and fruit that people bring him and gives away everything he does not need. He insisted on giving us some coconuts. He heals by saying a prayer to the god in his shrine and by the laying on of hands. I was much embarrassed when as I was leaving he asked me to give him a blessing. I told him I was not the proper person to do that, but he was insistent, and so, feeling hypo-critical and very foolish, with all those people looking on, I did what he wanted.

The Sufi. He lived in a little house in a poor quarter of Hydera-bad. It was almost a slum. There was a veranda, and we waited there to find out from our guide if the holy man would see us. Taking off our shoes before we entered, we were ushered into a smallish room, divided into two, as far as I could see, by mosquito-netting, and I surmised that the part we could not see was his sleeping apartment. The greater part of the space in which we sat was taken up by a sort of dais or platform, about eighteen inches from the ground, covered with cheap rugs, and on these was a rattan mat on which the saint sat. He was very old, very thin, with a ragged white beard; he wore a fez, a white cotton coat and white trousers; and his feet were bare. His eyes looked very large in the extreme thinness of his face in which the cheek-bones stood out above the sunken cheeks. He had long beautiful hands, but fleshless, and his gestures were profuse, graceful and expressive. Though so old and so frail, he seemed full of energy and talked with animation. He was cheerful. The expression of his face was very sweet and kindly. I do not know that he said anything remarkable. I know nothing of Sufism and so perhaps was more surprised than I should have been to hear him speak of the self and the supreme self in the same strain as the Hindu teachers speak. The impression I carried away was of a very dear, tender, kindly, charitable and tolerant old man.

A Holy Man. Sir Akbar Hydari sent his car to fetch him and at the appointed hour he entered the room. He was richly dressed and wore a great scarlet cloak of fine material. He was a middle-aged man, tall, of a handsome presence, and his manner was courtly. He spoke no English and Sir Akbar acted as interpreter. He talked fluently and well and his voice was sonorous. He said the things I had heard from others twenty times before. That is the worst of the Indian thinkers, they say the same things in the same words, and though you feel that it should not make you restive, for if they possess the truth, as they are convinced they do, and if the truth is one and indivisible, it is natural enough that they should repeat it like parrots, there is no denying the fact that it is irksome to listen interminably to the same statements. You wish at least they could think of other metaphors, similes, illustrations than those of the Upanishads. Your heart sinks when you hear again the one about the snake and the rope. Custom has too much staled it.

I asked him how I could acquire the power of meditation. He told me to go into a darkened room, sit on the floor cross-legged and fix my eyes on the flame of a candle, emptying my mind of every thought so that it was a complete blank. He said that if I would do that for a quarter of an hour a day I should presently have some extraordinary experiences. "Do it for nine months," he said, "then come back and I will give you another exercise."

That evening I did as he had directed. I took the time before I began. I remained in that state for so long that I thought I must have by far exceeded the quarter of an hour he had prescribed. I looked at my watch. Three minutes had passed. It had seemed an eternity.

A week or two ago someone related an incident to me with the suggestion that I should write a story on it, and since then I have been thinking it over. I don't see what to do. The incident is as follows. Two young fellows were working on a tea plantation in the hills and the mail had to be fetched from a good way off so that they only got it at rather long intervals. One of the young fellows, let us call him A., used to get a lot of letters by every mail, ten or twelve and sometimes more, but the other, B., never got one. He used to watch A. enviously as he took his bundle and started to read, he hankered to have a letter, just one letter, and one day, when they were expecting the mail, he said to A.: "Look here, you always have a packet of letters and I never get any. I'll give you five pounds if you'll let me have one of yours." "Right ho," said A. and when the mail came in he handed B. his letters and said to him: "Take whichever you like." B. gave him a five-pound note, looked over the letters, chose one and returned the rest. In the evening, when they were having a whisky and soda after dinner, A. asked casually: "By the way, what was that letter about?" "I'm not going to tell you," said B. A., somewhat taken aback said: "Well, who was it from?" "That's my business," answered B. They had a bit of an argument, but B. stood on his rights and refused to say anything about the letter that he had bought. A. began to fret, and as the weeks went by he did all he could to persuade B. to let him see the letter. B. continued to refuse. At length A., anxious, worried, curious, felt he couldn't bear it any longer, so he went to B. and said: "Look here, here's your five pounds, let me have my letter back again." "Not on your life," said B. "I bought and paid for it, it's my letter and I'm not going to give it up."

That's all. I suppose if I belonged to the modern school of story writers, I should write it just as it is and leave it. It goes against the grain with me. I want a story to have form, and I don't see how you can give it that unless you can bring it to a conclusion that leaves no legitimate room for questioning. But even if you could bring yourself to leave the reader up in the air you don't want to leave yourself up in the air with him.

I went to lunch with the heir apparent and his wife, the Prince and Princess of Berar. During luncheon the prince talked to me of my journey. "I suppose you've been to Bombay?" he asked. "Yes," I answered, "I landed there." "And were you put up for the Yacht Club?" "Yes," I said. "And are you going to Calcutta?" "Yes." "I suppose you'll be put up at the Bengal Club?" "I hope so," I replied. "Do you know the difference between them?" the prince asked. "No," said I innocently. "In the Bengal Club at

Calcutta they don't allow dogs or Indians, but in the Yacht Club at Bombay they don't mind dogs; it's only Indians they don't allow." I couldn't for the life of me think of an answer to that then, and I haven't thought of one since.

BENARES

BENARES. NOTHING CAN be more impressive than to saunter down the Ganges by boat in the evening just before the sun sets. It is thrilling to look at the city with the two minarets of the mosque standing up against the pale sky. A wonderful sense of peace descends upon you. There is a great silence.

Then in the morning before the sun rises you drive through the city, the shops still closed and men under rugs lying asleep on the pavement; a scattering of people are going down to the river, with brass bowls in their hands, for their prescribed bath in the sacred water. You get on to a houseboat, manned by three men, and slowly row down by the ghats. It is chilly in the early morning. The ghats are unevenly peopled. One, I don't know why, is crowded. It is an extraordinary spectacle, the throng on the steps and at the water's edge. The bathers take the ritual bath in different ways. For some of the boys it is a lark and they dive into the water, come out and dive in again. For some it is a ceremony that must be gone through as quickly as possible, and you see them make the motions of devotion mechanically and gabble through their prayers. Others take it solemnly. They bow to the rising sun and, their arms outstretched above their heads, utter their prayers with unction. Then, the bath over, some chat with their friends and you guess that the daily obligation offers an opportunity to exchange news and gossip. Others sit crosslegged in meditation. The stillness with which some of them sit is strangely impressive: it is as though in that throng they sat in a temple of solitude. I saw one old man whose face was decorated with great rings of white ash around his eyes, a broad oblong patch on his forehead and square patches on his cheeks, so that he looked as if he were wearing a mask. Many of the bathers, having taken their bath, carefully scrubbed and polished the brass bowl in which they were going to carry back to their houses the lustral water.

It is a moving, a wonderfully thrilling spectacle; the bustle, the noise, the coming and going give a sense of a seething vitality; and those still figures of the men in contemplation by contrast seem more silent, more still, more aloof from human intercourse.

The sun rises higher in the heaven and the grey light which had bathed the scene grows golden, and colour clothes it with a motley radiance.

THE TAJ

TAJ MAHAL. Notwithstanding my expectations and all the pictures I had seen of it, when I got my first and proper view of it, the view from the terrace of the gateway, I was overcome by its beauty. I recognized that this was the authentic thrill of art and tried to examine it in myself while it was still vivid. I can understand that when people say something takes their breath away it is not an idle metaphor. I really did feel shortness of breath. I had a queer, delightful feeling in my heart, as though it were dilated. I felt surprise and joy and, I think, a sense of liberation; but I had just been reading the Samkhya philosophy in which art is regarded as a temporary liberation of the same sort as that absolute liberation in which all Indian religion ends, so it may be that this was no more than a reminiscence that I transferred to my actual feeling.

I cannot enjoy the same ecstasy over a beautiful thing twice over, and next day when I went to the Taj again, at the same hour, it was only with my mind that I enjoyed the same sight. On the other hand I got something else. As the sun was setting I wandered into the Mosque. I was quite alone. As I looked from one end along the chambers into which it is divided I had an eerie, mysterious sense of its emptiness and silence. I was a trifle scared. I can only put what I felt into words that make no sense: I seemed to hear the noiseless footfall of the infinite.

MADURA

MADURA. THE TEMPLE at night. There is always a noise in India. People talk all day long at the top of their voices, but in the

temple they talk more loudly than ever. The row is terrific.
People pray and recite litanies, they call to one another, vocifer-
ously discuss, quarrel or greet one another. There is nothing that
suggests reverence and yet there is a vehement overwhelming
sense of the divine that sends cold shivers down your spine. In
some strange way the gods there seem to be near and living.

The throng is dense, men, women and children. The men are
stripped to the waist, and their foreheads, and often their arms
and chests, are thickly smeared with the white ash of burnt cow
dung. Many of them in the daytime, while going about their
ordinary affairs, wear European clothes, but here they have
discarded Western dress, Western civilization and Western ways
of thought. Here in the temple is the native India that knows
nothing of the West. You see them making obeisance at one
shrine or another and sometimes lying full length on the ground,
face downwards in the ritual attitude of prostration.

You pass through long halls, the roof supported by sculptured
columns, and at the foot of each column is seated a religious
mendicant. Some are old and bearded, some terribly emaciated,
some are young, brawny and hirsute. Each has in front of him a
bowl for offerings or a small mat on which the faithful now and
again throw a copper coin. Some are clad in red, some are almost
naked. Some look at you vacantly as you pass, some are reading,
silently or aloud, and take no notice of the streaming throng.
Sitting on the floor, outside the adytum, is a group of priests, the
fore part of their skulls shaven, the hair at the back tied in a knot,
rather stout, their hairless brown chests and their fleshy arms
streaked with white ash. One, a scholar and a noted holy man,
in a red turban, with bracelets on his arms, and a coloured dhoty,
with a grey beard and an authoritative manner, comes followed
by two or three pupils, utters a prayer at a shrine, and then, with
the dignity of a man who is respected, the way cleared for him
by his pupils, strides into the holy of holies.

The temple is lit by naked electric bulbs that hang from the
ceiling and throw a harsh light on the sculpture, but where they
do not penetrate render the darkness more mysterious. The
impression you take away with you, notwithstanding that vast,
noisy throng, or maybe because of it, is of something secret and
terrible.

When I was leaving India people asked me which of all the sights I had seen had most impressed me. I answered as they expected me to answer. But it wasn't the Taj Mahal, the ghats of Benares, the temple at Madura or the mountains of Travancore that had most moved me; it was the peasant, terribly emaciated, with nothing to cover his nakedness but a rag round his middle the colour of the sun-baked earth he tilled, the peasant shivering in the cold of dawn, sweating in the heat of noon, working still as the sun set red over the parched fields, the starveling peasant toiling without cease in the north, in the south, in the east, in the west, toiling all over the vastness of India, toiling as he had toiled from father to son back, back for three thousand years when the Aryans had first descended upon the country, toiling for a scant subsistence, his only hope to keep body and soul together. That was the sight that had given me the most poignant emotion in India.

IN TEXAS

WE WERE SPENDING the night at a small town in Texas. It was a convenient stopping-place for people driving across the continent, and the hotel was full. Everyone went to bed early. At ten o'clock a woman in one of the rooms put in a call to Washington, and in the frame house you could hear plainly every word she said. She wanted a Major Tompkins, but she didn't know his number; she told the operator that he was in the War Department. Presently she got on to Washington, and when the operator told her that she couldn't trace him, flew into a temper and said that everyone in Washington knew Major Tompkins. It was very important, she said, and she had to speak to him. She was cut off and in a few minutes tried again. She tried every quarter of an hour. She abused the local operator, what sort of a one-horse dump is this? She abused the Washington operator. She made more and more noise. Nobody could sleep. Indignant guests rang down to the office, and the night manager came up and tried to get her to be quiet. We listened to her angry replies to his mild expostulation and when, defeated, he left her she started once more to ring the exchange. She rang and rang. She shouted. Furious men in their dressing-gowns, dishevelled women in wrappers, went into the passage and banged on her door telling her to stop making so much noise so that they could sleep. She told them to go to hell with such variety of language as to excite the outraged indignation of the ladies. The manager was again appealed to and at his wits' end sent for the sheriff. The sheriff came, but he was no match for her and not knowing what else to do sent for a doctor. Meanwhile she rang and rang, screaming obscenities at the operator. The doctor came, saw her, shrugged his shoulders and said he could do nothing. The sheriff wanted him to take her to the hospital, but for some reason I couldn't understand, something to do with her being a transient from another state, and if she was crazy, as all these frantic people insisted, she might become a charge on the county, the doctor refused to act. She went on telephoning. She screamed that she must get Major Tompkins; it was a matter of life and death. At last she got him. It was four in the morning and no one in the hotel had shut an eye.

"Have you got Major Tompkins?" she asked the operator. "You're quite sure you've got him? Is he on the line?" Then with concentrated fury, spacing out her words to make them more emphatic: "Tell – Major – Tompkins – that – I don't – want – to speak – to him."

With that she banged the receiver down on to the cradle.

ALSO BY

W. SOMERSET MAUGHAM

THE PAINTED VEIL

Set in England and Hong Kong in the 1920s, *The Painted Veil* is the story of the beautiful but love-starved Kitty Fane. When her husband discovers her adulterous affair, he forces her to accompany him to the heart of a cholera epidemic. Stripped of the British society of her youth and the small but effective society she fought so hard to attain in Hong Kong, she is compelled by her awakening conscience to reassess her life and learn how to love. *The Painted Veil* is a beautifully written affirmation of the human capacity to grow, to change, and to forgive.

Fiction/Literature

ALSO AVAILABLE

Cakes and Ale
Christmas Holiday
The Moon and Sixpence
The Narrow Corner
The Razor's Edge
Theatre
Up at the Villa
A Writer's Notebook

VINTAGE INTERNATIONAL
Available wherever books are sold.
www.vintagebooks.com